Anthropocene Realism

Environmental Cultures Series

Series Editors:
Greg Garrard, University of British Columbia, Canada
Richard Kerridge, Bath Spa University, UK

Editorial Board:
Frances Bellarsi, Université Libre de Bruxelles, Belgium
Mandy Bloomfield, Plymouth University, UK
Lily Chen, Shanghai Normal University, China
Christa Grewe-Volpp, University of Mannheim, Germany
Stephanie LeMenager, University of Oregon, USA
Timothy Morton, Rice University, USA
Pablo Mukherjee, University of Warwick, UK

Bloomsbury's *Environmental Cultures* series makes available to students and scholars at all levels the latest cutting-edge research on the diverse ways in which culture has responded to the age of environmental crisis. Publishing ambitious and innovative literary ecocriticism that crosses disciplines, national boundaries and media, the books in the series explore and test the challenges of ecocriticism to conventional forms of cultural study.

Titles available:
Bodies of Water, Astrida Neimanis
Cities and Wetlands, Rod Giblett
Civil Rights and the Environment in African-American Literature, 1895–1941, John Claborn
Climate Change Scepticism, Greg Garrard, George Handley, Axel Goodbody, Stephanie Posthumus
Climate Crisis and the 21st-Century British Novel, Astrid Bracke
Cognitive Ecopoetics, Sharon Lattig
Colonialism, Culture, Whales, Graham Huggan
Contemporary Fiction and Climate Uncertainty, Marco Caracciolo
Digital Vision and Ecological Aesthetic, Lisa FitzGerald
Ecocollapse Fiction and Cultures of Human Extinction, Sarah E. McFarland

Ecocriticism and Italy, Serenella Iovino
Ecospectrality, Laura A. White
Environmental Cultures in Soviet East Europe, Anna Barcz
Fuel, Heidi C. M. Scott
Imagining the Plains of Latin America, Axel Pérez Trujillo Diniz
Literature as Cultural Ecology, Hubert Zapf
The Living World, Samantha Walton
Nerd Ecology, Anthony Lioi
The New Nature Writing, Jos Smith
The New Poetics of Climate Change, Matthew Griffiths
Radical Animism, Jemma Deer
Reading Underwater Wreckage, Killian Quigley
Reclaiming Romanticism, Kate Rigby
Teaching Environmental Writing, Isabel Galleymore
This Contentious Storm, Jennifer Mae Hamilton
The Tree Climbing Cure, Andy Brown
Weathering Shakespeare, Evelyn O'Malley

Forthcoming Titles:
Ecocriticism and Turkey, Meliz Ergin

Anthropocene Realism

Fiction in the Age of Climate Change

John Thieme

BLOOMSBURY ACADEMIC
LONDON • NEW YORK • OXFORD • NEW DELHI • SYDNEY

BLOOMSBURY ACADEMIC
Bloomsbury Publishing Plc
50 Bedford Square, London, WC1B 3DP, UK
1385 Broadway, New York, NY 10018, USA
29 Earlsfort Terrace, Dublin 2, Ireland

BLOOMSBURY, BLOOMSBURY ACADEMIC and the Diana logo are trademarks of
Bloomsbury Publishing Plc

First published in Great Britain 2023
This paperback edition published 2025

Copyright © John Thieme, 2023

John Thieme has asserted his right under the Copyright, Designs and Patents Act,
1988, to be identified as Author of this work.

For legal purposes the Acknowledgements on p. viii constitute an extension
of this copyright page.

Cover design: Burge Agency
Cover image © Mint Images Limited / Alamy Stock Photo

This work is published open access subject to a Creative Commons Attribution-NonCommercial-NoDerivatives 4.0 International licence (CC BY-NC-ND 4.0, https://creativecommons.org/licenses/by-nc-nd/4.0/). You may re-use, distribute and reproduce this work in any medium for non-commercial purposes, provided you give attribution to the copyright holder and the publisher and provide a link to the Creative Commons licence.

Bloomsbury Publishing Plc does not have any control over, or responsibility for, any third-party websites referred to or in this book. All internet addresses given in this book were correct at the time of going to press. The author and publisher regret any inconvenience caused if addresses have changed or sites have ceased to exist, but can accept no responsibility for any such changes.

A catalogue record for this book is available from the British Library.

A catalog record for this book is available from the Library of Congress.

ISBN: HB: 978-1-3502-9603-9
PB: 978-1-3502-9607-7
ePDF: 978-1-3502-9604-6
eBook: 978-1-3502-9605-3

Series: Environmental Cultures

Typeset by Newgen KnowledgeWorks Pvt. Ltd., Chennai, India

To find out more about our authors and books visit www.bloomsbury.com
and sign up for our newsletters.

Contents

Acknowledgements	viii
Introduction: Writing to the moment	1
1 'Weather as everything': Social realism in Barbara Kingsolver's *Flight Behaviour*	17
2 Seeking 'the perfect story': Metajournalistic realism in Helon Habila's *Oil on Water*	33
3 Apocalypse now? Visceral realism in Liz Jensen's *The Rapture*	45
4 Tracing genealogies: Circumstantial realism in Annie Proulx's *Barkskins*	57
5 'Trees are social creatures': Encyclopaedic realism in Richard Powers's *The Overstory*	69
6 It's not funny: Comic realism in Ian McEwan's *Solar*	87
7 'I used to be human once': Testimonial realism in Indra Sinha's *Animal's People*	95
8 Nordic noir: Urban realism in Antti Tuomainen's *The Healer*	103
9 'Boiling the frog'? Gradualist realism in James Bradley's *Clade*	113
10 'Everything change': Speculative realism in Margaret Atwood's *MaddAddam* trilogy	127
11 'Outside the range of the probable'? Picaresque realism in Amitav Ghosh's *Gun Island*	139
12 'Innumerable ommatidia': Multi-realism in Wu Ming-Yi's *The Man with the Compound Eyes*	155
Conclusion: A new realism?	171
Notes	177
References	191
Index	205

Acknowledgements

Begun during the time of the pandemic and completed in the summer of 2022 when the UK experienced its highest ever recorded temperature, this book has involved me in less face-to-face contact with friends and colleagues than any other I have written. This, though, has meant that the help of those who offered advice on major and minor issues, in person or at distance, has been more invaluable than ever. They include Patrycja Austin, Chun-yen Chen, Asis De, Maria-Sabina Draga Alexandru, Marta Dvořák, Jeanne Johnston, Owen Knowles, Chris Rolfe, Keely Saycell and Kathy Williamson. I am especially grateful to Ben Doyle, his colleagues at Bloomsbury and the series editors for their support and professionalism, and I owe a particular debt of gratitude to Scott Slovic, whose comments on the 'final' manuscript inspired changes and made this a better book than it would have been otherwise.

Introduction: Writing to the moment

This book examines some of the ways novelists writing in the age of climate change employ realist fictional modes to grapple with the challenges of a transformed planet. Historically, realist fiction has concerned itself with social *mores*, and in many of its more familiar iterations, it works to unravel the complications of plots in such a way that mysteries are solved and the social order is reaffirmed. So what happens to fiction when global warming and other consequences of Anthropocene behaviour disrupt supposed geological and meteorological norms, upend the very notion of a stable social order and unsettle epistemological assumptions about the situation of human and non-human life on earth? In this new context, realism seems all the more necessary, but the underlying foundations of earlier realist fiction have been shaken to the core and the genre faces the need to adapt to encompass the radically altered planetary situation. This book offers twelve case studies of ways in which novelists have addressed the problematics of writing fiction in the age of climate change.

Climate fiction – 'cli-fi' – has come to prominence as a genre distinct from sci-fi in the twenty-first century. The term was coined by the climate activist, Dan Bloom, in 2007,[1] to cover the growing body of novels that specifically deal with global warming and related issues, and to distinguish such writing from science fiction and eco-fiction more generally. Bloom has said, 'Sci-fi is mostly for escapism and entertainment. Cli-fi is about facing the reality of global warming via literature or movies' (Plantz 2015). Many science fiction devotees would, of course, disagree with this view of sci-fi, but certainly climate fiction's engagement with present and future catastrophes seldom opens the door for escapist readings and, through the medium of story, the genre fosters and augments climate literacy. Whether this engenders a significant change in its readers' behaviour is open to question, but at the very least cli-fi presents issues in a form, which, again in Bloom's view (Plantz 2015), is more likely to have an emotive impact than the facts and statistics of hard science.

This study considers the poetics of twenty-first century climate change fiction, offering close readings of novels written in realist modes and set in the 'long present', a term I use to cover the actual present, the near future and an historic past that interacts with the present. Clearly novels, such as Cormac McCarthy's *The Road* (2006) and Paolo Bacigalupi's *The Windup Girl* (2009), which are set in the future, have made a significant contribution to raising awareness of climate change and just as dystopian science fiction often offers allegories of the present – the disputed belief that the title of Orwell's *Nineteen Eighty-Four* (1949) involved an inversion of 1948,[2] the year in which it was completed, would, if true, offer a striking example of the point – futuristic cli-fi can provide red alerts of impending catastrophes. However, the immediacy of fiction set in the long present reduces the possibility of deferring engagement with the crisis on the grounds that it is a future threat rather than a here-and-now emergency, which has already changed the face of the planet and is continuing to wreak havoc on a daily basis. Bill McKibben, founder of the worldwide climate campaign group 350.org, put this particularly succinctly in the title of his 2010 book *Eaarth*, in which he claimed that the planet as humankind once knew it no longer exists. McKibben invoked the sense of wonder at life on the third rock from the sun that was felt by the astronauts of Apollo 8 as they experienced their first vision of what was to become known as 'Earthrise' but argued that their view of 'that stable secure place' was no longer tenable:

> *We no longer live on that planet.* In the four decades since, that earth has changed in profound ways …. We imagine we still live back on that old planet, that the disturbances we see around us are the old random and freakish kind. But they're not. It's a different place. A different planet. It needs a new name. Eaarth. Or Monnde, or Tierrre, Errde, оккучивать. (2010: 2–3; emphasis in original)

At the same time, he listed a host of influential public figures – among them Barack Obama, Ted Kennedy, Arnold Schwarzenegger, David Attenborough and Bill Clinton – who had referred to global warming as a future threat in speaking about the dangers that it posed for 'our grandchildren' (2010: 11–13),[3] before going on to ask how, with Arctic ice melting, the tropics expanding and the oceans becoming acidified, 'did time dilate, and "100 or 200 years from now" become yesterday?' (13). *Eaarth*, completed in 2009 (McKibben 2010: xiv), is roughly contemporary with some of the novels considered in this book, which embody a similar perspective, and Barbara Kingsolver, one of the most widely read of the writers discussed, explicitly acknowledges a debt to it, thanking McKibben and his 350.org colleagues for 'the most important work in the world' ([2012] 2013: 599). Awareness that global disaster is looming unless major measures are taken to combat climate change has, of course, increased very considerably since *Eaarth* appeared, particularly in the first years of the third decade of the twentieth century, but, now as then, the problem exists in the present. Powerful though the warnings about climate disaster in many dystopian novels are, they run the risk of kicking the can down the road as a problem that will impact on 'our grandchildren'. Without radical action that will surely be the case, but the grandchildren trope obscures the extent of the damage done yesterday and being inflicted on Eaarth's ecosystems today.

The fiction I discuss either engages with climate change as its central concern or as part of a preoccupation with a broader set of environmental issues that have emerged in the Age of the Anthropocene. As Margaret Atwood has memorably put it, 'Everything change' (Atwood 2015). So my entry-point is fiction about climate change, but this leads inevitably into a consideration of the effect that anthropogenic activity is having on Eaarth more generally. The fiction I discuss is all post-Millennial, but climate fiction has a longer genealogy and disquiet about a planet undergoing change because of anthropogenic behaviour can be found in texts that appeared centuries ago. One recent study of world literature traces concerns about climate issues back to foundational texts like *The Epic of Gilgamesh*, where, along with a pre-biblical narrative of the Flood, the human species can already be seen to be engaged in resource extraction (Puchner 2022: 25).[4] However, suggesting such a provenance runs the risk of failing to differentiate the global warming crisis of the last half century from earlier instances of environmentally damaging human interventions and, as the 2021 IPCC (Intergovernmental Panel on Climate Change) Summary for Policymakers puts it, recent 'human influence has warmed the climate at a rate that is unprecedented in at least the last 2000 years', with 'each of the last four decades [being] successively warmer than any decade that preceded it since 1850' (IPCC 2021: A.1.8, A.1. 2).

More obvious precursors of twenty-first century climate fiction include John Steinbeck's *The Grapes of Wrath* (1939), J. G. Ballard's *The Drowned World* (1962), Ernest Callenbach's *Ecotopia* (1975) and Octavia E. Butler's *Parable of the Sower* (1993). *The Grapes of Wrath* follows the enforced migration, from Oklahoma to California, of a family whose way of life is destroyed by the desertification of the dryland ecosystem in which they live, a situation that arises from a mixture of climate variation and human farming methods. Anticipated by John Wyndham's sci-fi classic *The Kraken Wakes* (1953), *The Drowned World* is set in a post-apocalyptic London, flooded as a consequence of the melting of the polar ice caps, a situation that recurs in subsequent novels about the inundation of the British capital, including Maggie Gee's *The Flood* (2004) and Liz Jensen's *The Rapture* (2009; discussed in Chapter 3). *Ecotopia* (1975; second edition 2014), which is more positive in orientation and which anticipates aspects of Richard Powers's *The Overstory* (2018; discussed in Chapter 5), is about a new Western American nation (comprising Northern California, Oregon and Washington) that has seceded from the rest of the United States and developed a society, which, as Callenbach put it in a 2004 Afterword to the novel, offers 'real alternatives to our present corporatist, militarist, ultracompetitive, oil-obsessed course' (Callenbach 2014: 170). Eerily prescient of changes that were to come in the years after its publication and narrated by a 'hyperempathetic' protagonist who experiences others' emotions and suffering as her own, *Parable of the Sower* is set in a dystopian 2020s California in which society has broken down and most of the population is struggling to survive in a parched environment where extreme violence is ubiquitous, now that 'people have changed the climate of the world' (Butler ([1993] 2019: 52).

It was, though, in the early years of the twenty-first century, with more widespread awareness of global warming and other threats to the planet generated by anthropogenic activity, that the number of cli-fi novels began to increase significantly, reaching a point where climate fiction demanded to be recognized as a genre in its own right, and this has been followed by the subsequent emergence of a body of critical commentary on the fiction, which is also playing a part in foregrounding issues and in some cases promoting activism to address the crisis.[5] As already indicated, the present book aims to make its own distinctive contribution to such criticism by focussing on Anthropocene fiction set in the long present and written in realist modes, in an attempt to forestall views that put the quest for solutions onto the back burner, because, to borrow a metaphor used in one of the novels discussed, James Bradley's *Clade* ([2015] 2017: 93–137), they fail to realize that the frog burns slowly.[6] It does so through close readings of a dozen representative twenty-first-century cli-fi novels drawn from various parts of the globe and written in a range of realist modes, some of which are conventional, some of which are innovative and some of which are a mixture of the two. These modes include metajournalistic reporting (Helon Habila's *Oil on Water*; 2010), a multi-generational saga (Annie Proulx's *Barkskins*; 2016), comic realism (Ian McEwan's *Solar*; 2010), visceral realism (Liz Jensen's *The Rapture*), testimony (Indra Sinha's *Animal's People*; 2007), encyclopaedic realism (Richard Powers's *The Overstory*) and Nordic noir (Antti Tuomainen's *The Healer*; 2010; trans. 2013). While some of these variant modes extend the bounds of realism, to a point where it is perhaps more appropriate to speak of a plurality of realisms, or a 'new realism', a form of fiction that subscribes to the conventions of realism, as developed in the eighteenth- and nineteenth-century European novel, but finds them stretched to breaking point and in some cases brings them into dialogue with other fictional modes, something which is particularly the case with the novels I discuss in Chapters 11, 12 and 13. None of the works discussed is a single-issue novel – they interweave dramatizing the climate threat with representations of the lived social experiences of individual human and non-human beings – collectively they attest to realism's vital role in communicating the present-day urgency of the crisis. The novels considered also vary in the extent to which they chart the international consequences of climate change engendered by practices such as deforestation, the melting of permafrost and the evaporation of water into the atmosphere because of rising temperatures, but patterns recur and, taken together, they provide a powerful indictment of the anthropogenic exclusivism that has created the worldwide crisis.

The long present mode of realism in which they are written is at its extreme in Annie Proulx's *Barkskins*, which begins in the late seventeenth century and ends in the early twenty-first, and James Bradley's *Clade*, which starts in an all-too-real present and inches forward, through a series of ten chapters, into a mid-twenty-first-century future. *Barkskins* opens with a very credible depiction of the historical settlement of 'New France' that particularly focuses on logging and the interaction between French settlers and members of the Mi'kmaw nation and subsequently traces the fortunes of two family lines and the timber industry through to an era in which the damage caused by deforestation is undeniable. *Clade*'s trajectory travels in the opposite direction and its narrative unfolds in a more indirect and less obviously linear manner, but it, too, employs a form of long-present realism that shows how the impact of climate change affects the lives of different generations of a family and its associates. In both of these cases realism is the bedrock on which the novel rests its climate narrative, though the elliptical mode of *Clade* is a world away from the protracted contingent detail of *Barkskins*, a novel that provides a striking example of what Roland Barthes terms 'the reality effect', the use of details, which lack any broader significance in a text and which are used as 'remplissages' ('fillers' [Barthes 1968: 84]) to create an impression of 'the real'.[7] Yet, different though their techniques are, both writers' approaches to realism can be seen as a response to the discursive challenges of writing about climate in the Age of the Anthropocene, challenges that are greater than those encountered by earlier environmental writers, such as the

Americans Aldo Leopold, whose work on wildlife management did much to reverse attitudes to wilderness as a site for exploitation, and John Muir, who was a moving force in the founding of Sequoia and Yosemite National Parks and a staunch advocate for the preservation of wilderness. For such pathfinders, the natural environment for which they campaigned was a tangible constant. The uniqueness of the phenomenon of human-induced climate change has unsettled this perception and for novelists the discursive corollary has been that realism has been stretched into hitherto uncharted territory. Earlier 'Nature' writing was usually dedicated to demonstrating the consequences of localized environmental situations; global warming has generated what Timothy Morton (2013) has termed 'hyperobjects', phenomena so vast and intangible that they are outside the realm of normal human comprehension and resist realist representation. This said, the effects of climate change are, of course, anything but abstract and intangible for those who suffer the consequences of floods, earthquakes and typhoons, and so, although hyperobjects may not readily lend themselves to realist representation, both the sudden catastrophic events and the slow attritional erosion caused by global warming demand a realist poetics that refuses to consign them to the too-difficult box of the intangible.[8] Wu Ming-Yi's treatment of the Pacific Trash Vortex, the gyre of floating micro-plastics in the North Pacific Ocean, in his novel *The Man with the Compound Eyes* (2011), which I discuss in Chapter 12, is highly relevant in this context. The Vortex may be a hyperobject, and it is not unreasonable to suggest that it is represented as such in the novel, particularly since one of the main protagonists, the Pacific islander Atile'i, is unable to comprehend it, but when it generates a tsunami that destroys Atile'i's homeland, the fictional island of Wayo Wayo, and wreaks havoc on the east coast of Taiwan, it is represented as anything but abstract. In this instance, the novel's complex admixture of modes confronts the intangible with a material reality.

Climate change challenges realist representation, then, and this challenge is central to one of the most probing books on the subject to have appeared to date, Amitav Ghosh's *The Great Derangement: Climate Change and the Unthinkable* (2016), a work which provides a powerful indictment of the carbon economy and other anthropogenic interventions that have contributed to global warming. Ghosh argues that beliefs about climate that rely on 'the calculus of probability' (2016: 23), the view that meteorological changes occur gradually, have become unsustainable, since the recent proliferation of extreme weather-related events has made the hitherto improbable the new norm. At the same time, *The Great Derangement* does something else: it engages with the poetics of representing climate change, with what Ghosh sees as *fiction's* limitations when it comes to depicting the meteorological shifts that threaten the planet's future. In a passage in the first section, entitled 'Stories', he focuses on the narrativization of climate change, extending his argument about reckless reliance on the calculus of probability to the realist novel. He maintains that the genre is built on a 'scaffolding' that prevents it from 'confront[ing] the centrality of the improbable' (23) in the form of sudden disasters that stretch the bounds of credulity by contradicting gradualist notions of meteorological change. *Pace* his own investment in realism in much of his fiction,[9] he attacks what he sees as the conventions of realist fiction and points to the fact that creative writers who have campaigned against global warming have generally avoided the form of the novel. He cites exceptions,[10] including three writers whose work is considered in the present book (Margaret Atwood, Barbara Kingsolver and Ian McEwan), but his basic premise is that the realist novel is unsuited to the representation of dramatic climatological events. He argues that 'the calculus of probability that is deployed within the imaginary world of a novel is not the same as that which obtains outside it' (23), adding that, 'within the pages of a novel an event that is only slightly improbable in real life – say, an unexpected encounter with a long-lost childhood friend – may seem wildly unlikely: the writer will have to work hard to make it appear persuasive' (24).

This seems to involve a contradiction in terms, since the realist novel is being taken to task for not engaging with what would not normally be considered realistic, at which point, one might say, it would not be a realist novel anyway! More than just this. Ghosh's view of the realist novel is questionable. From its inception, the so-called realist novel has, of course, incorporated improbabilities, including extreme weather events. In *Robinson Crusoe*, the novel often seen to stand at the fountainhead of English realism, the protagonist is a serial victim of troubled waters. Crusoe experiences several severe storms, in one of which the ship that he is on founders, before, like the novel itself, he is shipwrecked on his Caribbean desert island. And more generally it is one of the staples of novels such as *Don Quixote*, *Gil Blas* and *Tom Jones* that 'long-lost' characters turn up.[11] Of course, one may argue that such novels, self-styled 'histories', are parodies or comic-picaresque or anything but realistic, but to exclude them from the realist canon is to make Ghosh's contention valid through a form of circular reasoning: realism by definition does not step outside the bounds of probability; realism is inadequate, because it neglects the improbable. It seems more reasonable to concede that novels that do not obviously belong to fantasy genres, such as science fiction and the Gothic, frequently include what Ghosh calls 'wildly unlikely encounters'. Magwitch's return in *Great Expectations* seems perfectly credible within the novel's primarily realistic mode. So too do the reappearances of Mr Micawber in *David Copperfield*. To argue, as Ghosh does, that such events are 'wildly unlikely' in realist fiction, while they would only seem 'slightly improbable' in real life, seems tendentious to the point of being a reversal of how most people respond to the relationship between 'truth' and 'fiction'.

Interestingly, it is an issue that has a direct bearing on his own novel, *Gun Island* (2019), which I discuss in Chapter 11. Published after *The Great Derangement*, *Gun Island* is a work in which he appears to be offering his own sustained attempt at a serious novel that confronts the 'centrality' of the supposedly 'improbable' in the form of sudden extreme weather disasters. *Gun Island* can be read as a novel that provides at least a partial answer to the difficulties that Ghosh suggests face literary novelists, since it finds him moving between realism and fabulation. Nevertheless, the position he adopts on this subject in *The Great Derangement* remains questionable and so, while admiring the book's important contribution to climate studies more generally, I take issue with this particular aspect,[12] by arguing that 'realism', either in variants of its classic modes or in newly configured extensions of the genre, has been, and is, highly effective in representing the climate emergency. Ghosh's apparent ambivalence also foregrounds the fact that realism is a slippery category to define – as Kendall Walton puts it, it is 'a monster with many heads desperately in need of disentangling' (Walton 1990: 328; qtd. Furst 1992: 1) – and the changes wrought by climate change may be such that it needs to be reconfigured, something which Ghosh himself seems to be doing in *Gun Island*. I return to this in my conclusion.

Hitherto, most commentators on realism have demonstrated that it is predicated on a set of conventions and can never be an unmediated transcription of an external world. Nevertheless, *pace* the illusion inherent in a realist praxis, a form of strategic realism[13] seems crucial for any writer wishing to engage with the realities of the climate crisis: a strategic belief in mimetic realism reopens the possibility of fiction engaging with phenomena such as climate catastrophe in a materially grounded, ecologically ethical way, as a consciousness-raiser and a call to action.

So, this book concerns itself with 'realism' and by way of offering a prolegomenon to the use of the term in what follows and, again in Walton's words, 'separat[ing] a few strands from the snarl' (1990: 328), I begin with thumbnail sketches of two of the most influential bodies of what has been seen as realist fiction: the beginnings of the novel in eighteenth-century England and its efflorescence in nineteenth-century France. I contextualize this fiction with brief reference to some of the critical and theoretical commentary it has attracted.

For the man and woman in the street, what is real is, of course, usually taken for granted. The perceived physical environment is real: clouds and cuckoos are real; cloud cuckoo land isn't. Nevertheless, across the centuries realism has meant many things to many people and pre-Enlightenment and non-Western conceptions of what constitutes reality have often been diametrically opposed to the way the term has come to be understood in the West and in those parts of the world that have come under Western influence during the last four centuries. As I have been suggesting and as numerous philosophers, cultural theorists and critics – among them Plato, Aristotle, Coleridge, Benjamin, Adorno, Ricoeur and Derrida – have pointed out, there can be no direct access to an external reality, since language intervenes. Language is malleable and socially constructed and there is always the gap, central to post-Saussurean linguistics, between signifiers and signifieds, between the signs (mainly words) used to achieve signification and the concepts conventionally associated with them. Nevertheless there are various conventions that are common to what Eric Auerbach (1946) views as 'modern realism', what Ian Watt terms 'formal realism' (1957) and what Catherine Belsey (1980) and others refer to as 'classic realism'.

Seldom superseded, Auerbach's monumental *Mimesis: The Representation of Reality in Western Society*, which scrutinizes the discursive conventions inherent in the work of writers from Homer and the *Book of Genesis* to Virginia Woolf and Marcel Proust, stands at the headwaters of studies that anatomize the ways in which writers represent the reality of the worlds they depict, arguing that these are inevitably a product of the rhetorical conventions of their day. Most of *Mimesis* deals with ways of representing reality that predate the novel, but towards the end, when he discusses Stendhal, Balzac and Flaubert, Auerbach directly confronts the factors that gave rise to fictional realism. Here he argues that this kind of mimesis, 'modern realism', was a complete break with classical ideas of literary representation that involved a practice, predicated on distinct hierarchized 'levels of style', in which subjects were required to be treated in appropriate modes. The shift away from this legitimized the serious treatment of areas of experience that would hitherto have been considered low and therefore only suitable for representation in inferior modes. In Auerbach's words:

> When Stendhal and Balzac took random individuals from daily life in their dependence upon current historical circumstances and made them the subjects

of serious, problematic, and even tragic representation, they broke with the classical rule of distinct levels of style, for according to this rule, everyday practical reality could find a place in literature only within the frame of a low or intermediate kind of style, that is to say, as either grotesquely comic or pleasant, light, colorful, and elegant entertainment. ... And they opened the way for modern realism, which has ever since developed in increasingly rich forms, in keeping with the constantly changing and expanding reality of modern life. ([1953] 2003: 554)

So, in Auerbach's view, modern realism democratized the representation of reality, and the novel emerged as a genre that offered an empirical challenge to idealized Classical and Romance conceptions of narrative. Although his discussion of modern fictional realism takes up a comparatively small portion of his mammoth work, and *Mimesis* is predominantly European in its choice of case studies – it does not venture beyond Asia Minor and the ancient Near East – Auerbach's approach was seminal in demonstrating the extent to which notions of realism are perceived through the discursive lenses and intertextual assumptions of particular reading communities, and he shows how socio-economic shifts paved the way for the emergence of the realist novel. This is immediately apparent in the characteristics of the two bodies of fiction I am focusing on because of their foundational role in shaping modern notions of literary realism: the early eighteenth-century English novel and the nineteenth-century French novel. Like Auerbach, numerous subsequent commentators have seen nineteenth-century French iterations of realism as the high point of the genre, with many of them particularly focusing on Balzac's *Comédie humaine*, but the rise of the novel in England in the early eighteenth century provides an equally instructive instance of a corpus of prose fiction that moved away from Romance and Classical narrative constraints to reflect the socio-economic concerns of the day for a particular reading community.

In some respects, the classic study of the beginnings of realist English fiction, Ian Watt's *The Rise of the Novel* (1957), shares common ground with Auerbach. It views the emergence of the novel in England in the eighteenth century as a rejection of the traditional plots, usually drawn from mythology, legend or history, which had been the staple fare of earlier narrative, in favour of an approach that represented the particularities of individual experience, either contemporary or set in the recent past, in a mode founded on contingent detail. For Watt, this 'modern realism' ([1957] 1963: 12) had its roots in the anti-universalist epistemology of philosophers such as Descartes and Locke and, as he puts it, Defoe's 'total subordination of the plot to the pattern of the autobiographical memoir is as defiant an assertion of the primacy of individual experience in the novel as Descartes's *cogito ergo sum* was in philosophy' (15). In an age when neo-Classical orthodoxies continued to hold sway – later in the century, Samuel Johnson would write in *The Life of Cowley*, 'Great thoughts are always general, and consist in positions not limited by exceptions, and in descriptions not descending to minuteness' ([1781] 1986: 405) – the novel, in the hands of innovators such as Defoe and Richardson, true to its name, built its plots around 'novelty', a characteristic that Johnson viewed as the antithesis of generality, and which he dismissed as offering 'little hope of greatness' (405). Defoe in particular moved away from the neo-Classical general by offering his readers fictional biographies of contemporary or near-contemporary protagonists. He begins *Robinson Crusoe* by asserting that it is 'a just history of fact' ([1719] 1965: 25), but there are passages that stretch the bounds of plausibility beyond breaking-point, among them having barley unexpectedly shooting out of the ground in a climate which Crusoe acknowledges is 'not proper for corn' (94) and his finding penguins on his Caribbean island (123). These led to Defoe's subsequently being forced to backtrack and admit that the book was fiction, but he creates a convincing illusion of reality through an accretion of concrete detail. Similarly, he opens *Moll Flanders* by claiming in the preface that it is a 'genuine' autobiography, to be distinguished from 'novels and romances', and only fictionalized by a change of the protagonist's name and the use of 'modester words than she told it at first' (Defoe [1722] 1978: 28). While for most modern readers, such claims will appear spurious, much of Defoe's appeal to his contemporaries resided in his capacity for verisimilitude, his ability to conjure up a credible life-story through an accumulation of circumstantial information.

Richardson follows in the same secular Puritan tradition as Defoe, a tradition which signals its commitment to realism by turning away from the homiletic approach of earlier Puritan writers like John Bunyan, who also offers a degree of observed concrete detail in *Pilgrim's Progress* (1678) – rural Bedfordshire provided the inspiration for locations such as the Slough of Despond and the Land of Beulah (Foster 1901) – but deploys this in the service of religious allegory. Like Defoe, Richardson shifts the emphasis to supposed literal representation rather than allegory. His epistolary method involves a meticulous rendition of both material detail and subjective affect, but it also introduces a particular subset of realism through its use of letters, which he spoke of as 'written, as it were, to the *moment*, while the heart is agitated by hopes and fears, on events undecided' (Richardson [1753] 1812: ix; emphasis in original).[14] What Coleridge termed his 'close, hot day dreamy continuity' (1813) depicts social situations that are a world away from the Anthropocene fiction discussed in this book, but the present-tense immediacy of his writing, often mentioned by critics, though not always linked with the development of his particular form of realism, can be seen as an early precedent for writing to the moment that deals with 'events undecided', events which today could include climate change. From the beginning of *Pamela*, where in her very first letter the heroine tells her parents, 'O how my eyes run! Don't wonder to see the paper so blotted' (Richardson [1740] 1962: 1), Richardson highlights the here-and-now urgency of Pamela's situation. So, although the mixture of prurience and moralizing that characterizes his writing is remote from the concerns of cli-fi, the fictional mode that he developed represents that strain of realism that makes it an effective vehicle for depicting the situations of people living *in extremis* and uncertain about the future and, again with the caveat that Pamela's beleaguered situation is a far cry from the current exigencies of the climate crisis, the dramatic immediacy of his approach anticipates the use of the present in several of the novels discussed in this book. *The Rapture*, *Animal's People*, *The Overstory* and *Clade*[15] are all written, entirely or primarily, in the now-present tense, in a tense that might once have been termed the historic present, but which I prefer to call the now-present, since the temporal emphasis is far more on the current moment than a past time re-envisioned through a present-day lens. This, then, is how one strain of realism began in England. After Defoe laid the groundwork by placing individualism and a parallel absorption with contingent detail at the centre of his fiction, Richardson took this a stage further, using writing to the moment to encapsulate the psychological dilemmas of his characters.

In the hands of Defoe and Richardson, the claim to realism, the illusion that the events of an observed social world can be transcribed onto the printed page, seldom progressed beyond the level of assertion. In nineteenth-century France, it was developed more methodically in the work of writers such as Stendhal, Flaubert, Maupassant,[16] and, most persuasively, Balzac. They, too, avoided engaging with the gap between the external world and its representation in the linguistic medium of the novel, but their comments on their craft demonstrate more self-conscious awareness of their chosen role of chroniclers of bourgeois society. In the preface to the *Comédie humaine* (1842), his encyclopaedic fictional inventory of the Parisian *mores* of his day, Balzac presents himself as the secretary who would document the social history of his world, doing for France what no one had done for societies such as Rome, Athens, Persia and India:

French society was to be the historian, I had merely to be its secretary. ... By keeping to rigorous reproduction, a writer could become a more or less faithful, more or less felicitous, patient or courageous painter of human types, the narrator of the dramas of intimate life, the archaeologist of social property, the namer of professions, the registrar of good and ill. (Bouteron 1951: I, 7; qtd Furst 1992: 29)

'Rigorous reproduction': the phrase closes down the gap between the painter/writer's representation and the world he purports to portray, though the slightest hint of doubt about the feasibility of this project creeps in in the repeated use of the words 'more or less'. There had been no such hesitancy, when Balzac had described his practice in the earlier *Le Père Goriot* (1835), where he writes, 'mark this well: this drama is neither a fiction, nor a romance. *All is true*, so true that each one of you can recognise its elements in his or her own home, maybe in his or her own heart' (Bouteron 1951: II, 848; qtd. Furst 1992: 30; emphasis in original).[17] Here the sense of closure is complete: in the appeal to affect as well as in the assumption that an external reality, here domestic, can be captured for the reader.

Unsurprisingly, comments such as this, which underpin his fiction, have made Balzac's novels a happy hunting ground for theorists who have interrogated the assumptions inherent in classic realism and, following in the wake of Auerbach, two of the twentieth-century's most influential commentators on realism, György Lukács and Roland Barthes, have focused their discussions of the mode on his work. Like Ian Watt, who sees individualism as a defining characteristic of Defoe's work, Lukács, writing from a Marxist standpoint in *Studies in European Realism* (1950), stresses the economic infrastructure of Balzac's pictures of his social world. Viewing him as a novelist who may seem to be focusing on the individual alone, he argues that he displays a complete grasp of how capitalism operates in society. In this reading of Balzac, he is the novelist above all others whose realism 'uncovers every stage in the concrete process of "capitalization" in every sphere (the periodical press, the theatre, the publishing business, etc.) together with all the factors governing the process' (Lukács [1950] 1964: 49; qtd. Furst 1992: 100). As Pam Morris puts it, 'What Balzac's writing forces upon our attention is the clotted thingness that constitutes modern social space. And for Balzac every thing declares its monetary value' (Morris 2003: 61). Watt's account of economic man in Defoe's work is similar to what Lukács is arguing here, since it locates individual lives against a backdrop of socio-economic forces, and both writers are suggesting that realism is tied up with a materialist praxis, but while Watt *keeps* the emphasis on the individual, Lukács focuses on the ways in which

Balzac sees individuals as representative exemplars of the all-pervasiveness of capitalism.

Barthes also takes Balzac as his subject in *S/Z* (1970), in which he provides a detailed structuralist analysis of Balzac's novella *Sarrasine* (1830). He identifies 561 narrative units in *S/Z* and sees these as operating within five codes through which meaning is produced. With regard to realism, *S/Z* is at its most interesting when Barthes makes a distinction between two types of text, the 'readerly' and the 'writerly' ([1973] 2002: 4–5), the kinds of fiction that conceal their *modus operandi* and the kinds that lay bare the mechanics of their practice. He locates Balzac in the former category as a novelist whose fiction normalizes the socially constructed as aspects of an unchanging human nature. Hence the title of his vast project: the '*Comédie humaine*'. But for Barthes, who takes a less sympathetic Marxist-oriented view than Lukács, Balzac's fiction promotes a bourgeois ideology that encourages passive consumption on the part of readers, particularly since the text provides a closure that endorses the *status quo*. As Catherine Belsey puts it, *S/Z* demonstrates how classic realist fiction 'moves inevitably towards *closure* which is also disclosure, the dissolution of enigma through the re-establishment of order, recognizable as a reinstatement or a development of the order which is understood to have preceded the events of the story itself' ([1980] 1989: 70; emphasis in original). This takes one to the heart of the way in which narrative teleology works in realist fiction. Tracing a movement from problem to solution, it characteristically, though not always, develops as a linear sequence, in which the mystery of the beginning generates suspense – what Barthes refers to as the proairetic code ([1973] 2002: 19) – which is resolved in the dénouement. Tzvetan Todorov ([1971] 1977: 44–8) sees the detective story as a paradigm of this kind of hermeneutic progression, and it is easy to see how the genre's conventions are applicable in fiction more generally.[18] In *Great Expectations*,[19] for example, Pip assumes that Miss Havisham is his mysterious benefactor, only to discover that it is a very different kind of megalomaniac, the convict Magwitch, who is actually the source of his promotion into the gentry. The narrative stems from the scene in the graveyard and clues are offered at various points along the way, but it is only in the latter stages that Pip discovers the truth about his situation, after which the other issues on which the plot turns can be neatly resolved: Miss Havisham dies, Pip is re-united with Estella, and social order is restored, just as surely as it is in an Agatha Christie novel, when Hercule Poirot gathers all of the suspects together to reveal which one of them is the killer. This, then, is how the thrust towards closure informs 'readerly' fiction. 'Writerly' novels, such as Sterne's *Tristram Shandy*, a text which foregrounds its own processes at every juncture and which has been described by Viktor Shklovsky as 'the most typical novel of world literature', on the grounds that art forms cannot be explained 'in terms of their motivation to exhibit a mode of life' ([1929] 1968: 89, 88), function in a converse way, by opening themselves up to readers, so that they become participants in the process of making meaning. Extending the analogy with crime writing, one can say that writerly fiction invites its readers to play detective, first in identifying exactly what the crime is and then in becoming investigators, who play an active part in working out the solution.

Elsewhere, as mentioned above, Barthes has spoken of 'the reality effect', the use of details, which lack any broader significance in a text and which are used as 'fillers' (1968: 84) to create an impression of 'the real'. Such details clearly operate in an opposite way to those that serve as clues in the hermeneutic progress towards a solution, though, depending on the social context and the way readers respond to them, they can still serve particular purposes. Thus, Barthes implies that in Balzac the intended metanarrative is the comprehensive depiction of bourgeois society. One also needs to add that the extent to which readers are passive consumers varies enormously, and although realist fiction may encourage an unquestioning absorption of its premises, some will read against the grain – Barthes himself is clearly one such reader, since his interpretation of *Sarrasine* dissects it to a point where it begins to surrender up its status as a paradigmatic realist text – and at the opposite extreme metafictive texts such as *Tristram Shandy* can conceivably be read for whatever social or other 'realistic' content readers can find within them. In the early pages of Sterne's novel, Tristram reports that the local midwife has 'acquired, in her way, no small degree of reputation in the world', a world which is said to comprise a circle 'of four *English* miles diameter, or thereabouts, of which the cottage where the good old woman lived, is supposed to be the centre' ([1759–67] 2003: 12; emphasis in original). Such detail may seem incidental and out of keeping with the main tenor of the novel, but it is possible to read it as a comment on the limited parameters of the North Yorkshire social world into which Tristram is born, or possibly even a reflection on the condition of England in the mid-eighteenth century more generally.

So opinions as to what constitutes realist fiction will vary and there can be no all-embracing definition. That said, there is a degree of consensus about the conventions that inform it. These include verisimilitude, a primarily referential use of language, specificity in the rendition of time, place and character, a concern with the everyday behaviour of individuals in recognizable social worlds, and closure in the form of endings which pull the threads of story together, usually, though not always, as the completion of a causal trajectory which, as in the classic detective novel, moves from problem to solution and in so doing reaffirms the social order. Additionally, and this is only sometimes the case, realist fiction may turn to present-tense immediacy of the kind that Richardson introduced into English fiction and, when it does so, this usually has the effect of injecting a sense of urgency into the situations being depicted. Again, this facet of realist fiction makes it particularly well-suited to representing urgent environmental issues, but it is, of course, only one way in which the aesthetics of realist fiction serve as a fulcrum for increasing awareness and stimulating debate about the ethical issues associated with the climate crisis.

These, then, are some of the characteristics of classic realism. However, the current situation is taking realist fiction into new territory and, while I have expressed reservations about Amitav Ghosh's claims that climate novels have been thin on the ground and that literary fiction is ill-suited to representing the crisis, his position does highlight the extent to which realism is evolving in response to hitherto unprecedented situations. Twenty-first century climate novels reflect both the physical dangers and the epistemological uncertainty of living on Eaarth, a planet on which the comforting conclusions, the detective story-like solutions, of classic realism, are no longer sustainable. Increasingly, realist climate fiction engages with the ethical challenge of representing the threats to the environment and the transformation that it is undergoing by refusing to run the risk of deferring engagement with the crisis through the use of dystopian and other futuristic narratives. With the possible exception of Ian McEwan's *Solar* (see Chapter 6), the varied texts I consider in this book share a commonality of purpose in that they detail the consequences of anthropogenic climate change, doing so within a plurality of forms of realism that continue to be focused on the place of individuals in society, but which frequently interrogate the Anthropocene assumptions inherent in such a focus. I begin by discussing Barbara Kingsolver's *Flight Behaviour*, which is set in a social world that is every bit as 'realistically' realized as Balzac's Paris, but through its focus on species migration, extreme weather events and soil erosion makes it clear that contemporary forms of realism rest on shifting tectonic plates.

1

'Weather as everything': Social realism in Barbara Kingsolver's *Flight Behaviour*

This chapter views Barbara Kingsolver's *Flight Behaviour* (2012), one of the most widely read and critically acclaimed climate fiction novels to have appeared to date, as a work in the tradition of classic social realism. In her acknowledgements at the end of the novel, Kingsolver, who has degrees in biology, ecology and evolutionary biology (Ballard and Hudson 2003: 330), writes, 'The biotic consequences of climate change tax the descriptive powers, not to mention the courage, of those who know most about it' (Kingsolver [2012] 2013: 598). However, she herself rises to the challenge of depicting climate change in a novel by demonstrating its impact on one of the social worlds that she 'know[s] most about'. *Flight Behaviour* employs a proliferation of everyday detail to underpin unusual events, occasioned by changes in the weather, that are happening in an insular community in the American South, and by setting what would hitherto have been regarded as extraordinary occurrences against a background of the ordinary, the novel provides a highly effective, realistic account of how climate change is affecting lives on a local level. More than any of the other novels considered in this study, *Flight Behaviour* accommodates what could well have seemed amazing events – some of the local community speak of the action that opens the novel as a 'miracle' – within the confines of a realism that adheres to the conventions that I have outlined in the introduction: verisimilitude, a primarily referential use of language, specificity in the rendition of time, place and character and a concern with the everyday behaviour of individuals in recognizable social worlds. Only its ending, an ending in which a climate-induced disaster strikes, makes a significant departure from a classic realist praxis.

Foremost among the unusual events is the unprecedented migration of a population of North American monarch butterflies into a rural Appalachian environment, and Kingsolver connects the disruption of the millennia-old ecosystems of the monarchs to climate change. Along with this, the farming community of the novel is experiencing unparalleled rainfall and, anticipating concerns that I will look at more fully in relation to Annie Proulx's *Barkskins* and Richard Powers's *The Overstory* (in Chapters 4 and 5), this chapter shows how *Flight Behaviour* also interweaves a debate about the merits and demerits of financially motivated logging that may lead to soil erosion with the environmental issues that lie at its centre. In the first part of the chapter, I offer an account of how the mimetic realism of *Flight Behaviour* operates: through circumstantial detail, analogical language, particularly similes drawn from mundane aspects of the novel's social world, and satire. Thereafter I consider the various ways in which Kingsolver introduces climate crisis issues into the novel, arguing that her treatment offers a convincing example of realist fiction's capacity to 'confront the centrality of the improbable' (Ghosh 2016: 23). The chapter concludes with a reading of the ending, which has divided critical opinion, and an assessment of what it can be seen to portend for the climate future.

Like most climate change fiction, *Flight Behaviour* is not a single-issue novel. It is also an incisive portrait of a community in the American South, drawn by a writer who both satirizes its perceived shortcomings and displays an insider's understanding of the mindsets of its members, mindsets which in several cases display unswerving loyalty to the ultra-conservative views of its opinion-leaders. The beliefs of this community, climate change denial among them, are brought into dialogue with those of city-based America, and for the most part, this is a dialogue of the deaf, because the local population holds entrenched opinions, which are reinforced by confirmation bias.[1] At one point, the protagonist, Dellarobia Turnbow, who has grown up locally in the environs of Feathertown, the Tennessee town where the action is set, but whose enquiring mind sets her apart from most of her peers, reflects:

> Why did people ask Dear Abby [America's most renowned agony aunt] how to behave, or take Johnny Midgeon's [a local radio presenter's] words on which men in D.C. were crooks? It was the same on all sides, the yuppies watched smart-mouthed comedians who mocked people living in double-wides who listened to country music. The very word *Tennessee* made those audiences burst into laughter, she'd heard it. ... Nobody truly decided for themselves. There was too much information. What they actually did was scope around, decide who was looking out for their clan, and sign on for the memos on a wide array of topics. (Kingsolver [2012] 2013: 228; emphasis in original)[2]

So confirmation bias cuts both ways. In conversation with a group of scientific researchers, working for an entomologist who has come to study the phenomenon of the displaced monarchs, Dellarobia thinks, 'There were two worlds here, behaving as if their own was all that mattered. With such reluctance to converse, one with the other. Practically without a common language' (209). Kingsolver, with her background in biological sciences, clearly evinces a preference for the informed, scientific side of this debate.[3] However, her capacity for representing the psychology of 'redneck' America – Dellarobia uses the derogatory term more than once (58, 187, 221) and it does not grate in the way that it might, because she writes with insider knowledge – coupled as it is with the provision of a welter of scientific and other information about the migration of the monarchs and climate change, enables *Flight Behaviour* to go some way towards bridging this seemingly irreconcilable divide, which is not the least part of the novel's achievement.

Kingsolver's skill in bringing places and people alive through an accretion of persuasive realistic detail is everywhere apparent in *Flight Behaviour*. It informs her accounts of activities such as sheep shearing, vaccinating ewes and cutting and baling hay, and it particularly serves to characterize the *mores* of inward-looking 'Bible Belt' Feathertown, which views the nearby town of Cleary as 'enemy territory', because it has a college, an aspect that makes Dellarobia's husband Cub and her in-laws 'prickly, as if the whole town were given over to the mischief of the privileged' (421). Like so many small American towns, Feathertown has seen better days. Its 'mostly dead main street' (524) has lost its drugstore, hardware, diner and small grocery to the power of Walmart, and throughout incidental details attest to its poverty. Dellarobia wonders whether her son Preston will realize that the government form they send to his school will identify him as one of the 'free-lunch kids' (126), just as she has been before him. Alongside the visiting student researchers, she sees her 'leather-soled farm boots' as 'redneck-poor' (187). She feels terrible that she has to feed her 'perfect dog' on 'poverty rations', thinking he 'should apply for a position in a better household' (233). In each of these cases, and this is true of virtually the whole novel, carefully realized detail is mediated by Dellarobia's consciousness. A pre-Christmas visit to the local dollar store, where she has a heated argument with Cub over what they can afford, provides an extended set-piece of the same order: Dellarobia is chastened as she looks through a shelf of previously viewed DVDs, feeling these are analogous to 'previously chewed meals' (220), by the temptation to buy cheap binoculars, and more generally by a sense that she is 'child rearing in the under-privileged lane' (230). Through such contingent detail, Kingsolver assembles a telling picture of what it is to live within the economic constraints of Dellarobia's social bracket, and at the same time gives a strong sense of the limits it places on the aspirations of someone who can envisage more. So, through a process of strategic selection and through the use of Dellarobia as focalizer, what on one level operates as a 'neutral' representation of a rural Appalachian community also emphasizes its poverty and, as Debra J. Rosenthal (2020), who considers the novel through an 'eco-poverty lens', has argued, climate issues and poverty overlap in the novel. Where Dellarobia's own family is concerned, these come to a head in a division of opinion on whether to clear-cut the forest on the hillsides above the town, which would expose them to the risk of mudslides. With their livelihoods threatened, Cub's father, Bear, is strongly in favour of this.

There is the same eye for detail in Kingsolver's rendition of natural phenomena, particularly the 'endless rain' (24) that floods the book from beginning to end, to a point where it almost feels wet in the reader's hands. Seasons seem to have disappeared. At one point, Dellarobia struggles to remember which month of the year it is and, along with Cub, feels that it is 'no season at all. The season of burst and leaky clouds' (116). The rhythms of agricultural life have been disrupted by the rain: hay has to be bought from Oklahoma, because all the local crop has moulded (457); rains have led to the increased use of chemicals, from which Dellarobia and Cub's neighbours, now organic farmers, believe that their son has contracted cancer (281); sheep have had to be pastured on higher ground, though what constitutes higher ground is itself called into doubt by the torrential rains (456) and the notion of 'a freak storm' is equally elusive, since it is a new norm 'in a freak new world of weather' (571). The evidence accumulates. There is no sense of a future apocalypse, simply the ubiquitous meteorological assault on the environment in the here and now, and in a *Time* magazine interview she gave, when *Flight Behaviour* was published, Kingsolver said, 'Climate change is not some kind of abstract future threat here. It is literally killing our farm economy' (Walsh 2012).

All of this circumstantial detail makes for a vivid portrait of a community facing unprecedented challenges and too set in its ways to have the wherewithal to combat them. The plethora of literal description is further amplified by Kingsolver's deft use of similes, which remain very much within the realistic mode of the novel, since they are drawn from the everyday. At the outset, establishing the register that will be used to describe the weather and natural phenomena throughout, the narrative voice expresses the opinion that 'Whoever was in charge of weather had put a recall on blue and nailed up this mess of dirty white sky like a lousy dry wall job' (2–3). Subsequently, on a rare day of better weather, 'gray clouds scurr[y] away to parts unknown like a fleet of barn cats' (27), and trees that are losing their leaves in a November that demonstrates that the 'world of sensible seasons had come undone' are said, in a simile reminiscent of Eliot's famous conceit at the beginning of 'Prufrock',[4] to be 'like a chemo patient losing her hair' (67). When the novel's incessant rains generate a new creek, it has 'clots of foam … like dirty dishwater suds' (189) and, working with a pipette, an instrument that is new to her, Dellarobia likens it to a cake-decorating device that her mother-in-law, Hester, uses (330). In short, such analogies inform the style of the whole novel, locating everything in relation to the daily routines of Dellarobia's domestic life, and they culminate in a passage in which she looks back to her situation in the opening chapter, a moment when she was contemplating embarking on an affair with a telephone repairman, and remembers that her existence then 'felt about the size of one of those plastic eggs that panty-hose came in' (471).

Kingsolver's other main deviation from narrowly descriptive mimetic representation comes in her use of humour, much of which satirizes the blinkered mindset of Feathertown, a metonym for conformist Southern church-centred society, an environment in which, 'if people played their channels right, they could be spared from disagreement for the length of their lives' (357). Using the satirical eye of Dellarobia, who is something of an outsider in her own community, as an optic through which to view shortcomings in Southern society provides Kingsolver with a highly effective third-person angle of vision for poking fun at the foibles of Feathertown's inhabitants. Again, she achieves her most telling effects through realistic minutiae, as in passages such as the following:

> Dellarobia sensed troubled waters at the Café in Christ. Crystal Estep had parked herself at a table front and center, all done up for church, the waterfall of gel-stiffened curls cascading over her shoulders. A regular Niagara of blond highlights was Crystal, sitting alone with her breakfast, gazing at it with such earnest focus, you'd think she was on a first date with that Pepsi and glazed doughnut. (79)

Similarly, talking to the visiting student researchers about Hester's unwillingness to make allowances, she tells them, 'If she were an undertaker, she'd tell her clients to quit whining and walk to the cemetery' (210). At the same time, she does not see herself as exempt from the values of the community. Towards the end of the novel, she remarks, 'Christ on the cross …. The rebel flag on mudflaps, science illiteracy, that would be *us*' (544; emphasis added) and throughout she turns to biblical parallels, among them references to Moses, Isaiah, Job, Lot's wife and Noah to characterize her situation. Such references are prominent in the episode with which the novel opens and in numerous passages that link the torrential rains the community is experiencing with the biblical Flood.

In the opening episode, Dellarobia is diverted from her anticipated affair by an epiphany in which the trees she sees on the mountainside above her home seem to be ablaze with an orange glow, and, conditioned by the biblical discourse that is commonplace in Feathertown, she thinks of Moses's burning bush and Ezekiel's vision of God.[5] The epiphany quickly supersedes her thoughts of escaping from her humdrum life through the affair and, without being aware of what she is witnessing, she recognizes it as a life-changing phenomenon, 'not just another fake thing in her life's cheap chain of events' (21). The orange in the trees will turn out to be a population of monarch butterflies which have deserted their normal migrating patterns to overwinter on this Tennessee mountain,[6] but, although she has not witnessed a miracle, as first Cub and then the Feathertown community more generally will claim, her sense that she has been '*born again*' (113; emphasis in original) proves to be true in that her encounter with the butterflies propels her into a chain of events which is at odds with the norms of the world into which she has been socialized. She has descended from the mountain with the sense that while she has not had any 'words to put on a tablet … like Moses she'd come home rattled and impatient with the pettiness of people's everyday affairs' (30). Searching for terms in which to describe her feelings to her friend Dovey, she falls back on the words of 'Amazing Grace', 'I was blind, but now I see' (45), while telling Dovey that her experience has not been religious. The community, following Cub, is less reticent and quickly appropriate it into their habitual Christian rhetoric as a 'miracle', while the pastor Bobby Ogle calls on Dellarobia to 'covenant' (94) – she is irritated by the misuse of the word as a verb – with the church congregation.

Predictably, for the local community, the torrential downpours evoke the Old Testament Flood – at one point a character asks, 'What do you think of this weather? Should we start building an ark' (221) – and this trope, a staple of much climate fiction,[7] also informs Dellarobia's response. Rain seeping under her kitchen door makes her feel 'the times seemed biblical' (169), and with their house, 'becoming a boat, her family launched out to sea' (170), she ponders what Noah's wife would do in this situation. However, for her, the notion of a flood also has other resonances: her experience of seeing the butterflies on the mountain is repeatedly referred to as 'a lake of fire' (23, 32, 60) or 'a flood of fire' (77) and this oxymoron again has the effect of foregrounding the extent to which abnormal happenings are challenging what have appeared to be elemental norms. The novel's immersion in the everyday is well equipped for 'confront[ing] the centrality of the improbable' (Ghosh 2016: 23). In a conversation with Dovey – characteristically set against the mundane task of her straightening Dovey's hair, while they listen to country music – Dellarobia tries to explain how the butterflies have veered off course because their DNA has sent them the wrong way (264), adding that perhaps this is something they should be worried about. Here this is a tentative statement, but the link between non-human and human animals, embodied as it is in the novel's title – both Dellarobia and the butterflies are in flight – is clear from the outset, and throughout there are parallels between the behaviour of non-human and human species. Kingsolver does not go as far as some of the other novelists discussed in this study, most notably Powers and Sinha, in challenging the notion of Anthropocene primacy: human animals remain the main protagonists of her novel. However, the novel's analogies between the butterflies and people – not just Dellarobia, but also a group of human migrants who have come to Feathertown from the Mexican town of Angangueo,[8] where the butterflies usually overwinter – posits a level of interdependence that interrogates anthropocentric views of the relations between species.

The distinctively realistic form in which *Flight Behaviour* is written is, then, a mode that helps to make the intrusion of the seemingly extraordinary into the ordinary credible and this provides the context for Kingsolver's representation of climate change, which operates on various levels. In Greg Garrard's words, climate change 'becomes knowable in two closely-linked ways in Barbara Kingsolver's novel: through the protagonist Dellarobia's cognitive and affective development as a character; and through the brilliantly-conceived symbol of the monarch butterflies, whose migratory life-cycle has been disrupted by global warming in the novel's storyworld' (Garrard 2016: 302). This is a useful entry point for a discussion of how climate issues are dramatized in *Flight Behaviour*, particularly because of its emphasis on Dellarobia's awakening being both cognitive and affective. It can be extended by examining the various strategies Kingsolver uses to impart specific climate change information and considering how the novel represents the arguments that revolve around the issues of logging and soil erosion.

Realistic descriptions of the depredations caused by the weather are complemented by passages that juxtapose the attitudes of the largely uninformed and resistant local community with the scientific expertise epitomized by the visiting entomologist, Ovid Byron, and his team of researchers. Dellarobia stands between the two camps as the tearing-point of the novel, the uneducated but intelligent conduit, who is the reader's main viewpoint on climate issues, after she has been initiated by Ovid, who sees 'weather as everything' (440). From Ovid, she learns about the factors that appear to have caused the changed migratory patterns of the monarchs and also about climate issues more generally and, in dialogues with others, she becomes the medium through which they, and by extension the novel's readers, are informed about the consequences of global warming. These passages run the risk of being seen as narrowly didactic, since, unlike the details of rainfall and the first accounts of the butterflies on the mountainside, they convey climate information very directly, but the seamless way in which they are introduced into the characters' conversations with one another avoids this.

This range of dialogues begins with Dellarobia, who has been told about the monarchs by the Mexican refugees and has researched them on the Internet, treating Byron to a lecture on their migratory patterns! Unaware of his expertise, she is subsequently embarrassed when she discovers it is his specialism in the field that has brought him to Feathertown. The passage works well, because of the human interaction involved, while also serving the purpose of supplying the novel's readers with a potted summary of the butterflies' life cycles. It is the first of several passages that do this, communicating information with varying degrees of specialist jargon. Dellarobia is subsequently given a more detailed account of the changes in the monarchs' seasonal behaviour by Ovid and his assistant Pete, and this account broaches different levels of complexity by moving between laypeople's language and technical vocabulary. As she listens to it, Dellarobia's role makes her an interlocutor, whose position is akin to that of the novel's readers:

> It wasn't easy for her to stay on the train of the conversation, even if they were running it for her benefit. Pete explained that in recent years their studies had found the [monarchs'] range was expanding northwards. Meaning the butterfly generations had to push farther into Canada to find happiness, Ovid added helpfully, probably astute to the fact that in her pay grade a range meant a stove. (202)

Later Ovid will explain to her more pointedly that they are witnessing 'a bizarre alteration of a previously stable pattern …. A continental ecosystem breaking down. Most likely, this is due to climate change' (315), and she will subsequently translate what she has learnt from him about the butterflies' disorientation into simpler language still for Cub, who remains loyal to the radio presenter, Johnny Midgeon, in his denial of climate change. Dellarobia tells him, 'It's like if every

Friday you drove to Food King, but then one Friday you did the same as always, followed the same road signs, but instead of Food King you wound up at the auto parts store' (359–60). So in addition to dramatizing the effects of climate change, Kingsolver also conveys hard information about its consequences through conversations that employ a range of registers, most of which serve to explain the science in everyday terms.

Something similar happens in her representation of various groups who come to the mountainside, after the butterflies' presence there becomes national news. Among these are three young Californian activists, initially introduced as 'from some international group with a number for a name. Something-dot-org' (349). The group in question is Bill McKibben's 350.org and, as mentioned in my Introduction, in her Acknowledgements, Kingsolver pays tribute to McKibben and his colleagues for 'the most important work in the world, and the most unending' (599), particularly mentioning the insights she has gained from McKibben's *Eaarth*, published two years before *Flight Behaviour* in 2010 and a clarion call to take action to save what is left of the planet formerly known as earth. Dellarobia does not know what the organization's name means, until Ovid explains, telling her that 350 parts per million represents the number of carbon molecules the earth can hold, and still retain its normal balance (383), adding, like McKibben (2010: 15–16), that this has already been exceeded and the current figure is about 390 parts per million (384).[9] It is another instance of Kingsolver introducing climate 'facts' into the text without making such interpolation seem contrived or disjunctive. In this case, the lesson Dellarobia receives is more extended, but again Kingsolver sugars the pill by framing it as a dramatic dialogue, with Ovid explaining scientific details in accessible language and Dellarobia contributing, both supportively and sceptically, as a voice of questioning common sense, who mediates the science involved for the reader.

Others attracted to the mountain by news coverage of the butterfly phenomenon include a group of English girls who come to stage a sit-in against the logging and extend this into one against global warming, which takes the form of knitting monarch butterflies from old orange sweaters, solicited via the Internet. When Dellarobia tells Dovey about this, her account hovers on the edge of satire, but nevertheless the details enable Kingsolver to introduce recycling issues into the novel. So too, does the project of another environmentally aware visitor, a retired city-dweller named Leighton Akins, who is travelling around America trying to get people to sign a pledge to change their lifestyle, so as to restrict the damage they are doing to the planet. When he engages Dellarobia with the various categories of his pledge, the tone is again tinged with humour. Exemplary though his undertaking is in some respects, their exchange is again a dialogue between two mutually exclusive Americas, as it becomes clear that much of what he is proposing has little or no bearing on the lives of those like Dellarobia, who, enmeshed in rural poverty, are unable to forego what they have never had in the first place, or are already acutely aware of his proposed actions, since financial hardship forces them to practise them as a matter of course. He advocates taking Tupperware to restaurants to bring home leftovers; she hasn't eaten in a restaurant for two years. He proposes recycling old computers; she doesn't have a computer. He tells her to find her local 'reuse' stores; she has no need to *find* them. He recommends planning her 'errand route' to drive less; she replies, 'Who wouldn't do that? With what gas costs?' (451–3). In short, the various aspects of Akins' pledge, appropriate though they may be for reducing the carbon footprint of profligate city-dwellers, are largely irrelevant to the lifestyles of the rural poor, and there is a particular irony in this, since Akins has said earlier that he wants to bring his message to areas such as the Appalachians rather than to Portland or San Francisco, patronizingly adding, 'You people here need to get on board' (434–5). So, again, Kingsolver is at pains to point up the limitations of urban views of the rural south and to foreground the very different effects that climate extremes have on the two Americas.

Arguably the most compelling of the conversations that convey climate science information to the reader comes when Ovid talks to the manipulative television reporter, Tina Ultner. Tina has previously interviewed Dellarobia about the 'phenomenon' she has witnessed on the mountain and doctored the material she has gathered by twisting what Dellarobia has said, so as to present her as someone who was saved from a planned suicide by the vision of the butterflies. Like the townsfolk, she and her colleagues seize on the 'miracle angle' (359), because it makes a better story. Instead of providing accurate information, they, in Pete's words, produce versions designed to 'shore up the prevailing view of their audience and sponsors' (317), and in so doing cater to the 'official view of a major demographic' that is unsure about climate change and requires stories about 'environmental impact … to be made into something else' (318). Again, confirmation bias is at work. Dellarobia is keen to have the record put straight, to see the distorted version of the issues surrounding the monarchs' relocation replaced by scientific fact. So, when Tina returns for an in-depth follow-up to her misleading original piece, she takes her to Ovid, who has been reluctant to engage with a media, which, as he will say to Tina, is 'allowing the public to be duped by a bunch of damned liars' (509). His attitude towards the kind of coverage she embodies is very much in keeping with Kingsolver's comment in her earlier essay 'The Forest in the Seeds':

> The things we will have to know – concepts of food chain, habitat, selection pressure and adaptation, and the ways all species depend on others – are complex ideas that just won't fit into a thirty second spot. Evolution can't be explained in a sound bite.
>
> Even well-intentioned educational endeavors like carefully edited nature films, and the easy access to exotic animals offered by zoos, are tailored to our impatience. (Kingsolver [1995] 1997: 241)

Ovid displays antipathy to Tina's glib trivialization from the start of the interview, and as they talk the temperature gradually rises. Piece by piece, he dismantles the assumptions in her ill-informed questions. He laughs at her sound-bite approach, when she asks him to tell her 'in a nutshell' (502) what has brought the monarchs to the Appalachians, lets her know she has 'missed the boat' (505), when she states that there is still disagreement among scientists as to whether global warming is caused by humans, and, building to a climax, informs her that scientists who cast doubt on it work for the same public relations firm that previously tried to discredit the link between smoking and cancer: 'They went off the Philip Morris payroll and into the Exxon pocket' (509). This is the most vehement of *Flight Behaviour*'s statements about climate change denial; it is also Kingsolver's most forceful use of a dialogue to put climate change information across and again it demonstrates her skill in turning what, in the hands of another writer, might have been tendentious didacticism into compulsive human drama.

Climate change issues are also foregrounded in a dialogic manner in the debate about the merits and demerits of logging that runs through the novel. Dellarobia's father-in-law Bear's plans to clear-cut the mountain to avoid financial ruin divide opinion in his family and the community, since the short-term economic benefits this promises come with a disregard for the possibility of landslides that will be increased by logging. There is recent local precedent for landslides caused by the extreme rainfall, and further afield more devastatingly in the Mexican town of Angangueo, where the butterflies usually overwinter and from which the displaced family, who have lost their home to a flood and a landslide, has recently come to Feathertown. The divisions of opinion brought about by Bear's proposal reflect debates about global warming that were still very prevalent at the time when *Flight Behaviour* was published. The would-be loggers in the community, advancing a typical anti-climate change argument, claim that a local flood has been a once-in-a-century event (235–6). Dellarobia, sensitized to the dangers of logging, takes the opposite view and again Kingsolver uses her perspective to provide a nuanced picture of both sides of the argument. Although she is far more aware of the need to practise economies than Cub, as becomes clear during their exchange in the highly appropriate setting of the dollar store, she tells him that clear-cutting is likely to cause a landslide. The debate over the safety of logging continues for much of the novel, with Cub gradually coming to see the sense of Dellarobia's viewpoint. It only gets resolved towards the end, when the pastor, Bobby Ogle, a figure who is satirized but, with Kingsolver again providing a rounded portrait, is ultimately neither unsympathetic nor a stereotypical Southern minister, comes down on the side of the anti-loggers. Again, Kingsolver's success in conveying ecological issues emerges from her capacity to bring them alive through a realistic representation of viewpoints that reflect the varied mindsets, both conservative and progressive, of a particular Southern community.

That said, *Flight Behaviour* is far from parochial, and the concerns that are troubling Feathertown can be seen as a microcosm of issues affecting the entire planet. Kingsolver gestures towards this in her choice of chapter headings that speak to various levels of larger community. Chapters 5 to 9 particularly illustrate this. Expanding the frame of reference outwards, they move from 'National Proportions' to 'Continental Ecosystem' via 'Span of a Continent', 'Global Exchange' and 'Circumference of the Earth'. Kingsolver's use of these titles can be playful – 'national proportions' appears in the text of the chapter that has this heading when Dovey mimics a television voice to liken Dellarobia's first meeting with Ovid to an encounter with Barack Obama: 'In a scandal of national proportions, the president was seen flirting today with a sexy Tennessee woman wearing pajamas outside the home' (148) – but the novel also forges links between Feathertown and the wider world in other ways. While, again, its success comes from its vivid rendition of everyday particulars, these are not isolated from worldwide events and at the end, as Dellarobia watches a flood engulf her house, radio commentary locates this against a background of widespread 'Flood and weather warnings, disasters. Something beyond terrible in Japan, fire and flood' (591). So the ending situates the local catastrophe that is destroying the world Dellarobia knows against the Fukushima nuclear disaster of 2011. While operating on an almost exclusively local level, Kingsolver steers her readers towards seeing her microcosm as a metonym for the global effects of climate change.

Prior to this, the novel has already appeared to reach a conclusion, when Dellarobia decides to leave Cub and go to college in neighbouring Cleary, partly financing herself through a lab job that Ovid has found for her. In one sense this is the culmination of a process that has been gathering pace since she first met Ovid. The novel uses names emblematically and his first name, which evokes the author of *Metamorphoses*,[10] is highly appropriate in that he has a transformative effect on Dellarobia. The manner in which he speaks to her makes her feel she is 'a different sort of person. Someone she would like to carry on being' (357), and when they first meet, he suggests a different possible provenance for *her* name, which brings with it the sense of an alternative possible identity for her. Her mother has named her after a wreath made from pine cones and acorns mounted on a polystyrene base, but he as it were elevates her by telling her Della Robbia was an Italian Renaissance artist. Now, in what looks like it may be the conclusion, she is about to break with the life she has known, leaving the solid unimaginative Cub, to join the ranks of college-educated America. This is disappointing in one sense, since it perpetuates the division between the two Americas, by suggesting that escape is the only road to self-realization for a questioning individual like Dellarobia; there is no possibility of finding fulfilment within a farming community like Feathertown. That said, it provides a fitting conclusion to that aspect of the novel, which, as Linda Wagner Martin sees it, operates as a *Bildungsroman* (2014: 1–20). It is not, though, the novel's last word, and what follows is both more ambivalent and more satisfying as a culmination of the novel's response to climate change.

In the closing section, the flood motif that has coursed through the whole novel provides a climax as the threatened deluge becomes a vivid reality, and the novel ends with Dellarobia, marooned on a hummock, surrounded by water and feeling that, like Columbus, she has become 'a tiny island nation of one' (592–3). Her fate uncertain, she looks down on her house which is fast becoming immersed. Her isolation is reminiscent of the trope of the last person in the world that is frequently used in post-apocalyptic fiction,[11] but here it is deployed in a situation that remains very much in the present and within the bounds of circumstantial realism. Critics have, however, debated exactly what happens at the end. Disagreeing with Linda Wagner-Martin's view (2014: 197) that Dellarobia dies, Debra J. Rosenthal writes, 'I understand the ending to indicate that Dellarobia survives and thrives' (2020: 280). Adeline Johns-Putra has no doubt that Dellarobia is facing 'impending death' (2017: 22–3) and takes Timothy Clark to task for suggesting that she survives, a view that he ties in with the comment that the ending involves a 'pointed *disjunction* between the individual character's story and the fate of the insects that would have made the text more provocative as a climate change novel' (Clark 2015: 178; qtd.

Johns-Putra: 23; italics in Clark's original). In Johns-Putra's view there is just 'such a disjunction – in Dellarobia's death and the butterflies' awakening' (23). These differing views raise two crucial questions: does Dellarobia perish, and what, in a climax that raises questions about the Anthropocene domination of the planet, is the relationship between her fate and that of the butterflies? Although the overwhelming majority of the monarchs have perished in the cold weather, a small colony has re-established itself in the dead peach orchard of the family that lives next door to Dellarobia and Cub, and this suggests the possibility of renewal for a fragment of the original vast population.

The novel is, in fact, very explicit in what it says about the butterflies and how their fate relates to Dellarobia's, and this leaves one wondering how perceptive critics such as Johns-Putra and Rosenthal, with their opposed viewpoints, have managed to misread it. Looking at the surviving butterflies, Dellarobia feels a sense of affinity:

> Their numbers astonished her. Maybe a million. The shards of a wrecked generation had rested alive like a heartbeat in trees, snow-covered, charged with resistance. Now the sun blinked open on a long impossible time, and here was the exodus. *They would gather on other fields and risk other odds, probably no better or worse than hers.* (597; emphasis added)

So the future is uncertain for both Dellarobia and the butterflies. Human and non-human protagonists stand the same chances of survival, and, amid the disaster, there is a ray of hope. Dellarobia looks up to the sky as the butterflies take flight 'to a new earth' in 'a merging of flame and flood' (597) that rekindles the vision of the novel's opening. It would be reductive simply to say that this challenges the Anthropocene order, but nevertheless the conclusion confirms the symbiotic relationship that has been inherent in the shared 'flight behaviour' of Dellarobia and the butterflies from the outset. In Serenella Iovino's terms, the novel belongs to 'what we can call an *interspecies literature*, a literature in which the representation of non-human animals or of the natural world is not hierarchically oriented, or not exclusively presented in an anthropocentric perspective' (2010: 44; emphasis in original). It is, needless to say, difficult for a human author to write from the perspective of a non-human animal, a subject I will explore further in my discussion of Richard Powers' *The Overstory* (in Chapter 5) and *The Man with the Compound Eyes* (in Chapter 12), and *Flight Behaviour* continues to use Dellarobia as the focalizer to the end, but nevertheless the relationship between human and non-human animals is conveyed in a manner that is not hierarchically loaded.

As I have been arguing throughout this chapter, *Flight Behaviour* succeeds because of the deftness with which Kingsolver handles particulars, and this holds true to the end. At the same time, through the use of references such as the allusion to Fukushima, the text lends itself to the possibility of a metonymic reading, in which the specifics of Dellarobia's small world represent planetary forces. If one interprets *Flight Behaviour* in this way, what conclusions about climate change, then, may reasonably be inferred from the ending? The answer would seem to be that, while the environment is rapidly being overtaken by the adverse effects of climate change, some form of renewal remains possible. In her *Time* interview, Kingsolver put it like this: 'I think every one of us operates in our various modes of denial. It's how we survive. We're made that way. You asked if I'm hopeful. I would say I'm not optimistic but I am hopeful because hope is a renewable option' (Walsh 2012). So, as has been the case with many climate activists, both at the time of the novel's publication and more recently, the message of gloom and doom is tempered by a ray of hope. The novel's ending suggests that disaster is with us and it is almost too late, but not quite if we act now. When *Flight Behaviour* appeared, there was arguably more need to combat climate denial, but the underlying issues have remained largely the same and Kingsolver's ending remains highly contemporary because it is open.

2

Seeking 'the perfect story': Metajournalistic realism in Helon Habila's *Oil on Water*

This chapter deals with the effects of oil excavation and extraction on climate in the global South, with particular reference to Helon Habila's *Oil on Water* (2010), a novel about the ruinous effects of a multinational company's exploitation of oil resources in the Niger Delta. After a very brief introduction to the genre of 'petrofiction', it offers a close reading of *Oil on Water* that pays particular attention to the distinctive mode of realism employed in the novel.

Again, Amitav Ghosh provides a departure-point. In his stimulating essay, 'Petrofiction: The Oil Encounter and the Novel', in which he reviews Abdelrahman Munif's *Cities of Salt* and *The Trench* (Ghosh [1992] 2005; Munif 1984 and 1987), Ghosh laments the dearth of fiction on the subject of oil, a claim that he returns to in *The Great Derangement* (2016). Just as he argues that literary fiction is ill-suited to the portrayal of climate change, he sees oil as a commodity that is resistant to artistic representation, in this case not simply in the form of the realist novel. In *The Great Derangement* he says, 'For the arts, oil is inscrutable in a way that coal never was: the energy that petrol generates is easy to aestheticize – as in images and narratives of roads and cars – but the substance itself is not. Its sources are mainly hidden from sight, veiled by technology, and its workers are hard to mythologize, being largely invisible' (Ghosh 2016: 74–5).

Earlier, in 'Petrofiction', he had offered similar explanations for the paucity of fiction about oil, arguing that 'the territory of oil is bafflingly multilingual ..., while the novel, with its conventions of naturalistic dialogue, is most at home within monolingual speech communities (within nation-states, in other words)' (Ghosh [1992] 2005: 142) and also suggesting that the 'displaced, heterogeneous, and international' world of oil frustrates the novel's penchant for 'luxuriating in a "sense of place"' (142). The argument seems dubious. Although it is clearly the case that oil transactions frustrate the boundaries of nation-states, the excavation and extraction of oil usually takes place in a particular country's territory or its coastal waters, and where literary representation is concerned, there are no obvious obstacles to oil's 'territory' being described in a single language (Ghosh himself does this), even though migrant labour is often employed in the industry, particularly in the Middle East.

Ghosh's claim also needs qualification in other ways. Munif apart, well-known novels such as Upton Sinclair's *Oil!* (1926–7) and Edna Ferber's *Giant* (1952)[1] are centrally concerned with oil, and Ghosh's own novels *The Circle of Reason* (1986) and *The Glass Palace* (2000) also include sections about the oil encounter. Beyond this, there are numerous other fictions that appeared before Ghosh's essay, which deal with the oil encounter. An article by Graeme Macdonald (2017) on *Cities of Salt* and Mackay Brown's *Greenvoe* (1972) mentions Rafael Jaramillo Arango's *Barrancabermeja* (1934), Ken Saro-Wiwa's short-story collection A *Forest of Flowers* (1986)[2] and Linda Hogan's *Mean Spirit* (1991), as well as *Cities of Salt* and *Greenvoe*, along with examples of the genre that appeared after the first publication of Ghosh's essay, such as Rilla Askew's *Fire in Beulah* (2001), Charles Red Corn's *A Pipe for February* (2002) and Habila's *Oil on Water*, which is just one of a number of novels that deal with the exploitation of oil resources in the Niger Delta.[3] So, although one could argue that, given oil's omnipresence in twentieth- and twenty-first-century societies, it remains underrepresented, there are numerous novels in which it does play an important role.[4]

'Petrofiction' is, then, a distinct sub-genre in its own right, albeit one which overlaps with cli-fi, because recent petronovels invariably represent the toxic effects of the carbon economy, particularly on the social imaginaries of non-Western communities. And in novels, such as Martinican Patrick Chamoiseau's masterpiece *Texaco* (1992, trans. 1998) and Nigerian-born Chris Abani's *GraceLand* (2004), in which oil is not ostensibly *the* central subject, it remains the pivot on which the plot turns, because the impact of the nation's oil economy is seen to weigh heavily on the lives of its socially dispossessed subalterns, whose environments are changed beyond recognition or who are internally displaced into 'new urban spaces' (Balkan 2015: 24).[5] Additionally, there are numerous novels, including *The Circle of Reason* and *The Glass Palace*, where oil figures prominently in sections that successfully demonstrate the 'displaced, heterogeneous, and international' world of oil, since migrant labour plays a key part in its extraction.

Ostensibly, Habila's *Oil on Water* is concerned with a very particular world: the landscape of the Niger Delta, which is suffering such major environmental damage from multinationals' oil exploitation that its microclimate has changed. This change may be local, but the damage being inflicted can also be read as a metonym for the consequences of anthropocentric, and more specifically Western, neocolonial economies that threaten the future of the planet generally and the global South in particular. At one point in the novel, the protagonist watches the film *Waterworld* (1995), in which the Earth has been almost entirely submerged as a result of the melting of the polar ice cap, and the characters, headed by Kevin Costner playing the part of 'a hated mutant, with gills and webbed feet' (Habila [2010] 2011: 101),[6, 7] live their entire lives on the water, dreaming of dry land. This post-apocalyptic setting is in direct contrast to that of *Oil on Water*, where the action is firmly rooted in the early twenty-first century and exemplifies the realist turn in climate fiction, albeit not without including postmodern metafictive passages, and this negates any possibility of seeing the issues it raises as futuristic fantasy about disasters yet to come. Habila's waterworld belongs to the here and now.

Oil on Water documents the impact of oil extraction and production in the Niger Delta through the eyes of a young reporter, Rufus who journeys into territory contested by various groups of militants and the army in search of the missing, assumed kidnapped, wife of an expatriate oil engineer. The search for the woman does not, however, turn out to be the main concern of the novel. Looming larger is Rufus's quest to forge meaning from the increasingly surreal world in which he finds himself. He is travelling with a once-famous, but now disgraced, older journalist, Zaq, whose decaying condition seems to complement that of the landscape, and when he asks Zaq what they seek, he is told that 'the story is not always the final goal'. This, Zaq tells him, lies in the 'meaning of the story', something that is only discovered by a 'lucky few' (5) and, like Rufus, who is puzzled by this remark, *Oil on Water* embarks on a quest to salvage meaning from the detritus of a landscape of polluted waters, abandoned oil equipment and deserted villages. In the later stages of the novel, Rufus and Zaq dig up a shallow grave on an island, Irikefe, which is centred on a religious shrine, maintained by a community of worshippers who seem apart from the moral collapse engulfing the region. The grave supposedly contains the body of the missing expatriate wife, but it turns out to be empty, and this in itself frustrates the possibility of a neat resolution of their quest at this point. The ensuing action, which has the worshippers telling Rufus and Zaq that a purification ritual of indeterminate length has to be performed, because they have desecrated a grave, further underscores the elusiveness of meaning, and the whole episode replaces expected presence, albeit presence in the form of a corpse, with an absence that has to be sanctified. So, while the mode of narration remains essentially realistic, Rufus and Zaq find themselves moving into hyperreal existential terrain.

When *Oil on Water* first appeared, reviewers related it to *Heart of Darkness*[8] and, although the seemingly mandatory necessity to compare any African river journey with that in Conrad's novella can prove reductive, there is an appropriateness here, since, like Conrad's Marlow, Rufus finds the culmination of his quest for a missing European is not what he expected, and the failure to achieve closure leaves a semantic vacuum. The 'meaning' of the story inheres in something else, in finding a way to make sense of the 'dense, inscrutable mist' (210) that pervades the atmosphere of the region and serves as a trope for the psychological haze that Rufus has to penetrate in order to understand the significance of the events he is experiencing. The novel begins with him in a mental fog, a fog of memory, through which he tries to reconstruct the happenings of an oil-related tragedy in his past. His father is guilty of having set fire to a barn full of drums containing oil, which, readers will later learn, he has been selling illicitly, and of killing or maiming a quarter of their small town's population, including Rufus's sister, Boma, whose face is left seriously scarred, and his friend John's father, who dies. The details are sketchy – they become clearer later in the novel – but this sets the tone for what will follow. The mental fog of this opening gives way to an actual fog that is enveloping the landscape and the canoe in which Rufus and his companions are journeying upriver. So the personal and the social overlap as Rufus struggles to make sense of both his own situation and the realities of the misty landscape through which he is travelling. *Oil on Water* is, then, an interrogative text, written in a realist mode that has affinities with the postmodern detective novel, a genre in which solutions to the mysteries being investigated remain elusive, and uncertainty is at the heart not just of Rufus's situation, but also the liminal predicament of the Ogoni villagers, who inhabit the Niger Delta and who are said to 'endure the worst conditions of any oil-producing community on earth' (108). Caught between multinational companies, the government, which is heavily reliant on oil revenues, and the various groups of militants, they are faced with having to choose between complicity in the oil economy and attempts to preserve their increasingly impoverished ancestral way of life.

As well as resembling a postmodern detective novel, Habila's spare account of the devastating effects that oil production has had on the Niger Delta has strong affinities with the related genre of investigative journalism, and using Rufus as the novel's focalizer provides Habila with a highly appropriate mode for reporting on the social and economic effects of the oil exploitation that has polluted vast swathes of the Niger landscape and waterways. So, although *Oil on Water* is not actual journalism, its use of a reporter as its narrator renders its distinctive form of present-day realism metajournalistic. Rufus has been inspired many years before, by hearing Zaq lecture on the role of 'journalists as conservationists [who] scribble for posterity', and 'maybe once in a lifetime [come across] a transcendental moment, a great story only the true journalist can do justice to' (73). The novel's approach to its story involves a similar impetus. It, too, speaks to conservation issues, both through its providing a record of older communal ways that are being eroded by the oil economy and through its attack on the despoliation of the environment. Later in the narrative, Zaq will suggest to Rufus that they should return to the state capital, Port Harcourt, complete with 'what is almost a perfect story. A British woman kidnapped by local militants who are fighting to protect their environment from greedy multinational oil companies' (135). The 'almost' is significant, since it seems clear that such a version would fall short of the once-in-a-lifetime great story Zaq has mentioned earlier. Habila's novel engages with narrative elements that could be shaped into a story of the kind that he is now speaking about, but it takes a different direction. Interestingly in this context, in a reading at the Library of Congress (Habila 2012), Habila spoke about how the novel had started life as a screenplay for a 'sensational' film based on the violence and kidnapping of foreign oil employees in the Niger Delta region in 2007 and provisionally entitled *Blood Oil*, by analogy with the Sierra Leonean-set Hollywood thriller *Blood Diamond* (2006).[9] However, his own primary concern was, he said, with the environmental damage being done to the region, which had led to the wholesale dispossession of farming and fishing communities in the course of a single generation. The upshot was that, when he submitted his first draft of the script, it became clear that he and the movie company involved had divergent views on what the film's focus should be and so they went their separate ways. Subsequently, he refined his material, which had involved a year's research, including interviewing inhabitants of the Delta region, into the novel that became *Oil on Water*.

This divergence is mirrored in the text itself, where the almost perfect story that Zaq proposes is similar to the movie company's expectations. As suggested above, initially readers are likely to assume that the quest to find the kidnapped wife is the central focus of the plot – Rufus himself imagines he will be writing an 'overwrought tale of ... daring adventure' (78) – but as the narrative develops, such a reading becomes unsustainable. The 'local militants ... fighting to protect their environment from greedy multinational oil companies' (135) belong to rival groups, some of which are self-serving, and they are engaging in turf wars rather than joining forces against the common enemy. Similarly, many of the region's villagers, enticed by the promise of the material benefits that will accrue from oil exploration and extraction, have been complicit in the exploitation of their environment, while the 'kidnapped' wife, Isabel Floode, has in fact left her husband, who has been having an affair with their maid, and run off with their driver, who is the maid's fiancé. So very little in the plot is as it may initially seem to be.

In short, the opaqueness and indeterminacy surrounding both the characters and the action appear to negate the possibility of the almost perfect story about kidnapping by environmentally sensitive militants that Zaq will later propose. The novel depicts a complex array of compromised actions that are a world away from this. Rufus still clings to the idea that the perfect story may be within his grasp and dreams of 'fashion[ing] a headline that would be worthy of such a great story, the perfect, inevitable headline, the one that gets your story on the front cover, an inch high' (146–7), but finds himself drawn into a world of uncertainties and blurred ethics that seem to rule out the possibility of any such narrative. The mode of *Oil on Water* mirrors this, operating as a self-reflexive narrative about the problem of constructing a story from the polluted murkiness of the oil-ruined landscape and waters and the human degradation that trails in its wake. Again then writing realist fiction in the Age of the Anthropocene propels the genre into new territory. From the first, Rufus's experience of the Niger Delta is traumatic and, although the account of his journey propels the present-day action forward in a linear manner, the narrative is disrupted by time-shifts and multiple backstories, which are integral to the action since they humanize the predicaments of the characters and show how they have arrived at their present situations. Habila has spoken of his own concern, as a third-generation Anglophone African writer, to tell individual stories rather than offer broad-based accounts of the state of the nation or its historical past after the fashion of pioneering first-generation novelists such as Chinua Achebe, who once famously wrote that he would be content if his work 'did no more than teach [his] readers that their past – with all its imperfections – was not one long night of savagery from which the first Europeans acting on God's behalf delivered them' (Habila 2012; Achebe 1988: 30). Needless to say, Achebe's characters are vividly individualized and any gap between his practice as a novelist and Habila's is at best a matter of degree, since synecdoche is at work in both cases: both novelists draw vivid portraits of individuals that have broader significance – in Habila's case in *Oil on Water*, illustrating the plight of the Ogoni people.

Habila's backstories move between being highly personalized and taking on broader communal relevance, but again there is seldom a clear distinction between the individual and the social, and also again, the stories are a narrative element whose importance is foregrounded through explicit metatextual references. In Zaq's lecture that has inspired Rufus, he has said that 'the best stories are the ones we write with tears in our eyes, the ones whose stings we feel personally' (135) and building on this, Rufus adds, 'To be a great reporter required a lot of suffering, a lot of back story' (135-6). Habila offers just such an approach in the novel, bringing his characters' situations alive through the use of backstories that document their past suffering. In addition to interpolating details of Rufus and Boma's earlier lives, the novel provides information about Zaq's rise to fame as a crusading young journalist whose articles brought about social change. Foremost among these articles has been a series entitled 'Five Women', which has narrated the stories of girls from the country drawn into prostitution when they come to Lagos. Written as an attempt to show the social change that Nigeria is undergoing, again a project that mirrors what *Oil on Water* is doing, these articles have triggered a strong emotional response from the public, which in turn has prompted action from politicians, international organizations and charities. For a time, Zaq's byline has been 'a magic formula' (123), but he has subsequently fallen from grace as a consequence of having had cocaine discovered in his luggage by British customs when he was entering the country with one of the women whose situation he had previously championed. Now his fiancée, this woman has had several liaisons with rich men in the interim, and the implication is that she has been behind Zaq's being found responsible for carrying the drug. He has served a prison sentence for this in the UK, but more significantly this episode has led to his decline.

This, then, is the backstory behind the situation in which Rufus finds Zaq, now a shadow of his former self, as they set out on their journey to try to find the missing Isabel Floode. It typifies the seemingly endemic corruption in which idealists trying to bring about a better Nigeria become enmeshed. Other backstories in *Oil on Water* show a similar loss of idealism and are more directly linked to the impact of the oil economy. Among these, the realistic detail lavished on the story of an itinerant doctor offers a particularly telling instance of the pernicious effects of oil. The doctor relates how, as a younger, more principled man, he was posted to a Delta village, where his attempts to educate the inhabitants and to minister to their health needs proved ineffective in the face of their poverty and desire for the material benefits of 'that fire that burns day and night' (91). Their wish was granted two years after his arrival, when commercially viable quantities of oil were discovered on the edge of their village and, now calling it 'the Fire of Pentecost' (92), they turned the spot where it burned into a quasi-religious site. The doctor's warnings of the dangers of oil pollution went unheeded, and a year later the village was suffering the consequences in the form of dying livestock and withering crops. Unable to persuade the villagers of the risks they were being exposed to, he submitted water samples containing high levels of toxins to the oil company, which paid him for these results but did not take any action. Subsequently, when people started dying, he took blood samples and sent them to the government, which filed them away, and then to NGOs and international organizations, which published his findings, but failed to influence the government to act, even though more people were dying. The main force of this detailed mini-history emerges not from the information about the lethal effects of oil production and the government's ignoring its impact on ordinary people's lives, but from the doctor's account of how it has affected him personally. He feels complicit in the exploitation that is being perpetrated and now travels from village to village, trying, with little success, to make communities 'in thrall to the orange glare' (92) aware of its deadly effects. Now, in the present, he appears seedy and overweight, and Rufus sees him as a man whose physical appearance is a correlative of the decadence he has encountered in the region.

A more communal backstory is told by Chief Ibiram, the leader of a settlement to which Rufus and Zaq are taken in the first part of the novel. He tells the tale of how he and his clan once lived in a close-knit, paradisaical village, where they were 'happily insulated from the rest of the world by their creeks and rivers and forests' (38), and unlike their neighbours, initially resistant to the oil companies' attempts to buy their land. In time, some of the village's families succumbed to the financial inducements offered to them, while the former chief, who refused to sell their land, was thrown in jail for purportedly supporting the militants. In jail he wasted away and died, allegedly after signing a contract to sell the village land to an oil company. Drilling began, and Ibiram and those of the villagers who had not sold out decided to leave, becoming refugees who have lived in five different places since departing from their ancestral village.

So Habila portrays an environment in which virtually all the characters have backstories of traumas brought on by the oil encounter, and beyond this by the murky sociopolitical world of Nigeria at large. As both narrator and protagonist, Rufus is the point where these various stories converge and, complementing what he is witnessing at first hand, the various told tales make him aware of the full extent of the disaster that is taking place in the Delta. The stories flesh out the situations he encounters and, as he listens to them, the text brings them alive as metajournalistic interviews, similar to those Habila conducted when researching the novel (Habila 2012).

As in *Heart of Darkness*, the most important part of the action takes place in the narrator's mind. Conrad's Marlow's journey into the interior is a voyage into terrain that challenges his view of existence. He tells his listeners:

> Going up that river was like travelling back to the earliest beginnings of the world, when vegetation rioted on the earth and the big trees were kings. An empty stream, a great silence, an impenetrable forest. The air was warm, thick, heavy, sluggish. There was no joy in the brilliance of sunshine. The long stretches of the waterway ran on, deserted into the gloom of overshadowed distances. (Conrad [1902] 1980: 48)

Rufus has a very similar response to the landscape through which he is travelling in the early stages of his river journey:

> After a while the sky and the water and the dense foliage on the river banks all looked the same: blue and green and blue-green misty. The whole landscape was now a mere trick of light, vaporous and shape-shifting, appearing and disappearing behind the fog. (Habila [2010] 2011: 4)

Both narrators undergo a journey of initiation, then, but there is a major difference in their attitudes towards their surroundings. Marlow sees himself as entering a primeval, pre-human landscape, only to learn that the *tabula rasa* of his imagination has in fact been penetrated by Western interference.[10] Rufus is aware from early on that he is travelling through an environment that has been ruined by neo-colonial human intervention. It is clear from the outset that the exploitation of the oil reserves of the region is dramatically changing not just the landscape but also its microclimate and the psychology of its inhabitants, as can be seen in the following passages:

> Soon we were in a dense mangrove swamp; the water underneath us had turned foul and sulphurous; insects rose from the surface in swarms to settle in a mobile cloud above us, biting our arms and faces and ears. (9)

> We were as soundless as a ghost ship, the roar of our motor muffled by the saturated air. Over the black, expressionless water there were no birds or fishes or other sea creatures – we were alone. (10)

Oil on Water: Habila's title succinctly encapsulates his novel's central concerns. In a reversal of the calming connotations associated with the phrase 'pour oil on troubled waters', the text represents the damage that oil is doing to the waters of the Niger Delta. Oil is all-pervasive: in a trope that embodies the title, a village well plays host to 'Something organic, perhaps human', but now 'dead and decomposing …, its stench mixed with that unmistakable smell of oil' (9);

a patch of grass is 'suffocated by a film of oil, each blade covered with blotches like the liver spots on a smoker's hands' (9); fish stocks are dwindling in the toxic river (17); gas flares are killing bats and other flying creatures (129). The deadly explosion caused by Rufus's father issues from factors beyond the company's control, since, as Rufus explains at the very beginning of the novel, although 'it was not a pipeline accident …, it might easily have been one, like in countless other villages' (3). An army Major douses a group of captive militants with petrol, threatening to set them alight and taunting them with the words, 'By the time I'm through with you, you'll hate the smell of it, you won't take money that comes from oil, you won't get in a car because it runs on petrol. You'll hate the very name petrol' (55). In short, the noxious presence of oil is everywhere, and, as Rufus is again told in the closing pages, the story of the consequences of 'the oil on the water' (210), not that of the supposed kidnapping and whereabouts of the missing Isabel Floode, is the one that he has to write. Earlier, Zaq has instructed him to inform people of the gravity of the situation and he commits himself to doing this, putting the larger issue of the destruction of the environment first, in much the same way as the novel demotes the obvious journalistic story of the quest to find and rescue Isabel to the sidelines in favour of a wide-ranging realistic depiction of the devastating impact of oil on individual lives. Again, then, a metanarrative element is to the fore: the way in which the story is to be told becomes the story.

Oil on water. While oil is the substance that is ruining the ecosystem of the Delta, water, in its unpolluted form, represents the possibility of a purer, organic environment. Rufus remembers how, in their youth, he and Boma used to go crab-catching in the sea, which seemed to offer the promise of a fulfilling life: 'Barefoot and underfed we may have been, but yet the sea was just outside our door, constantly bringing surprises, suggesting a certain possibility to our lives' (26). In the present action of the novel, water is altogether more ambiguous, but polluted though it is in many places, it can still be a source of renewal. Its potential for regeneration is hinted at throughout the novel, particularly in connection with the worshippers at the shrine on Irikefe Island who believe in 'the healing powers of the sea' (127), and at one point there is a nod towards a mythical water spirit who embodies various aspects of water. When soldiers capture Rufus and Zaq from one of the villages that they visit in the first part of the novel, the boats on which they take them away, *Mami Wata 1* and *Mami Wata 2*, are named after a mermaid-like water spirit, widely celebrated in West Africa and beyond. Habila does not expand on the possibilities suggested by the use of this name, but in Nigeria, Ghana and elsewhere, Mami Wata is represented in a plethora of ways. She can be a protective figure, linked with the healing sacred aspects of water and a conduit to material success through commerce, but she is also sometimes represented as a deadly siren-like figure, luring people to their doom (Drewal 2008), and this ambivalence is in keeping with the representation of water in the novel. The aquatic world of the Delta has been polluted by the activities of the oil industry, and many villagers have been co-opted into the new economy it has brought into being, but uncontaminated water continues to symbolize a pure organic existence, independent of Western and corrupt Nigerian government intervention.[11] Such purity is a thing of the past, but at the end of the novel, at the same time as Rufus is contemplating the actions of a group of militants who are sabotaging an oil refinery, he likens Chief Ibiram and his people to 'a fragile flotilla, ordinary men and women and babies, a puny armada about to launch itself once more into uncertain waters, braving the darkness in order to get to the light' and watches Boma joins a group of Irikefe worshippers in the water at 'a place of healing' (216). There can be no return to an uncontaminated, pre-contact ecosystem, but there is at least a tentative flicker of hope that enough remains of the older organic world of water to make renewal possible. Meanwhile Isabel Floode will return home, and in a fortnight her experience in the forest will be no more than a story to dine out on. She and her husband have ultimately been no more than bit-players in the tale that Habila has told, a tale that offers a more nuanced metajournalistic response to the exploitation of the subaltern population of the Niger Delta than the adventure story Zaq has suggested they should be writing. With little of the sensationalism that such a story might have contained, *Oil on Water* documents the tragedy of the Ogoni people and the damage to the region's ecosystem from its new human-induced microclimate in a cumulatively persuasive realistic mode. The novel has repeatedly foregrounded the question of how the story should be told. Ultimately, it answers this by subsuming its potentially postmodern indeterminacy within the framework of Rufus's quasi-journalistic narrative of what is happening in the region.

3

Apocalypse now? Visceral realism in Liz Jensen's *The Rapture*

When Liz Jensen reviewed Barbara Kingsolver's *Flight Behaviour* for *The Guardian*, three years after her own novel *The Rapture* (2009) had been published, she began by posing one of the central questions facing cli-fi novelists: 'Climate change: the spectre hanging over every child, is the single most urgent issue of our times – and a challenge to any novelist. But how to write fiction about the Earth's storm-filled future without a whiff of the pulpit?' (Jensen 2012). In *The Rapture*, at a time when recognition of cli-fi as a discrete genre was in its infancy, following Dan Bloom's coinage of the term just two years before the novel's publication, she had offered her own distinctive take on what a climate fiction novel might be in a psychological thriller that eschews 'the pulpit' and is primarily realistic, but introduces elements that smack of the paranormal. This chapter assesses the originality of the novel's narrative technique, the interaction of its apparently paranormal elements, for which a possible scientific explanation is provided, with its predominantly realistic mode, and its effectiveness as a call for climate activism.

In the years that followed the publication of *The Rapture*, Jensen was to become involved with campaigns to combat the climate crisis, and in 2019 she was a co-organizer of the 'Writers Rebel' group that held its first event as part of Extinction Rebellion's 2019 October uprising. The following year, after participating in a Zoom discussion on 'the role of storytellers in shaping the narrative and communal imagination towards action and engagement with the climate crisis' (Jensen 2020) as part of Wales Climate Week 2020, she again addressed the issue of *how* fiction could contribute to climate activism when she was asked by the Environment Editor of *Wales Arts Review*, Holly McElroy, about the effectiveness of post-apocalyptic dystopian novels in promoting climate change awareness. McElroy specifically raised the question of whether the reliance on fear that characterizes such novels makes them ineffective in motivating engagement with climate issues and referred to Jensen's advocacy of hope as a means of empowering people to take action to combat climate change. Jensen's response was, and is, highly relevant to her stance in *The Rapture*:

> The hopeful climate change novel is set in the near or distant future, it's full of ingenious, humorous people, living lives both utterly different and uncannily similar to those we live today, against backdrops that are far more luscious, varied and vertical than the landscapes we know.
>
> But I'd still like to come to the defence of dystopian fiction because I believe that it is also a path to hope. In positing worst-case scenarios, dystopian fictions are red flags. And without red flags – specific, embodied warnings of what might happen if things take a certain course, how can we picture the dangers we must avoid? (Jensen 2020)

The Rapture is set in the *near* future, just a few years after the date of the novel's publication, at a moment recognizably close to the present. The Copenhagen climate summit, which was held in December 2009, at the end of the year in which the novel was published,[1] is said, with predictable foresight, to have 'failed to deliver' (Jensen 2009b: 33), and the 2012 London Olympics are also a thing of the past, leaving the stadium free to provide a setting for the climax of the novel. At the same time, the action of *The Rapture* moves towards apocalypse and so, while this is not in the *distant* future, it serves as a 'red flag' alert to 'the dangers we must avoid'. Its vision of apocalypse in the near future and the '*uncanny*' (39; emphasis in original) clairvoyant powers that one of the two main protagonists, the psychotic teenage matricide Bethany Kroll, possesses are aspects of the novel that may appear to transgress the bounds of realism, narrowly defined, but the world in which it is set is recognizably in the long present of the early twenty-first century and in most respects its mode remains within the confines of classic realism, in that it adheres to verisimilitude, employs a referential use of language and is specific in its rendition of place, character and time.

Written in the present, a convention employed by certain novelists from early on in the English realist tradition, *The Rapture* communicates a particularly strong sense of the *immediacy* of the climate crisis. As discussed in my introduction, when the Puritan originators of the novel in England were tentatively laying the groundwork for a realist fictional praxis, Samuel Richardson stressed the importance of 'writing to the moment' ([1753] 1812: ix; Carroll 1964: 326) as a means of injecting dramatic immediacy, and, while Jensen's concerns and settings are a world away from the prurience of his claustrophobic interiors, her technique is similarly committed to that aspect of formal realism that engages with extremities in the present. The opening words of *The Rapture* convey a sense of mounting emergency by ramping up the actualities of the effects of global warming in England at the end of the first decade of the twenty-first century and projecting a reality that could be seen to be just around the corner:

> That summer, the summer all the rules began to change, June seemed to last for a thousand years, The temperatures were merciless: thirty-eight, thirty-nine, then forty in the shade. Old folk collapsed, dogs were cooked alive in cars, lovers couldn't keep their hands off each other. (Jensen 2009b: 3)[2, 3]

As the plot unfolds, there are numerous references to meteorological and geological disasters around the globe, where 'maverick weather [is] becoming the norm' (4), but, looking at a rural English landscape at one point in the novel, the narrator Gabrielle Fox says that it is 'unimaginable' that a major cataclysm can overtake an environment like this: 'There is no room for catastrophes in such a world. They cannot gain entry' (267).

Nevertheless, the novel concludes with Southeast England being devastated by an apocalyptic tsunami. So nowhere, it seems, is exempt from the possibility of catastrophe, and on one level the narrative refutes Amitav Ghosh's view that the realist novel is unsuited to addressing climate change because it is built on a 'scaffolding' that prevents it from 'confront[ing] the centrality of the improbable' (Ghosh 2016: 23) in the form of sudden disasters that stretch the bounds of credulity by contradicting gradualist notions of meteorological change. However, the gradualist effects of climate change and sudden disasters are not incompatible and Jensen also represents its steadily developing, all-pervasive consequences. Readers are repeatedly reminded that the seasons are changing – 'five years ago, the British seasons made some kind of sense. Not any more' (54) – and everyday life is affected by global warming: 'Venturing outside is an ordeal, something one must gear up to, armed with drinking water, sunglasses, cream, headgear' (124).

Much of the action pivots on the relationship between the violent Bethany, who is said to have a Nostradamus-like gift for predicting the future, and Gabrielle, a paraplegic who has been assigned to Bethany as her psychotherapist in Oxsmith, the maximum-security psychiatric hospital for adolescents where she has been placed, after stabbing her mother to death in a frenzied screwdriver attack, which has culminated with her ramming the screwdriver into her mother's left eye. Both protagonists are struggling to come to terms with trauma, and there is clear overlap between psychiatrist and patient. Bethany is initially completely unresponsive to Gabrielle's attempts to understand her, but it will transpire that her hostility has its roots in her childhood: she has been driven to the murder as a response to being tortured by both of her fanatical Christian fundamentalist parents and appears to be repressing knowledge of her act. The police psychiatrist who has examined her has commented, 'Elective amnesia as a form of denial, or refuge, is not uncommon among those who have experienced trauma' (11). Gabrielle, who has been involved in a car accident for which she feels guilty and which has left her wheelchair-bound, grapples with her own demons, mental and physical. At the outset, she says, 'Psychic revolution, worlds upended, interrogation of the status quo, the eternal proximity of Hell' are 'subjects close to [her] heart' (4). A specialist in art therapy, she has a print of Frida Kahlo's 'Autorretrato con Collar de Espinas' ('Self-Portrait with Necklace of Thorns') and strongly identifies with the Mexican artist, who like her was left wheelchair-bound after a car accident, but comments, 'She's an appalling role model. I am a Petri dish of nascent manias, many no doubt as poisonous as those that swarmed in Kahlo's head' (32). So, although she has not resorted to extreme violence, Gabrielle too is suffering from inner trauma, and, with the novel foregrounding the psychic as well as the physical disorder generated by the changed weather, the turbulence felt by both characters can be seen as a correlative of the anthropogenic climate turmoil that is threatening planet earth and specifically the Anthropocene order.

There is no real rapprochement between therapist and patient, but their situations, both of which are mapped onto the climate crisis, link them closely. Bethany's capacity to predict meteorological and geological disasters is complemented by her ability to see inside Gabrielle's mind and exploit her vulnerability, which is as much emotional as physical, by preying on her weaknesses. At the same time, Gabrielle quickly realizes that she needs Bethany, and when she is later suspended from her position at Oxsmith, she reflects that Bethany remains her 'job', saying that she 'is all I have left' (260). Nevertheless there is no sentimental resolution of their relationship. Talking about Bethany in an interview, Jensen has said that she 'set out to make her journey a very small one ... she doesn't really change very much', adding that if she attracts more sympathy as the novel goes on, 'It's the reader who does the emotional work of growing to like Bethany' (Jensen 2009a). Bethany remains psychotically dangerous, on a trajectory that will lead to suicide, and it becomes clear that there is no easy solution to her disturbed state of mind, any more than there is a simple answer to impending climate disaster.

Gabrielle wonders, 'Am I projecting my own internal dramas on the social landscape. or is there actually an atmosphere of recklessness in these long, overheated summer weeks?' (45) and the novel poses the same question, suggesting an affirmative answer to both supposed alternatives. In addition to overt remarks that link the psychological and the meteorological, there are various verbal echoes that develop parallels between the changes in the climate and the protagonists' personal situations. For example, words from the novel's opening sentence ('That summer, the summer all the rules began to change') are picked up when Bethany eventually tells Gabrielle about the circumstances that led to her stabbing her mother, and Gabrielle responds, saying 'Your mother's job was to protect you. That's what parents are supposed to do. … I can understand how you'd feel that the rules had changed', a sentiment with which Bethany for once concurs, repeating the words, 'The rules changed' (275). Here there is no suggestion of a direct causal connection, but the novel does draw explicit parallels between the disasters that Bethany predicts and the condition of her brain. At Oxsmith, she is being treated with electroconvulsive therapy (ECT) that gives her grand mal seizures, epileptic-like fits that are artificially induced and a side-effect of the electric force that is administered to her is that it seems to provide her with the power to foretell disaster. If this is so, the ECT provides a scientific explanation for what would otherwise be seen as paranormal. A parallel is drawn with van Gogh,[4] who in paintings such as his 'Starry Night' is said by the character Frazer Melville, a physicist with whom Gabrielle has a relationship, to have 'liked turbulence' and 'captured it in an almost scientific way' (99). Later this is developed with reference to a scientific paper which has argued that the production of van Gogh's most turbulent paintings coincided with his periods of psychotic anxiety and speculated that his epileptic fits may have given him 'a unique understanding of the physics of flow' (132). The suggestion in the paper is that the paintings reflect turbulence '*with a realism consistent with the way that a mathematic model characterises this phenomenon*' (131; emphasis in original). So, if this is correct and if it can be applied to the connection between Bethany's ECT treatments and her predictions, then there is at least a tenuous scientific explanation for what would generally be regarded as paranormal. Offering this possible explanation allows the novel, then, to stay within the realms of the possible, to retain at least a toehold on the empirically real. Beyond this, Gabrielle's predecessor as Bethany's psychotherapist at Oxsmith, Joy McConey, believes that 'She's not just predicting things! She's making them happen!' (95). Whether or not this is the case, Bethany is twinned with the series of disasters that she predicts with unerring accuracy. These include an earthquake that devastates Istanbul, destroying ten thousand buildings, among them the Blue Mosque, and a hurricane that strikes Rio, toppling the statue of Christ the Redeemer that overlooks the city, another quintessential landmark in another iconic city. Sceptics say some such events were likely and her prophecies could be based on information gleaned from Google, but the burden of evidence is against this, since, unlike Nostradamus, she provides precise dates and times which turn out to be true.

So *The Rapture* walks a tightrope between carefully nuanced, credible projections of a future that is just around the corner and, in both the personal and public spheres, schlock horror elements – the screwdriver in the eye; the fall of the statue of Christ the Redeemer – that maximize dramatic effects and push realism to its limits. Is it, then, reasonable to view it as realistic cli-fi? A comparison of its style with that of Barbara Kingsolver's *Flight Behaviour* (see Chapter 1) is instructive, particularly because some aspects of Jensen's prose have affinities with Kingsolver's. There is the same meticulous eye for detail and the same capacity for rendering weather phenomena through the use of tropes drawn from the everyday: in *The Rapture* thunder is said to be on 'a spin-and-tumble cycle' (60); a 'fierce sunball hangs low over Rio, French-kissing it, upending day and night' (80), as the hurricane approaches the city; in the dénouement 'the sun's glint giv[es] the air the translucency of a troubled onion glaze' (302). So, up to a point, the prose of *The Rapture*, like that of *Flight Behaviour*, is carefully rooted in day-to-day specifics, but even when it appears to be at its most 'neutral', it is more heavily laden with a sense of a world succumbing to entropy and decay than is the case in Kingsolver's novel. This can be seen in a passage such as the following, in which Gabrielle describes what she sees as she navigates her way through streets in the town outside which Oxsmith is situated. She uses her lightweight wheelchair,

> to trundle along the pedestrian area of Hadport, with its tiny boutiques selling candles and wind-chimes and horoscope jewellery and over-packaged soap, then into the shabbier side-streets of kebab outlets and newsagents, then past the cinema, the sports centre, the bird-spattered statue of Margaret Thatcher, and the elderly, pony-tailed New Ager selling fluffy worm-puppets on long strings. (34–5)

This is England in miniature, England in decline, an England in which even the New Ager is old, and as the episode continues, the scene is set in a climate change context by one of the novel's numerous references to the all-pervasive heat:

> After the downpour and the gales, the sun is back, a relentless fireball. The heat is abrasive, a hair-dryer with no off switch. Surfaces glitter in the shimmering

air. Everyone is wearing sunglasses. I can't think of the last time I saw anyone's eyes in daylight. (35)

The hair-dryer metaphor domesticates the hitherto abnormal, in a manner not unlike Kingsolver's use of such tropes in *Flight Behaviour*, but it accentuates rather than normalizes the harshness of the new meteorological 'rules' and this is typical of the style Jensen uses to convey a sense of the changes occasioned by global warming. In much the same vein, the passage that follows the 'spin-and-tumble cycle' metaphor cited above continues by referring to a view of the sky as 'operatic, the arms of the white windmills revolving intently in the distance, forked lightning cracking over the ink-pool of the sea, trees straining at the roots, their canopies stirred up like seaweed, sometimes a filament whipping off to become a missile' (60) and throughout the novel's prose resonates with the same high-decibel intensity.

Towards the end, Gabrielle says that when she had earlier been talked 'through the various stages of rapid climate catastrophe … it seemed too theoretical to be terrifying. But now the knowledge is visceral' (323–4), and this can be read as a self-referential comment on the novel's own practice, which provides its readers with a similarly visceral initiation into the potentially cataclysmic consequences of climate change. Jensen's style is, then, ultimately very different from that of Kingsolver, who achieves her effects by dramatizing how a disaster assaults the everyday in an almost matter-of-fact register. There is no such reticence in *The Rapture*, where Jensen has Gabrielle speak of having 'a visceral urge to draw' (61), and this makes for a narrative that is awash with nightmare imagery and hyperbolical language. When Gabrielle watches news coverage of the effects of the earthquake that strikes Istanbul, she writes:

> The pall of dust is clearing to reveal a choked wasteland, desolate as a hundred thousand Ground Zeros, dwarfing anything I have seen or could have imagined, a smoking, smouldering bleakness that stretches for kilometre upon kilometre […] Mosques, their domes popped open like puffballs, gape up at the sky. Thousands of people are entombed in rubble. (142)

Again, this is typical of the novel's taut, no-holds-barred style, and there is a welter of similarly supercharged language, when the tsunami, one of a 'vicious cycle', strikes in the eschatological climax, where 'the ocean [is] on fire', 'the sun's glare roasts the planet' and global warming has 'gone psychotic' (324). Climate apocalypse is happening now.

All of this is very pertinent to Jensen's question, 'How to write fiction about the Earth's storm-filled future without a whiff of the pulpit?' *The Rapture* steers well clear of one kind of pulpit, in that it excoriates millenarist Christian fundamentalism. It does, however, embed its eschatological theme in an eschatological form, suggesting that, in Frank Kermode's oft-quoted words, 'no longer imminent, the End is immanent' ([1967] 2000: 25). Bethany clearly feels the End is within her, since she constructs a narrative of self in which she has died and her body is 'slowly putrefying' (11), and in the climax she makes this immanent belief an actuality when she jumps to her death from a helicopter, in which along with Gabrielle and a small group of climate science experts she is escaping from the disaster that is engulfing Southeast England. In much the same way the novel moves at an accelerating pace towards the inevitability of an apocalyptic conclusion, with the implicit suggestion that this represents the climate change future. The immanent moment of the present is part of a plot-driven teleological structure.

Bethany's prophecies of apocalyptic events emanate from her own very individual psyche, but the novel also portrays apocalyptic thinking as being at the heart of the group thinking of two very different movements that are gaining followers in the wake of a global economic crash, suggestive of the banking crisis of 2007–8: the 'Faith Wave' and the 'Planetarians'. The Faith Wave is an American-originated fundamentalist group which now has 50,000 churches in Britain. Bethany's abusive father, Leonard Krall, has become a convert to it and as an evangelical preacher, who promotes a Manichean form of Christianity, sees Bethany as quintessentially and irredeemably evil and humanity more generally as being divided between those who will be damned and those who will be saved. This is associated with The Rapture, a millenarian strain of the Faith Wave, which promises the faithful that they will be transported straight to Heaven, when Armageddon strikes after a seven-year period of 'Tribulation' in which humankind will be punished for its sins. However, the disaster at the end is of a different order from the Revelations-inspired rhetoric of those caught up in the Faith Wave and close to that of the Planetarians, a group committed to a more scientifically founded form of eschatological thinking, which sees impending apocalypse in ecological rather than theological terms. Its spiritual leader is a renowned environmentalist, Harish Modak, who is a fierce critic of the Age of the Anthropocene and predicts that humanity is set to undergo either a new mass extinction or an extreme marginalization. Bethany's predictions have something in common with both groups. The discourse in which she frames them owes much to her upbringing. Like her father, who cites biblical authority for the coming of the Rapture, she draws on the Book of Revelation, along with Ezekiel and Thessalonians, but at heart she is completely at odds with her father's views, and, although she does not express allegiance to any particular ecological movement, she is said at one point to be 'singing from the same hymn-sheet' (58) as Harish Modak and the Planetarians.

The culmination of the climate disasters that Bethany predicts is triggered by a methane-induced catastrophe that results from an energy company's negligent exploitation of sub-oceanic hydrates. Jensen has said in an interview that she chose this, because she wanted a 'dramatic effect' from an event that could plausibly happen in the present rather than something that would affect our grandchildren and, talking to a geologist about the sudden global warming that led to an extinction fifty-five million years ago, she learnt that this had been caused by a series of earthquakes that released methane from the seabed (Jensen 2009a). Now at a time when people were turning to methane, referred to in the novel as 'the most dangerous greenhouse gas of all' (Jensen 2009b: 187), for energy, drilling for it was running the risk of unleashing 'the worst of the worst' kind of environmental disaster, something which could make 'tar sand look like a children's tea party' (Jensen 2009a).[5] Within the novel itself, the dangers of frozen methane are fully spelt out, when Gabrielle trawls the Internet for information and through conversations she has with experts. In much the same way that Dellarobia learns about the change in the monarch butterflies' seasonal migrations from Ovid Byron in *Flight Behaviour*, Gabrielle receives specialist knowledge from a number of authorities. In addition to Harish Modak and Frazer Melville, Kristin Jonsdottir, an Icelandic geo-palaeontologist, and Ned Rappaport, an Australian climatologist, are enlisted to provide information about the dangers threatening the planet, and this background is integrated into the text with no real 'whiff of the pulpit', providing answers to the kind of questions that many readers will be asking. Thus Ned Rappaport tells Gabrielle – and the novel's readers – that, while properly handled, methane could provide a solution to the world's energy problems, the companies drilling for sub-oceanic hydrates are 'playing Russian roulette' (212) and Kristin Jonsdottir explains that miscalculations could lead to a build-up of pressure that would unleash 'huge amounts of ... frozen methane' (227).[6]

Having laid the groundwork for the apocalyptic climax that Bethany has been predicting, in the closing stages of *The Rapture*, Jensen deserts the nuanced and realistic representation of climate issues, disability and trauma that has informed most of the narrative. This is replaced by a headlong rush towards a dramatic finale, as Gabrielle, Bethany and the small group of experts try, in the best traditions of that kind of thriller that relies on a few individuals to save the world, to avert disaster. Following a series of scenes that privilege suspense-based action, the novel reaches a climax in an iconic location, another staple of many action thrillers:[7] in this case the 2012 London Olympics Stadium, a venue which has offered hope to Gabrielle as she has watched the Paralympics while in rehab shortly after her accident. Now, though, the stadium has been appropriated by followers of the Faith Wave, thousands of whom have come to hear preachers such as Leonard Krall declare that the moment of the Rapture has arrived.

Jensen's prose remains compelling and few readers will deny that *The Rapture* is a page-turner, but its ever-quickening pace leans heavily on sensationalism, and this raises the question of whether the thriller elements run the risk of undermining the climate change message. Discussing the novel, along with Hamish MacDonald's *Finitude* (2009), Timothy Clark comments that 'extreme environmental scenarios unfold with a kind of remorseless logic whose effect of protest is undone by their aesthetic logic of increasing suspense, in which horror merges with a kind of gripping excitement' (2015: 182). In Clark's view, the novel's attempt at activist fiction is compromised by its increasingly graphic descriptions of catastrophe and its increasingly dream-like immersion in a form of Schadenfreude. So does *The Rapture* weaken its effectiveness as a climate change novel by employing thriller elements in a manner designed to generate the maximum amount of tension, at the expense of a realistic engagement with the climate present? Does it destroy credibility? Within the novel, Gabrielle raises a similar genre-related question in a conversation with Ned Rappaport. Talking about Bethany's visions, she acts as a spokesperson for empiricism, when she comments, 'How empiricists – and I include myself – disdain anything that smacks of the supernatural, of manipulative TV series, of low-budget believe-it-or-not, of strange-but-true' (225). Bethany's prophecies could be said to fall into this category and, as in her earlier novel, *The Ninth Life of Louis Drax* (2004), where the comatose boy protagonist is shown to be capable of inhabiting the minds of others, Jensen appears to be intent on suggesting to her readers that there are more things in the human mind than are dreamt of in their psychology.

The aspects of *The Rapture* that revolve around the conceit of Bethany's prescience do, then, seem to transcend the boundaries of realism, though, as indicated above, there is a quasi-scientific explanation for them in the suggestion that her ECT treatments may be a catalyst, in a manner similar to van Gogh's supposedly seeing visions as a product of his epileptic fits, and this speculative thesis is bolstered in scenes set in a remote Norfolk farmhouse where Bethany is given high-voltage treatments to help her release more information about the impending disaster. Pushing the envelope in this way threatens to undermine the credibility of the novel but leaves readers free to decide for themselves whether the putative explanation that is proffered is acceptable. Arguably, Clark's comments are harder to answer, since they involve a critique of the generic mode of the novel, particularly in its final stages, where the use of 'increasing suspense' is part of a more general commitment to formulaic thriller conventions, common to both fiction and film, namely mounting tension, an iconic setting and reliance on a few individuals to avert disaster. Now, with the stadium and the Faith Wave followers about to be engulfed by the rapidly approaching tsunami, in the best traditions of disaster movies where those who have engaged the audience's sympathies survive the general cull, the small band of characters – Gabrielle, Bethany and the various earth scientists – is allowed to escape by helicopter. As they do so, Gabrielle panics that she is losing her wheelchair, but even this is saved.[8] Thousands are about to die, but this is outweighed by the fact that the main characters escape.

Bethany will fulfil the death wish she has expressed throughout by jumping from the helicopter, and the other survivors face the prospect of eking out an existence in 'Bethanyland', a desolate post-Anthropocene world, which in Helen E. Mundler's words offers 'no hope of future redemption' (2012: 158). The oil rig responsible for the methane disaster has been named Buried Hope, and with the characters facing a daily 'rude, clobbering battle for survival and the permanent endurance of regret, among the ruins of all we have created and invented' (Jensen 2009b: 341), the future looks close to hopeless. This view is, however, partly offset by the fact that the paraplegic Gabrielle is pregnant by Frazer Melville, who is gripping her in his arms as Bethany falls to her death. Her pregnancy is rendered all the more poignant, since she has previously miscarried, but there is no movement towards a 'feel good' happy ending. Gabrielle has no illusions about the 'new earth' that awaits them. She sees it as a world she wants 'no part of. A world not ours' (341). Nevertheless, it is the world the child she is carrying must enter and, as is often the case in climate fiction, the trope of the child speaks to the climate future,[9] which is envisaged in terms of a diminished human condition. Harish Modak's thinking on the end of the Anthropocene era is relevant here. He has spoken of the human arrogance that believes the species will last forever, and he is an adherent of 'the notion of Gaia, the planet as a self-regulating organism with its own "geophysiology"' (36),[10] but the ending of *The Rapture*, unlike some of the other novels discussed in this book (particularly *The Overstory*, *Animal's People* and *The Man with the Compound Eyes*), remains locked within an exclusivist anthropocentric vision of a human society where 'there will be no green fields … no safe place for a child to play' (341). The novel is, then, far from hopeful and it dissipates some of its force through succumbing to the 'aesthetic logic of increasing suspense', but its visceral realism enables it to provide a powerful 'red flag' warning of the apocalypse that is looming *now*.

4

Tracing genealogies: Circumstantial realism in Annie Proulx's *Barkskins*

Annie Proulx's *Barkskins* (2016) is a multi-generational historical saga, which opens in 'New France' (later Québec, the Maritime provinces of Canada and parts of the north-eastern US) and which follows the fortunes of two families, the Sels and the Duquets (later Dukes) from the late seventeenth century to the early years of the twenty-first century. As such, it belongs to the long present of environmental fiction, in this case demonstrating continuities between the *past* and the present. The human and non-human genealogies that it traces – evolutions in forestry practices and attitudes towards trees, along with the changing nature of forest itself, are central to the novel – offer a loose causal explanation of one aspect of anthropogenic climate change, though this is only fully articulated at the end of the novel. Earlier it appears in sporadic, often overobvious statements, such as when an advocate of reforestation explains, 'The day will come, ... though it be difficult for you to believe, when timber is scarce and becomes more valuable than we can project', a comment which is underscored when the narrative voice adds, 'It forced the Board to think in new ways, on a scale of decades rather than months or a few years. Very frightening stuff' (Proulx [2016] 2017: 574).[1]

Barkskins opens with René Sel and Charles Duquet, two very different French émigrés, arriving in the New World in 1693 to work as *engagés* (indentured labourers), charged with the task of clearing an area of forest for their *seigneur*, Monsieur Trépagny, who sees it as his mission 'to subdue this evil wilderness' (17). In return they are to receive their own consigned plot of land after three years' service. They respond to their situation in diametrically opposed ways. Duquet runs away from the harsh treatment that he receives at Monsieur Trépagny's hands and nearly dies in the forest, but he survives to found an entrepreneurial dynasty, which over the course of the years will become a major player in the timber business, both nationally and internationally. René (Proulx calls him by his Christian name, a familiarity which she does not extend to Duquet) is much more attuned to the land. He remains a logger and marries a woman from the Mi'kmaw nation, whose culture is predicated on living 'in harmony and gratitude' (51) with nature, and their lineage, without always being overtly dedicated to environmental issues, is generally sensitive to maintaining an ecological balance. Through the course of the several hundred pages that follow, the stories of the two men's descendants alternate in a braided narrative that juxtaposes an anthropocentric linear account of material development, which, particularly in its nineteenth-century sections, resonates with the expansionist beliefs of Manifest Destiny, and a depiction of an animist way of life that challenges human exclusivism. While the two histories are not completely discrete, the Duke line of descent is primarily concerned with the unsustainable exploitation of natural resources, particularly timber, while the Sel family line, which is entwined with the way of life of the indigenous Mi'kmaw people, lives closer to nature, though Mi'kmaw beliefs and customs are shown to be suffering from attenuation as family members are increasingly assimilated into 'whiteman' culture.

Proulx's vast and sprawling novel develops these two histories using a technique which at its best, in passages such as the following, works within those conventions of realist fiction that conjure up a plausible rendition of events by using a register founded on deftly realized concrete particulars:

> They had a reckless style and could outhowl wolves. Duquet needed every paddling skill he had learned for some of the wild water they ran, between rock ledges that squeezed the canoe through violent chutes, and in one extraordinary place between two towering cliffs that leaned toward each other, narrower than the river so that the sky was a rock-edged slice. When they emerged from the pinching canyon the river hurled itself into a maelstrom. (66–7)

Similarly, when Proulx expounds on René's brother Achille's attitude towards the physical properties of different kinds of axes and different chopping styles, she writes in a vein reminiscent of the materialism that informs Defoe's *Robinson Crusoe*,[2] a foundational work for realism in the English novel and, as I have written elsewhere, 'a text in which everything can be assigned a material value, in terms of its weight, worth or magnitude' (Thieme 2001: 55). Proulx's use of discriminating detail to convey a sense of reality can be seen in passages such as the following:

He had several axes, including an old one that had belonged to René. Hard use had worn away much of the cutting-edge metal and the thick remnant dulled quickly. He wanted an American falling ax with a heavy poll and, if he had enough money, a good goose-wing hewing ax. … He thought of René and his inimitable chopping style. At this moment in among the big pines he missed him and wished they were cutting together again. Every chopper had his own way of doing the work, but René had been notable for quick light strokes with his very sharp ax; he could go on chopping for hours without tiring. As a boy Achille had found it difficult to chop in rhythm with him. (198)

Like much of the text, this appears to be carefully researched[3] and given its relevance to one aspect of the activities of the barkskins,[4] who, as the title indicates, have a central role in the novel, it is very germane. That said, detail is not always used effectively in *Barkskins*. The novel often suffers from its immersion in minutiae that do little or nothing to advance either the action or the environmental agenda that lies at the heart of the text. A sentence such as, 'Particularly was he irked by the example of William Wentworth, a growing power in New Hampshire whose wife produced sons as a shingle maker rived the shakes from a bolt of cedar' (127), appears to have little purpose, other than to display archaic word order ('was he irked'), presumably to suggest that *this* is how people talked in the early eighteenth century, and to provide the opportunity to introduce the vivid simile that links childbearing with the shingle maker's art. The Wentworths themselves remain ciphers who do not play a significant role in the action, and this is typical of the novel's penchant for introducing characters who swell its cast list, but have no more than walk-on parts. In the words of one of its early reviewers, Adam Mars-Jones, 'unnamed people without a connection to the narrative somehow earn a place in the text' (2016), and, as another reviewer, Anthony Cummins, put it, 'Of the dozens of characters featured in these pages, many are little more than names, with some introduced only to show how they die' (2016). On a single page Proulx manages to kill off a cook in the Chicago household of a branch of the Duke family, who has not been a major presence in the novel – 'Mrs Trane was gone, a victim of dropsy that made her legs swell to the size, shape and color of Boston harbor seals. She had suddenly fallen dead on the floor while kneading bread dough' (526) – replace her with a new cook, who will be equally undeveloped, with the seemingly self-sufficient comment that she 'was proficient enough' and let her readers know that other duties are being performed by a retainer who 'kept things in repair, tended the horses and yard, got drunk and roared on Saturday night' (526). The use of readily disposable characters is complemented by throwaway details that fail to rise above the level of anecdote. In the same paragraph, a 'distant New Brunswick cousin' arrives to take charge of the household, telling everyone 'freely and often that nothing in Chicago could compare with the virtues of New Brunswick' (526). The main purpose of such incidentals seems to be an attempt to convey to readers that this is how it was in that particular place at that particular moment in time. Otherwise, gratuitous information is introduced to lend an air of authenticity to the novel's evocation of the historical past.

Something similar happens when Proulx takes Jinot Sel, a nineteenth-century descendant of René and Mari, the Mi'kmaw woman he marries, to New Zealand/Aotearoa and, along with some persuasively realized information about the country's trees, introduces her readers to a smattering of Māori words:

> The dominant building was near the wharf, a trader's huge *whare hoka*. Next to this warehouse stood a chandler's shop ornamented with an old anchor for a sign. Two shacks leaned off to one side. The larger bore a sign that said NEW ZEALAND COMPANY. The houses of the *pakeha* traders and government men ranged along streets terracing the hillside. Behind a screen of distant trees was the Maori village – *pa* – fenced round with poles; farther back loomed a fantastic tangle of ferns, trees, creepers and exotic fragrances, a fresh world. (422; emphasis in original)

The insertion of Māori terms – two of the three are also rendered in English and so, one might argue, are effectively redundant – smacks of ethnographic local colour, and one has the sense of a writer, away from her usual terrain, unable to restrain herself from unloading researched information to provide an aura of authenticity, but without taking sufficient pains to make it relevant to the plot.[5] The local colour takes precedence and when, on the next page, readers are told, 'Mr Bone showed off some of his Māori words and amazingly, this man [a waiting Māori chief], his brown face a map of curled and dotted tattoos and clad in a sinuous flaxen cloak that tickled his ankles, understood some of the compromised phrases' (423), it is difficult not to relate this to Proulx's own 'compromised' introduction of Māori terms.

Proulx's use of contingent information, whether it is related to forestry, the fur trade, fishing, the drawing rooms of the Duke family or the habitus of Māori life, seems to be designed to create what Roland Barthes terms 'l'effet de réel' ('the reality effect'), the use of details which lack any broader significance in a text and which have been introduced as 'remplissages' ('fillers') (Barthes 1968: 84) to create an impression of 'the real'. For Barthes this is a challenge to his attempt to provide a comprehensive analysis of the structural elements that make up a narrative, but nevertheless a facet of the text that cannot be ignored. For readers who are less concerned with such structuralist taxonomy, the problem remains. Where *Barkskins* is concerned, it leaves one wanting to ask, 'What is the point of description which, whether or not it carries conviction for particular reading communities, appears to be introduced to validate the 'reality' of the narrative by including information that is extraneous to any of the central issues with which the novel is concerned?'

Barthes develops his position in relation to passages in Flaubert's story 'Un Coeur simple' ('A Simple Story') and *Madame Bovary*. He begins by focusing on a detail from 'Un Coeur simple', in which Flaubert writes that in a room occupied by one of the characters, 'un vieux piano supportait, sous un baromètre, un tas pyramidal de boîtes et de cartons' ('an old piano supported, under a barometer, a pyramid heap of boxes and cartons' [Barthes 1968: 84; my translation]). Subsequently, he argues that the depiction of Rouen in Flaubert's masterpiece 'est soumise aux contraintes tyranniques de ce qu'il faut bien appeler le vraisemblable esthetique' ('is subject to the tyrannical constraints of what must be called aesthetic verisimilitude' [Barthes 1968: 86; my translation]). In neither case, in Barthes' view, is there any relation to an external reality of the kind suggested in accounts of realism, which see it as operating through mimesis. The piano, barometer, boxes and cartons are gratuitous details; Rouen is conceived as a painting, an artistic construct that enables the novelist to parade a few refined metaphors. It is not difficult to come up with caveats to Barthes' comments – he himself says the piano could be seen as a marker of the bourgeois standing of its owner – and ultimately both the significance and plausibility of any passage of fiction will depend on its readers' responses – but his argument about 'realistic' detail that is effectively self-validating, since its primary function is to create an illusion of realism, by being irrelevant to the main issues of the text, remains persuasive. And this has resonance when one comes to consider the role of what strikes readers, such as the two reviewers quoted above, as unfocused circumstantial detail in *Barkskins*.

The proliferation of summary deaths in *Barkskins* is arguably the most striking aspect of its use of perfunctory detail and in passages such as the following, the novel seems to be revelling in the licence it allows itself to kill off characters with unseemly haste:

> The question of heirs began to disturb Lavinia's sleep when Cyrus and his family, as well as many Chicago people high and low, fell ill with typhoid. Cyrus perished in great pain with intestinal perforations. The children went one by

one and finally Clara, demented with grief and helplessness, fashioned a knotted loop in a heavy shell-pink silk scarf, stepped off a chair set on the dining room table and hanged herself from the chandelier. (534–5)

Such passages, which led one reviewer to describe *Barkskins* as a 'Baedeker of doom' (Garner 2016), inform the whole novel. What is one to make of such culling? Given that the novel spans numerous generations, it is of course inevitable that the death count will be high, but something more seems to be involved. Several of the deaths are particularly grisly and suggest a fixation not just with mortality, but also with the view that life is nasty, brutish and short. Even when the record of a character's passing is handled more gently, as is the case when Mari Sel dies, it remains cursory: 'One bright May morning Mari answered her long-dead sisters, who called her as owls call' (57). When Proulx was asked in an interview whether the abundance of arbitrary misfortunes and unexpected ailments that occur in *Barkskins* indicated that the characters were subject to the forces of a fate that was outside their control, she replied in the affirmative, adding that accidents were common in earlier times, particularly for those engaged in logging (Owens 2016). The death rate among both loggers and the rivermen who transport timber down the region's waterways in the novel is particularly high, but characters also die from a range of illnesses, shipwrecks and accidents in domestic surroundings, not to mention murder and suicide.

The best justification for this seems to be that, although the novel has a vast human dramatis personae, its most enduring and memorable protagonist is the forest, a constant amid the transient people that clutter its pages. Following Ursula K. Heise's comment that 'epic-style narratives over the last century have tended to shift the major narrative actants from individual human characters to collective and sometimes nonhuman actors' (2019: 301), one commentator has argued that *Barkskins* employs just such a collective protagonist (Nolè 2020). Arguably the forest is the most important element in this shift away from the individualism on which the English novel was founded, when writers like Defoe turned away from neo-Classicism's emphasis on the generality of experience and adopted the individualistic form of the autobiographical memoir. Now, the suggestion is, the wheel has come full circle and the anthropocentrism inherent in the novel centred on human individuals needs to be supplanted by a collective, in which the human animal is just one of many species. Proulx's main focalizers remain human, but their frequently short-lived lives are played out against the backdrop of the forest. From the outset its towering presence is said to have a 'narcotic effect' (5) on the newly arrived *engagés*, René Sel and Charles Duquet:

> Here grew hugeous trees of a size not seen in the old country for hundreds of years, evergreens taller than cathedrals, cloud-piercing spruce and hemlock. The monstrous deciduous trees stood distant from each other, but overhead their leaf-choked branches merged into a false sky, dark and savage. ...
>
> The forest had many edges, like a lace altarpiece. Its moody darkness eased in the clearings. Unknown plants and curious blossoms caught their eyes, funereal spruce and hemlock, the bright new-growth puffs at the tips of the pine branches, silvery tossing willow, the mint green of new birch – a place where even the sunlight was green. (4–6)

And this initiation into a new world is contextualized when their employer, Monsieur Trépagny, tells them, 'It is the forest of the world. It is infinite. It twists around as a snake swallows its own tail and has no end and no beginning' (5). At the same time, Monsieur Trépagny makes them aware that the native population is spiritually at one with the forest and, although he himself is battling to subjugate it, he suggests that failing to respect it is tantamount to sacrilege: 'When an alder branch tore Duquet's jacket, he swore in a low voice. Monsieur Trépagny heard him and said he must never curse a tree, especially the alder, which had medicinal powers' (6). Here, as elsewhere, Proulx is at pains to celebrate the distinctive qualities of particular trees, among them white birches, maples, redwoods, spruce, willows and cedars, as well as alders, and when, later in the novel, Jinot goes to New Zealand, Proulx waxes lyrical about the kauri tree, while towards the end she expands further to enumerate a range of tropical hardwood trees, which fall victim to 'the great onslaught on tropical forests', in which the expanded Duke company plays a leading role, 'taking all they could' as 'part of the new colonialism' (659).

At the end of the novel, Proulx appends family trees for the Sels and the Dukes, but these spill awkwardly across double pages and, in keeping with the novel's tendency to shuttle between different minor characters in a manner that will tax the memory of all but the most retentive readers, do more to confuse than to clarify the tangled farrago of human family relationships. Meanwhile, actual trees figure in the text in less complicated ways, enjoying a longer life-span than humans, and the time-scale of the novel enables Proulx to move from an account of the settler obsession with clearing the land to an explicit indictment of the Anthropocene exceptionalism, present from the first, that treats forests as commodities. Reflecting the dominant attitudes of the periods in which it is set, the novel, particularly in the Duke sections, travels from an account of the settlement of New France, which at times evokes narratives of how the American

West was won (in the later stages, the Duke business empire actually expands westward), to a contemporary critique of the materialism that is plundering the environment for short-term gain. Throughout, the despoliation of the forest is accompanied by the acculturation of the Mi'kmaq, but nevertheless their worldview offers a challenge to post-Enlightenment humanity's solipsistic separation of itself from the natural world's other species and, as Ben de Bruyn suggests, *Barkskins* offers the human animal an object lesson in 'learning to be a species' (2016). This emerges as a major concern in the attack on the Anthropocene that Proulx mounts in her closing pages, but it is present from the very beginning of the book in an epigraph she takes from Lynn White Jr's classic essay 'The Historical Roots of Our Ecological Crisis', which concludes, 'Before one cut a tree, mined a mountain, or dammed a brook, it was important to placate the spirit in charge of that particular situation, and to keep it placated. By destroying pagan animism, Christianity made it possible to exploit nature in a mood of indifference to the feelings of natural objects' (White 1967: 1205; Proulx [2016] 2017: ix). When the novel begins, this underlies numerous passages that represent the Mi'kmaw's spiritual response to the fauna and flora of their region and anthropocentric notions of species exclusivism are particularly undermined by references to the Mi'kmaw belief in therianthropic figures, such as Chenoos (cannibalistic ice giants) and loup-garoux (were-wolves), which erode human/animal binaries.[6]

As it moves towards a conclusion, *Barkskins* has a group of professionals coming together to replant forests and rescue polluted rivers, an activity which is presented as a contemporary development of the age-old Mi'kmaw reverence for the environment. Now, though, in a globalized world, they are joined by 'the children of indigenous forest residents' (706) from numerous countries, particularly native peoples from Asia and Latin America, who are seen as those best equipped to accomplish the task of healing. However, despite this emphasis on the role to be played by the descendants of indigenes, Proulx stops short of suggesting that there can be a return to an idealized pre-Columbian past. The central character in the closing pages, Sapatisia Sel, who has immersed herself in the study of botany and ecology, is a firm believer in the age-old Mi'kmaw ways of living in harmony with the rest of nature, but has no illusions about the possibility of being able to revive them in a world, in which pesticides, exhaust particles and acid rain have changed the very nature of the forest. She says, the plants that provided herbal remedies in the past 'grew in a different world ... surrounded by strong healthy trees, trees that no longer exist, trees replaced by weak and diseased specimens' (696).

The ending draws many of the novel's earlier strands together, albeit while extending them into more general commentary on climate change that runs the risk of descending into a vein of homily that is less persuasive than the earlier descriptive passages that have dramatized the consequences of deforestation. This is ratcheted up a further notch when, in the last couple of pages, Sapatisia travels to Greenland with a group of ice scientists and experiences an epiphanic shock, as she sees that the polar ice that she has assumed is an immutable part of the earth's make-up is melting rapidly. Previously, she has dismissed reports that the loss of biodiversity is a consequence of global warming as alarmist. Now she has to ask herself whether the planet is facing omnicide and the novel concludes with her questioning if the work of reparation is futile:

> 'What can I do but keep on trying? But what if it was all for nothing? What if it was already too late when the first hominid rose up and stared at the world? No!' What she and so many others were doing was working, it had to work. So many people trying to repair the damage, so selfless many of them caring and trying. And the forests themselves trying to grow back. (713)

The shift in this passage from human to arboreal agency is interesting. While Sapatisia is the main focalizer for Proulx's final peroration, trees have been at the heart of the novel throughout, outliving the humans that come and go through its pages, and perhaps *this* justifies the almost casual way in which people are killed off. As in Richard Powers' *The Overstory* (discussed in the next chapter), where this line of thought is developed in a more sustained way, there is the suggestion that human existence is ephemeral in comparison with the complex longevity of trees. Now, though, the overlapping ecosystems that make up the natural world are threatened by anthropogenic climate change.

Earlier Proulx has largely confined herself to the issue of deforestation and, lengthy though the novel is,[7] she said in one interview that she felt that any broader engagement with climate change would have been beyond its compass and her capacities: 'After several decades of thinking and observation I wanted to write a story about climate change. That subject was too large and difficult (for me, anyway) to serve as the foundation for a novel. So I chose to write about one facet of climate change – deforestation' (Clay 2017). However, in another interview she was less reticent about the extent to which *Barkskins* engages with the climate crisis, saying that 'rather than calling it an environmental novel I think of it more in the sense of a writerly nod to human interplay with climate change, what some in the humanities and arts are beginning to think of as a cultural response to the environmental changes we have inherited in the so-called

Anthropocene'. This follows on directly from her saying, that for her, 'the chief character in the long story was the forest, the great now-lost forest(s) of the world. The characters, as interesting as they were to develop, were there to carry the story of how we have cut and destroyed the wooden world' (Leyshon 2016).

These remarks help to counter the comments I have made above about her perfunctory erasure of characters. If one sees the novel's humans not as protagonists, but as bit players in a text that is primarily concerned with the decimation of the forest and the concomitant climate tragedy, then what may seem gratuitously circumstantial can be seen to be part of a different genealogy, a genealogy concerned with the longevity of forests, which is now under threat, not the transient transfusions of human bloodlines and the capitalist commodification of nature. *Barkskins* remains a tale of two human families, but, read simply as such, it descends into a series of short stories that are handled with varying degrees of success. Read teleologically as an indictment of deforestation and, in its conclusion, as a cautionary summons to action in the present, it is altogether more satisfying as a climate change novel, even if its range is restricted and its structure meandering. A mantra repeated by character after character in the novel, especially those in the Duke family line, is that forests 'replenish themselves' (96); they are 'everlasting' (96), 'infinite and permanent' (364), but by the end of *Barkskins* it is clear that sustainability and reforestation are essential to the future of the planet, and Proulx's rhizomatic trajectory has reclaimed trees from being seen as exploitable commodities. In the early stages, even René Sel never questions the need to clear the land, and his attitude is directly contrasted with the Mi'kmaw perspective of his wife, Mari:

> They stood opposed on the nature of the forest. To Mari it was a living entity .... She believed the interminable chopping of every tree for the foolish purpose of 'clearing the land' was bad. But that, thought René, was woman's talk. The forest was there, enormous and limitless. The task of men was to subdue its exuberance, to tame the land it grew on – useless land until cleared and planted with wheat and potatoes. It seemed both of them were subject to outside forces, powerless to object in matters of marriage or chopping. (50–1)

Confirmation bias leaves both characters locked within their community's beliefs, but the novel transcends these mindsets by successfully representing both the chopping mentality of the settlers, and the reverence for the natural world engrained in Mi'kmaw ways of thinking, and the conclusion looks forward rather than backward as Sapatisia advocates 'approach[ing] questions from the viewpoint of the forest' (705). *Barkskins* ends, then, by both emphasizing the gravity of the climate crisis, particularly when Sapatisia experiences the melting of permafrost in the Arctic at first hand, and by entering a plea for reforestation to combat the damage that, it is now apparent, has been chronicled from the opening chapters. Proulx's preoccupation with the 'realist effect' muddies the water along the way, but if this has convinced readers of the verisimilitude engrained in her long trawl through the history of post-Columbian responses to New World timber, then perhaps this is a reasonable price to pay for the concluding coda, which is a clarion call for a movement towards a post-Anthropocene climate praxis.

5

'Trees are social creatures': Encyclopaedic realism in Richard Powers's *The Overstory*

The *Booklist* reviewer of Annie Proulx's *Barkskins*, Donna Seaman, referred to it as 'nothing less than a sylvan *Moby-Dick*' (2016), a comment that is even more appropriate as a description of Richard Powers's *The Overstory* (2018) since Powers's encyclopaedic novel goes further still in doing for trees what Melville's *magnum opus* did for whaling.[1] That said, *The Overstory*'s representation of the interaction between humans and non-human species is very different from Melville's account of Ahab's predatory pursuit of the white whale. Margaret Atwood has said, '*Moby Dick* as told by the White Whale would be very different ("Why is that strange man chasing me around with a harpoon?")' (1972: 74), which suggests one way of reversing the anthropocentric stance of Melville's novel, but although Powers's narrative is concerned with illustrating trees' agency, and particularly their role in maintaining ecological balance, *The Overstory* does not offer any sustained attempt to use them as focalizers. It does, however, do so in a section at the very beginning of the novel,[2] in which a woman 'in a park above a western city after dusk' – presumably the character, Mimi Ma, who will be seen in such a spot at the end of the novel[3] – listens to a tree 'saying things, in words before words' (Powers [2018] 2019: 3) and these utterances are extended into a chorus of tree voices, which sets the tone for what will follow by telling her, 'Your kind never sees us whole' and listing some of trees' innumerable contributions to earth's well-being: '*Creating the soil. Cycling water. Trading in nutrients. Making weather. Building atmosphere. Feeding and curing and sheltering more kinds of creatures than people know how to count*' (4; emphasis in original). Similarly, in the introductory section to the third of the novel's four parts, 'Crown', trees emit a series of explicit messages concerning climate change: black spruces '*put it bluntly*: Warm is feeding on warm. The permafrost is belching. The cycle speeds up', and '*Noisy aspens and remnant birches, forests of cottonwoods and poplars, take up the chorus*: The world is turning into a new thing' (443–4; emphasis in original). *The Overstory* is arboricentric throughout, but in the main body of the narrative, with the exception of passages such as these, the novel uses human focalizers – nine people, whose lives are entwined with trees in various ways. This entwining is conveyed through an interplay between dramatized action, particularly as seen in the struggle of environmental activists to prevent loggers from destroying ancient Redwoods in California, and reflective passages, especially those in which Powers uses his character Patricia Westerford, a pioneering plant biologist, as a mouthpiece to relay the beliefs of 'new forestry'.[4] Gradually, the initially discrete lives of the human characters begin to intersect, though some never meet and even the unifying cause of trying to prevent the logging of ancient trees in episodes based on events that took place during the so-called 'Redwood Summer' of 1990[5] only brings five of them together. As Patrycja Austin puts it, the novel 'breaks the convention of following the story of an individual protagonist in his or her self-development and focuses on multispecies encounters, communication, and care' (2020/21: 25–6). Its trajectory displays an increasing sense of interconnectedness – among trees, among the human characters and between trees and the planet's many other species – and a vast amount of evidence is marshalled to make the case that 'trees are social creatures' (153) that collaborate as collective units, networking together underground and nurturing all forms of sentient life, including human beings. As such trees emerge as life-forms, which, although they are endangered by anthropocentric exclusivism, particularly manifest in deforestation and climate change, act as the lynch-pins of reciprocal ecosystems, which are the antithesis of the economically driven, short-term human activity that is inflicting major damage on non-human animals and plants, as well as *homo sapiens*.

The Overstory is, then, an encyclopaedic introduction to dendrology and particularly, to borrow the title of one of the texts that has influenced Powers, to 'the hidden life of trees' (Wohlleben [2015] 2017). Yet, despite the proliferation of realistic researched detail within its pages, unlike Annie Proulx's *Barkskins* (see Chapter 4), which offers a comparable attempt at a wide-ranging portrayal of arboriculture, the novel avoids succumbing to the Barthesian reality effect, the introduction of details, which lack broader significance and appear to have been brought in solely to create an illusion of 'the real'. Here, directly or indirectly, everything contributes to the central purpose of demonstrating the crucial role that trees play in sustaining life on earth. The tree references included in sentences such as, 'But the clerk sells him an orange, a chocolate bar, and a cup of coffee, three priceless tree treasures that get him to the public library' (234) and 'The smell of her red cedar pencil elates her' (276–7) appear incidentally, but they typify the way the novel deploys contingent particulars to show that trees are ubiquitous. Elsewhere casually introduced information goes further in conveying the message that trees are life-sustaining, as when the Vietnam War veteran, Douglas Pavlicek informs two strangers he encounters in a roadhouse, that they are living in the 'Age of Wood' and tells them that, in addition to putting 'Lotta greenhouse gases … to bed', trees are used in the manufacture of shampoo, shatterproof glass, toothpaste, shoe polish, ice-cream thickener, buildings, books, boats and furniture' (231).

It is impossible, in a discussion such as this, to convey the *cumulative* force of the huge amount of detail that informs *The Overstory*'s engagement with trees. One can only give a sense of how its essentially realistic, and at times quasi-factual, technique operates by offering a summary of ways in which Powers demonstrates trees' pivotal role in virtually every aspect of life on earth. At one point, in language suggestive of animist Native American discourse, Patricia Westerford addresses a western red cedar as a 'Long Life Maker', and thanks the tree for the numerous everyday essentials it provides: 'the baskets and the boxes … the capes and hats and skirts … the cradles. The beds. The diapers. Canoes. Paddles, harpoons, and nets. Poles, logs, posts. The rot-proof shakes and shingles. The kindling that will always light' (170). Later in the novel, she offers a similar, slightly more specialist inventory of products that come from trees, when she delivers a lecture at a conference on 'Home Repair'. On this occasion, she mentions, 'Waxes, fats, sugars. Tannins, sterols, gums, and carotenoids. Resin acids, flavonoids, terpenes. Alkaloids, phenols, corky suberins', and goes on to suggest that the creative capacities of trees are constantly expanding: 'They're learning to make whatever can be made. And most of what they make we haven't even identified' (565). Elsewhere, readers are told about trees that 'migrate' and trees that 'remember the past and predict the future' (368). They learn that there are 'so many substances in woodland pharmacies that no one has yet identified' (275), that Californian sequoia are 'five times larger than the largest whale' (331) and, a point that is made on numerous occasions in the novel, that the longevity of many tree species makes human existence, and by extension, the Age of the Anthropocene, no more than a passing moment. Towards the end, in a familiar trope, the history of life on Earth is likened to a single day, in which '*modern man shows up four seconds before midnight*' (592; emphasis in original).[6] In Patricia's lecture she puts the matter particularly succinctly, when she shifts the emphasis away from the view that man is the measure of all things,[7] by saying '*This is not our world with trees in it. It's a world of trees, where humans have just arrived*' (530; emphasis in original). She also refers to the probability of a sixth

Great Extinction, after which trees are likely to return, as they have after each of the previous such events: 'Five times at least, she says, the tree has been dropped, and five times it has resprouted from the stump. Now it's toppling again, and what will happen this time is anybody's guess' (611). Meanwhile, as a safeguard to ensure the rebirth of trees in a future world, Patricia starts a seed bank as a botanical ark 'to preserve those tens of thousands of tree species that will vanish in our lifetimes' (408). The importance of this project is underscored in the title of the final part of the novel, 'Seeds', which is the culmination of the tree-focused progression that has been developed in the titles of the novel's previous parts: 'Roots', 'Trunk' and 'Crown'. Now, at a moment in the novel when activism against logging has proved abortive and the majority of the human protagonists have suffered fates (death, disfigurement, serious illness and imprisonment among them), which seem to be a trope for the failure of individuals to reverse the damage humankind has inflicted on the planet, hope is rekindled in the form of seeds that may germinate in the future. Like trees, seeds are said to have a longevity that can far outlive humans: A two-thousand-year-old Judean date palm seed has been found in Herod the Great's palace on Masada and campion seeds buried under permafrost in Siberia have begun to grow again thirty thousand years later (489). So Patricia's seed bank, preserved in the vaults of a Colorado mountain, is an attempt to ensure the continuation of life, whatever lies ahead,[8] and its future is made more secure, when it 'becomes a legal person' (408). Previously, in another challenge to Anthropocene exclusivism, the issue of the judicial rights of plants has been the subject of contrary opinions. The psychologist Adam Appich, as yet unreconstructed with regard to awareness of the nurturing, social nature of trees, brushes aside what he terms 'plant personhood', when his research advisor tells him that 'we're living at a time when claims are being made for a moral authority that lies beyond the human' (297). In contrast, the property lawyer, Ray Brinkman 'wants trees to be rewarded for their intellectual property' (309) and another lawyer, the father of Olivia Vandergriff, who at the outset of the novel is herself a student of actuarial science, rebuffs her comment that 'You can't own the rights to a living thing!', by telling her 'You can. You should. Protecting intellectual property creates wealth' (202).

Each of the novel's nine human protagonists is connected with a particular tree, and in the first part, 'Roots', they are introduced in separate chapters that open with a reproduction of a nineteenth-century steel engraving of the species with which they are associated. Thus, the very first chapter links the artist Nick Hoel with a chestnut, which is the sole survivor, on his family's Iowa farm, of a blight that has killed all the chestnuts in the Eastern United States. The Hoel Chestnut takes on an iconic status as a *'sentinel tree'* (12; emphasis in original), a landmark in its neighbourhood, and its growth across a period of eighty years is captured in animated motion in a flip-book made up of a series of photographs taken by members of different generations of the family. Again, this suggests the enduring qualities of trees. Similarly, Douglas Pavlicek's life is saved, when his plane is shot down over Cambodia, by a banyan tree that breaks his fall to earth. Made up of 2,000 trunks and with origins that the novel traces back 300 years to the moment when a wasp laid eggs that fertilized the green fig for which they were destined, the banyan is said to be 'a sacred tree bigger than some villages' (102) and under its influence, when Douglas subsequently discovers the extent of clear-cutting in North America, he becomes a life-long convert to the cause of reforestation. These are just two of the characters' links with particular trees. Among the others, Mimi Ma, the daughter of a Chinese Muslim immigrant and a woman from the American South, is associated with the mulberry tree that her father cultivates as a silk-farm; Adam Appich, the youngest of four siblings, each of whom has their own tree, is fascinated by the variety of life in a maple; Neelay Mehta, the brilliant paraplegic son of an Indian Silicon Valley programmer, is inspired by a Queensland Bottle Tree in the Inner Quad of Stanford University and Patricia Westerford, whose career will involve researching many species of trees, is especially linked with Douglas-firs: 'an ecosystem unto themselves, hosting more than a thousand species of invertebrates. Framer of cities, king of industrial trees, that tree without which America would have been a very different proposition' (178).

The remaining three protagonists, whose respect for trees is less obvious at the outset are, nonetheless, also linked with specific trees. Introduced with the sentence, 'They're not hard to find: two people for whom trees mean almost nothing' (80), the couple Ray Brinkman and Dorothy Cazaly, are swiftly found tree connections: Ray becomes an oak when he plays Macduff in an amateur production of *Macbeth* and travels across the stage as part of the branch-bearing forces that migrate from Birnam Wood to Dunsinane to defeat Macbeth; Dorothy is connected with a particular tree in a more immediately physical way, when she crashes her car into a parkway linden. Lastly, Olivia Vandergriff is associated with a *Ginkgo biloba* (Maidenhair) tree, which she has passed by night after night, without ever noticing it. It is left unnamed in the chapter which introduces Olivia, but a reference to it as 'a singular tree that once covered the earth – a living fossil, one of the oldest, strangest things that ever learned the secret of wood' (183) and the steel engraving heading to the chapter that introduces Olivia establish its identity, which will be confirmed when she later adopts the name of 'Maidenhair'.

These, then, are the trees with which *The Overstory*'s main human characters are associated. The novel also makes reference to numerous famous trees, relating some of the trees that figure in its action to these. Among the famous trees that are mentioned are the historic Hundred-Horse Chestnut on Mount Etna (11), reputedly the oldest chestnut tree in the world, Old Tjikko (277), the Norway spruce in Fulufjället National Park, Dalarna, Sweden, whose root-system is more than 9,000 years old, and mythical trees such as the Buddha's Bo Tree, *Ficus religiosa* (232), a portal to Enlightenment, and Yggdrasil, the World Tree of Norse mythology. The Hundred-Horse Chestnut is linked with the Hoel chestnut. For Patricia, Old Tjikko teaches the lesson that the world is not made for human utility, while the Bo tree evokes the Buddha's words: 'A tree is a wondrous thing that shelters, feeds, and protects all living things. It even offers shade to the axmen who destroy it' (277). Yggdrasil is seen as an archetype for the Redwood 'Mimas' (327–30), in which Olivia and Nick live for months to stop its being felled by loggers, and Mimas is also linked with the Buddha, when trunks growing out of its main line are said to be 'shooting up parallel like the fingers of a Buddha's upraised hand' (330). In short, Mimas is invested with mythical overtones as it becomes the World Tree, but at the same time the contingent details of Olivia and Nick's tree-sit, partly based on the experience of Julia 'Butterfly' Hill,[9] who occupied an ancient 55-metre-high Redwood she named 'Luna' for two years, are realized in concrete realistic terms. Like Julia Hill, an account of whose tree-sit appears in her book *The Legacy of Luna* (2000), Olivia and Nick anthropomorphize the tree by giving it a pet name. Also, like Hill, they embark on their occupation as a stopgap measure to prevent the tree's being chopped down and end up staying for a protracted period, and they are threatened by a helicopter, which in their case, unlike that of Hill, who photographed and outlasted an intimidating helicopter that she would later describe as causing a 'cyclone' (Hill 2000: 82), forces them down from the tree.

The Overstory's encyclopaedic range of reference also involves an extensive use of intertexts, relating to tree lore and ecological issues more generally. This is particularly embedded in the thinking of landmark American environmentalists such as Aldo Leopold, whose work on wildlife management did much to reverse earlier attitudes to wilderness as a site for predation and exploitation, and John Muir, who was a moving force in the founding of Sequoia and Yosemite National Parks and a staunch advocate for the preservation of wilderness. Both are invoked on several occasions in *The Overstory*. Muir was associated with Ralph

Waldo Emerson and, beginning with the first of the novel's epigraphs, taken from Emerson's 'Nature' – 'The greatest delight which the fields and woods minister, is the suggestion of an occult relation between man and the vegetable.' (Emerson [1836] 1911: 4; Powers [2018] 2019: ix) – Transcendentalist intertexts also play a prominent role in situating *The Overstory* in relation to classic American Nature discourse. Thoreau figures on several occasions, most notably when Neelay undergoes an epiphany, as he realizes that Mastery, the globally popular virtual reality game he has devised, is 'rotten at its core', because it is founded on the premise of ever-expanding, pyramidal growth that lacks an 'endgame' (512). He comes to this realization as a result of reading Patricia's book, *The Secret Forest*, which draws on the writing of Suzanne Simard, on whom Patricia's character is loosely based,[10] and Peter Wohlleben's *The Hidden Life of Trees*, and imagining an on-screen chestnut, reminiscent of the Hoel chestnut, undergoing a 100 years of coming to maturity in twenty seconds, 'like a scene in a hand-cranked kinetoscope' (543). The passage is dense and not without ambivalence: it goes on to invoke 'old chestnut words of extinct Transcendentalism' (543), so the screen image of an actual tree and the notion of an 'old chestnut' as a hackneyed piece of information merge. Overall, though, the sense seems to be that a return to the Transcendentalist reverence for nature, however 'extinct' it may initially seem to be, needs to supersede the imperialist acquisitiveness that is endemic in Mastery. Neelay's future-world needs to be informed by an earlier American philosophy that promoted a harmonious relationship with Nature. Just as the image of the screen chestnut contains continuities that have begun a hundred years earlier, Neelay is effectively putting the clock back, when, conflating two separate passages, he turns to Thoreau's writing for inspiration and, wresting them from their original prose contexts, re-envisages them as quasi-poetic mantras:

> The gardener sees
> only the gardener's garden.
> The eyes were not made
> for such grovelling uses as they
> are now put to and worn out by,
> but to behold beauty now invisible.
> MAY
> WE
> NOT
> SEE
> GOD?

(Powers [2018] 2019: 544; Thoreau [1849] 1961: 325, [1862] 1996: 58)[11]

Other nineteenth-century figures mentioned in *The Overstory*, who had affinities with Transcendentalism, include Whitman – '*A leaf of grass is no less than the journey-work of the stars*' (Powers [2018] 2019: 9; emphasis in original; Whitman ([1855] 1957: 51) is cited in the opening pages – and the legendary nurseryman Johnny Appleseed (John Chapman), described here as a 'crazed Swedenborgian' (200). Olivia feels she is treading in Johnny Appleseed's footsteps, as she travels west, guided by voices that are leading her to a new life. Sleeping in an Indiana parking lot 'that was once an orchard full of unpredictable apples' planted by Johnny Appleseed, she thinks of the 'arcane magic' of his hand that 'transformed a swath from Pennsylvania to Illinois into fruit trees' (202).

The Overstory also includes an extensive range of non-American intertexts, among which two are particularly central. James Lovelock's *The Revenge of Gaia* (2006)[12] is referred to directly by Douglas in a conversation with Adam in which they look back on the apparent failure of their earlier activism (539), and long before this, a passage from Lovelock's *Gaia: The Practical Science of Planetary Medicine* (1991), quoted as one of the epigraphs, has helped to set the tone for the whole novel: 'Earth may be alive: not as the ancients saw her – a sentient Goddess with a purpose and foresight – but alive like a tree' (Lovelock 1991: 12; Powers [2018] 2019: ix).[13] Complementing this, and arguably the most pivotal of all the novel's intertexts, are references to Ovid, which, with their emphasis on transformation and the fusion of species, radically undermine the notion of human exclusivity. On Patricia's fourteenth birthday, her father gives her a copy of *Metamorphoses*, which from the moment when she reads the first sentence, '*Let me sing to you now, about how people turn into other things*' (147; emphasis in original), leaves her feeling that, though the stories are 'odd and fluid', they are also 'somehow familiar'. Most tellingly, imbued with sentiments that are in tune with Lovelock's Gaia hypothesis, she also finds that 'the fables seem to be less about people turning into other living things than about other living things somehow reabsorbing, at the moment of greatest danger, the wildness inside people that never really went away' (147).

Elsewhere, I have written about pre-Enlightenment and postcolonial representations of the figure of the therianthrope that reverse the demonized ways in which it is generally seen in post-Enlightenment Western contexts, where it characteristically appears in incarnations such as the vampire and the lycanthrope, and I have argued that such reclamations of the figure strike at the heart of the notion that humans are superior to other species (Thieme 2017). As part of that argument, I focused on the erosion of animal-human binaries embodied in the protagonist of Indra Sinha's *Animal's People* and in the present book, I return to Sinha's novel to examine this transgression in the context of localized climate change (see Chapter 7). In *The Overstory*, the use of a number of therianthropic tropes offers a similar interrogation of the Anthropocene: protesters blocking a road in Oregon don animal costumes and engage in a carnivalesque dance that reminds onlookers of the first books they ever read, in which 'all things were possible and real' (290). Similarly, at one point during her stay in Mimas, Olivia, here referred to by her forest-name of Maidenhair, is said to be dancing 'like some mythic beast' (324). At the same time, the animist poetics of *The Overstory* go beyond the therianthropic in their challenge to a view of species in which humanity stands at the pinnacle of the chain of being. Early on, tree trunks are likened to elephant trunks (117) and more generally there is an erosion of the distinction between humans and trees. As a young girl, Patricia feels that trees are 'the lost kin of humans' and, linking the human with both flora and fauna, she makes 'twig creatures' (141) from parts of trees. Later, when her father gives her the copy of *Metamorphoses*, she is fascinated by the myths in which people become trees – Daphne, Cyparissus and Myrrha among them. She is especially moved by the story of Baucis and Philemon, an old couple, who, alone in their town, extend hospitality to Jupiter and Hermes, when the gods visit them in disguise. For this, the two gods reward them by granting them a form of immortality, which allows them to live on after death intertwined with one another as trees – an oak and a linden. This particular arboranthropic (my coinage, by analogy with therianthropic) conjunction is played out in the novel in its account of the relationship between Ray and Dorothy. Related to an oak and a linden from the moment when they first appear, they are particularly linked with Baucis and Philemon in the conclusion, when Ray dies and Dorothy reads the story of the Greek couple in another book by Patricia, *The New Metamorphosis* (620). Speaking to Ray's corpse, Dorothy tells him that she will be with him soon. So the suggestion is that the harmonious union they have struggled to achieve as humans will now occur through their metamorphosis into intertwined trees. And the assumption of tree identities is also transformative for each of the characters who protest against logging in the central action. Olivia, who has been drifting through college without a clear sense of purpose and who has narrowly escaped death when she accidentally electrocutes herself, reinvents herself as Maidenhair, Douglas enjoys a similar kind of resurrection as Doug-fir, Nick is reclaimed from years of near-isolation, when he is inspired by Olivia and joins her in the forest protest as Watchman, and Mimi and Adam develop new identities as Mulberry and Maple.

The network of interconnecting traces that links the characters with both trees and one another is intricate, but throughout metamorphosis, in which trees play a crucial role, is central. It opens up new possibilities for the main characters, who in one way or another have been scarred by their pasts. Besides sharing connections with particular trees, they are linked by experiences of being seen as social outsiders or having become estranged as a result of suffering family tragedies. As a child, Adam realizes this most clearly. Hearing his mother whisper, 'He's a little socially retarded', he decides he is happy not to be 'regular': 'There's something wrong with regular people. They're far from being the best creatures in the world' (59). He develops broad interests in flora, fauna and fossils, has an instinctively anti-Anthropocene viewpoint, while still a boy, and 'doesn't *get* people' (67; emphasis in original). Neelay is described as 'only borderline human' (142): he has Asperger's syndrome and is left wheelchair-bound after he falls from an oak tree. Nick returns home from an art exhibition to discover that his parents and grandmother have died in a gas accident, and he becomes a semi-recluse for the two decades that follow. Mimi's father, who has been a guiding force in her life, commits suicide. As already mentioned, Olivia accidentally electrocutes herself and Douglas is left crippled after he is saved from death by the banyan tree. Ray is largely blind to environmental issues until, late on in the novel, he has a major stroke, which leaves him semi-paralysed and barely able to communicate. Patricia suffers from both impaired hearing and vision and does not speak until she is more than three years old, but from her earliest days her supposed impediments gift her with an awareness of animism that grows into an absorption with botany, as her father inducts her into the knowledge that 'nothing is less isolated or more social than a tree' (144). Later, when the value of her research is called into question, she contemplates suicide and this is the fate she chooses for herself at the end of her 'Home Repair' lecture, seeing it as a positive act of reconciliation with the earth.

The significance of the commonalities in the various back stories of the characters becomes clear in the 'Home Repair' lecture, in which Patricia argues that social outsiders have a particular affinity with the environment, especially with trees. Out of step with habitual ways of perceiving the world, they emerge as characters who share knowledge of trees' unique capacities. So what she says at this point does not simply reinforce the evidence for trees' cooperative intelligence. It also indicates the extent to which the novel's ensemble cast comes to share an environmental awareness that runs counter to the unquestioned assumptions of the majority of humankind:

'My whole life, I've been an outsider. But many others have been out there with me. We found that trees could communicate, over the air and through their roots. Common sense hooted us down. We found that trees take care of each other. Collective science dismissed the idea. Outsiders discovered how seeds remember the seasons of their childhood and set buds accordingly. Outsiders discovered that trees sense the presence of other nearby life. That a tree learns to save water. That trees feed their young and synchronize their masts and bank resources and warn kin and send out signals to wasps to come and save them from attacks. …

'Men and trees are closer cousins than you think. We're two things hatched from the same seed, heading off in opposite directions, using each other in a shared place.' (566–7)

In this context, Adam's research into human predictability, which may seem tangential to the novel's main concerns, emerges as centrally relevant. From a young age, he is absorbed with 'confirmation bias, and the conflation of correlation with causality – all these faults, built into the brain of the most problematic of large mammals' (61). As a high-school senior, he realizes, from reading a book entitled *The Ape Inside Us*,[14] that humans invariably act in accordance with 'legacy behaviors and biases' (76), inherited from an earlier stage of evolution. As an adult, he becomes a social psychologist, exploring whether 'legacy cognitive blindness will forever prevent people from acting in their own best interests' (294). As a lecturer, in the context of telling his students about the world's having lost half of its six trillion trees as a consequence of human intervention, he draws on the work of theorists such as Durkheim and Foucault to explain to them that the very notion of 'reason' is a recent invention. On this level, the thinking remains relatively obscure. It takes on a more everyday complexion, when, in pursuit of his research on the issue of whether group loyalty interferes with reason, he first encounters Olivia and Nick in Mimas. Like Patricia's later lecture, the dialogue that ensues between them juxtaposes the gap between outsiders who are 'immune to consensual reality' (400) and those who act in accordance with group loyalty. Olivia takes the initiative with Adam, when she asks him questions about human beings' depletion of the world's limited resources, and then provides her own answer, which undermines the basis of thinking that lies at the heart of most Western economies: 'Exponential growth inside a finite system leads to collapse' (401). The immediate context is the logging activity against which they are protesting, but the wider implications for climate change are clear when Olivia supplements her claim with details of the rate at which resources are being exhausted, pointing out, for example, that the demand for wood has tripled in their lifetime.

This, then, is an outline of some of the ways in which *The Overstory* demonstrates the essential role that trees play in regulating balanced and self-sustaining ecosystems and I have gone into some detail, in order to illustrate how Powers's technique operates, through the accretion of supporting facts. This ensures that the argument is forcefully conveyed, but the didactic elements of the novel mean that there is a danger that polemic will overwhelm fiction. So the question needs to be asked: *The Overstory* is nothing if not a *roman à these*, but how does its mass of information about the centrality of trees to life on earth work *as fiction*, and what implications does this have for climate change? While the novel has been widely acclaimed by prize juries,[15] and elicited responses such as Ron Charles' *Washington Post* review entitled 'The most exciting novel about trees you'll ever read', in which viewing *The Overstory* as 'a monumental companion' to Annie Proulx's *Barkskins*, he wrote that it 'soars up through the canopy of American literature and remakes the landscape of environmental fiction' (Charles 2018), it has also had detractors, who have felt that the gravitas of its message has eclipsed its ability to succeed as literature.[16] Most trenchantly, in a *Sunday Times* review of Powers's subsequent novel, *Bewilderment* (2021), which also talked about *The Overstory*, Claire Lowdon took the view that the two novels exemplified the dangers inherent in 'intelligent fiction that bravely tackles the most urgent topic of our day', saying 'these books are aesthetically impoverished. Characterisation is crude; dialogue constantly veers between the functional and the sentimental. … What a shame it would be if the climate crisis were to create a monoculture of worthy, single-minded tracts, such as Powers's' (Lowdon 2021).

This leads back to Amitav Ghosh's claim that literary fiction is incapable of representing climate change.[17] Within *The Overstory*, Powers addresses the issue when he has Ray, now paralyzed, assert:

> To be human is to confuse a satisfying story with a meaningful one, and to mistake life for something huge with two legs. No: life is mobilized on a vastly larger scale, and the world is failing precisely because no novel can make the contest for the *world* seem as compelling as the struggles between a few lost people. (477–8; emphasis in original)

In many ways, *The Overstory* itself provides a portrait gallery of people, who could be considered 'lost' in a conventional sense, because they find themselves at odds with societal norms, but these nonconformist individuals' struggles go beyond human interaction and *are* concerned with 'the contest for the world', specifically with regard to the consequences of deforestation. Additionally, the fate of trees such as Mimas generates considerable dramatic tension. So, as Barbara Kingsolver wrote in her review of the novel, 'In the end, *The Overstory* defies its own prediction about fiction's limits, making the contest for the world feel every bit as important as the struggles between people' (Kingsolver 2018).

The relevance of particular forms of fiction is also foregrounded within *The Overstory*, when Adam reads a novel 'about privileged people having trouble getting along with each other in exotic locations' (414) and ends up throwing the book against the wall. And, as it were countering such fiction, classic realism claims a space in *The Overstory* in the books shared by Ray and Dorothy, who over the course of a period of years, work their way through *The Hundred Greatest Novels of All Time* (477), particularly immersing themselves in reading classic nineteenth-century doorstoppers, such as *Anna Karenina*, in which Dorothy finds a parallel with her own situation – she reads the novel to Ray with 'no hint that art and life have enrolled in the same drawing class' (478) – and *War and Peace*. So the issue of whether literary fiction continues to be meaningful in the era of climate change is very much to the fore, and the predominantly realistic mode of *The Overstory*, along with its sustained use of the present tense as the narrative moment of the novel, suggests it is. In the words of another reviewer of the novel, Powers's 'magnum opus attempts the maximalist grand narrative of the classic Victorian novel, as the title, *The Overstory*, suggests. Shattered by Modernism, and scattered by Post-Modernism, perhaps it is time for its rehabilitation and return in an atomised age when people are seeking stories that make sense of the world around us' (Manwaring 2019). The banyan-like intertwining of the different characters' stories represents a departure from some versions of realism, but taken separately, each of them can be read as a realistic novella, centred on the common theme of an awakening from cognitive blindness through an induction into the indispensable role played by trees in the maintenance of life on earth. Together these entwined stories work in a manner similar to a nineteenth-century grand narrative. Quite apart from the inventory of information about trees' characteristics and capacities, the novel tells a series of tales, whose narrative momentum injects tension into the unfolding accounts of the characters' symbiotic relationships with trees and, most importantly, in so doing it enacts the message that a psychic transformation is both necessary and possible. Each of the characters' awakenings contributes to the collective epiphany that the novel offers its readers, as it sensitizes them to the hidden life of trees.

The most dramatic of the individual characters' awakenings, and it is the element in the novel that comes closest to departing from realism, occurs when Olivia returns to life after her electrocution, and having 'died' for just over a minute. Born again, she has a sense of being guided by 'presences – the only thing to call them' – that remove 'her blinders and let her look *through*' (196; emphasis in original). Powers is, though, simply representing a mental condition – there is no intrusion of actual otherworldly beings into the narrative – and, as Olivia puts it herself when she first meets Nick, 'Maybe it's all my subconscious, finally paying attention to something other than me' (221). Rebirth is a trope, associated in Olivia's case with the call to action to combat deforestation and climate change, and it is a trope that is central to the novel's agenda, since, although not all of the protagonists become activists, they are all awakened to the need for an altered way of looking at life, to breaking with the cognitive blindness which, Adam's research argues, afflicts most people. Radically changed in her own outlook, Olivia becomes an inspiration to Nick, reclaiming him from ten years of squatting in the Iowa home where his relatives have been gassed. She has something of the same effect on the more sceptical Adam, when he joins them in Mimas, and is the central figure in the action against the timber companies' operations. Twice Powers writes, 'The best arguments in the world won't change a person's mind. The only thing that can do that is a good story' (420, 607 [emphasized on p. 607]) and the first time these self-referential words are spoken, they are directly connected with Olivia. They are introduced in the context of a gathering around a campfire in Oregon, in what the assembled group of Native Americans and outsiders who have come together there have named 'THE FREE BIOREGION OF CASCADIA' (416)[18] and they are followed by Olivia citing *her* story as a quasi-religious parable about renewal:

> Maidenhair tells that story that the rest of the campfire knows by heart. First she was dead, and there was nothing. Then she came back, and there was everything, with beings of light telling her how the most wondrous products of four billion years of life needed her help. (420)

This is endorsed by a member of the Klamath Nation, who offers a benediction and tells the gathered group that everything that is happening, namely the imminent death of the forest, has long been known to his people. As in *Barkskins*, Native America is seen as a repository of animist wisdom, to which corporate America is blind.

Olivia is unfailingly optimistic in her belief that the novel's small group of transgressive eco-warriors can successfully prevent the clear-cutting of old forest, but her accidental death, when the group's attempt to save trees by blowing up a resort site goes wrong, seems to negate the possibility of her kind of idealism effecting change, and *The Overstory* is far from sanguine about the possibility of reversing the catastrophic effects of deforestation. Nevertheless Olivia's last moments suggest that this is unfinished business. Through a process of thought transference, she puts the words '*Something's wrong. I've been shown what happens, and this isn't it*' (438; emphasis in original) into Mimi Ma's head[19] and she dies, seemingly associated with Mimas in a phrase that moves beyond the human – 'an animal falling from a great height' – though not before telling Nick 'This will never end – what we have. Right?' (440).

Olivia's transformation after her rebirth is the most overt response to a call to action in the novel, but, as mentioned above, each of the characters undergoes an awakening: Nick and Adam through their contacts with Olivia; Ray and Dorothy, when they adopt a chestnut tree in their St Paul backyard as the daughter they have never been able to have,[20] and allow the yard to go wild; Douglas, whose roadhouse encounter with the two strangers takes place near the town of Damascus, Oregon (229), an appropriate location for a man who undergoes a Pauline conversion after a tree saves his life, and who will again be saved by trees later in the novel (483); Neelay, when he abandons the aggressive competitiveness of Mastery in favour of a game based on 'growing *the world*, instead of yourself' (517; emphasis in original). Patricia is less obviously in need of an epiphany to induct her into an awareness of the extraordinary capacities of trees, since from her earliest childhood she has been attuned to the natural world. However, she enters a further phase of existence, when during her 'Home Design' lecture, she moves beyond any notion of Anthropocene superiority. She informs her audience, which includes Neelay and Mimi, who have not met her, but who have been inspired by *The Secret Forest*, about the properties of the 'suicide tree', *Tachigali versicolor* (569), a tree which sacrifices itself so that the soil is enriched for new seedlings. Then she follows its example. Remembering the opening lines of *Metamorphoses*, '*Let me sing to you now, about how people turn into other things*' (583; emphasis in original), she makes herself one with the earth by poisoning herself with plant extract.

From one point of view, the novel offers a catalogue of tragedies: by the end Olivia, Ray and Patricia are dead, Adam and Douglas are in jail, Neelay's skeletal body is wasting away; and Dorothy, like Philemon in the Ovidian tale, expects to join Ray soon. This may suggest the failure of all their endeavours to combat deforestation and climate change, but the novel is not altogether pessimistic about the future of life on Earth. Patricia sees her suicide as a movement into another phase of being, which will help sustain the planet. Positing a possibility similar to that raised by James Bradley in *Clade* (see Chapter 9), Neelay imagines artificial intelligence continuing to expand its knowledge exponentially, to 'learn what life wants from humans' (608) and, acutely conscious of his own mortality, he feels 'he would rather be here, launching the start of the rehabilitation, than live in the place his learners [robots] will help repair' (606). Two of the participants in the logging protests remain at large in society, albeit in danger of being apprehended and punished for their part in supposed ecoterrorist activity, and along with Neelay, they are the main focalizers for the closing pages of *The Overstory*. Ultimately, Mimi proves to be the character most obviously concerned with a received form of spiritual Enlightenment. As a young woman, she inherits the most precious objects her father has brought from China: three jade rings depicting trees that represent the spiritual attributes of past, present and future and a scroll that has a series of portraits of arhats, beings who have passed through the four stages of Enlightenment and reached perfection. The message of the scrolls is most obviously Buddhist, but their provenance, as an heirloom in Mimi Ma's family, involves a syncretism that transcends the religion. Early on in the novel, when her father is about to leave China, *his* father refers to him as 'A Moslem from the land of Confucius, going to the Christian stronghold of Pittsburgh with a handful of priceless Buddhist paintings' (33) and further back the family have Persian ancestors. Mimi herself is absorbed into corporate American society as a ceramic engineer, but in the latter stages of the novel she assumes another identity, reinventing herself as an alternative therapist. Close to the end, she comes across the image of a tree on her phone, and is amazed to see 'a ring of figures [that] sits on the brink of enlightenment' (602). She recognizes that the image is Nick's work, and in a further moment of illumination, she realizes that she is viewing 'her arhats, in the exact postures from the scroll – their robes, their hunched shoulders, their protruding ribs, the smiles across their sardonic faces' (602). So Nick, who has spent time in her house sketching, while others in their group were planning attacks, has come to share her vision of the scrolls. This is a prelude to a moment, when at midnight in San Francisco Mission Dolores Park, with a 'pine standing in for a Bo, Mimi gets enlightened' (621). The passage harks back to the beginning of the novel, and again trees are talking to her, speaking about an apocalyptic future which is associated with transformation and rebirth. Several of the strands come together, as the trees reiterate their capacity for photosynthesis, their underground networks and the multiple ways in which seeds germinate. The passage reaches a climax in a pantheistic passage that combines echoes of the *Book of Revelation* with suggestions of the attainment of Nirvana:

> The fires will come, despite all efforts, the blight and windthrow and floods. Then the Earth will become another thing, and people will learn it all over again. The vaults of seed banks will be thrown open. Second growth will rush back in, supple, loud, and testing all possibilities. Webs of forest will swell with species shot through in shadow and dappled by new design. .... Once *the real world* ends. (622; emphasis in original)

Nick, who is living in the northern forest, has the last word, literally, when he puts together a massive wooden installation, in which pieces of dead pine, spruce, willow and birch have been assembled to form a single word. Large enough to be visible from space, this piece of environmental artwork simply reads 'STILL' (624). It is a message to be decoded by the 'learners' who are Neelay's heirs and also, of course, by the novel's readers, who may, like the robots, make connections and see it as an assertion that trees will survive, irrespective of the fate of humankind. The novel ends with a voice at the base of the trees repeating Olivia's dying words, 'This *will never end*' (625; emphasis in original).

So, despite its pessimism over humanity's future, *The Overstory* ends on an upbeat note, and more generally its encyclopaedic accumulation of information about trees leaves its readers with an open invitation to move beyond Anthropocene exclusivism: to change the ways they look at trees and their attitudes to the climate crisis. Its sustained use of mimetic realism incorporates a mass of persuasive information about trees' self-regulating ecosystems, which functions as a manifesto for an urgent reassessment of humanity's relationship with the natural world, but it also tells a series of dramatized stories, which complement its archive of tree lore. The comment that 'the best arguments in the world won't change a person's mind. The only thing that can do that is a good story' underpins Powers's technique, and ultimately the novel's narrative 'overstory', layered on top of its numerous other concerns, is what brings it alive. At the heart of its trajectory has been the way the lives of its diverse characters change as a result of their encounters with trees and the power of the novel's story encourages its readers to follow suit. Just as Barbara Kingsolver dramatizes the urgency of the climate crisis by homing in on butterflies, Richard Powers does so by making trees the centre of an environmental epic.

6

It's not funny: Comic realism in Ian McEwan's *Solar*

In this chapter, I consider Ian McEwan's satirical novel *Solar* (2010) as a late arrival in the English comic realist tradition that was established in the eighteenth century by novelists such as Henry Fielding and Tobias Smollett. After a brief discussion of the foundations of this form of realist fiction, which focuses on Fielding's precepts and practice, I debate whether McEwan's use of comic realism in *Solar* is successful in representing climate change in the Age of the Anthropocene. Although the comic realist novel is well suited to the satirical exposure of social failings and as such, judiciously handled, it could be an ideal genre for foregrounding the aberrations that have led to the crisis, its effectiveness in *Solar* is, I suggest, questionable.

As outlined in the introduction to this book, Erich Auerbach viewed modern realism as a departure from the classical tenet that subjects should be treated in literary genres appropriate to their content. Classical poetics were predicated on a hierarchical view of genre, which placed epic at the top of the pyramid, as a form appropriate for housing the encyclopaedic content of heroic nationalist works such as the *Iliad* and the *Aeneid*, and which, in Auerbach's words, 'assigned' tragedy to the 'high style' and comedy to 'the middle or humbler style' ([1953] 2003: 564). Auerbach saw the shift away from this classification of genres as opening a portal into a new form of mimesis, 'modern realism', which was concerned with the representation of everyday social life, of the kind that one finds in the work of writers such as Stendhal and Balzac. Such matter had hitherto usually been associated with comedy and prior to the appearance of a body of writing on social realism in nineteenth-century France, in England in the eighteenth century, the Puritan realism of Defoe and Richardson (discussed in the introduction) had been complemented by an aesthetic that placed comedy at the centre of its appeal to realism. Its most significant early exponent in the form of the novel,

Fielding, was steeped in the Classics and particularly engaged with the issue of revisionist generic classification. First in *Joseph Andrews* (1742) and then more fully in *Tom Jones* (1749), he both aligned what he called his 'new province of writing' ([1749] 1969: 88) with the Classics, and distanced his work from them by referring to *Joseph Andrews* as a 'comic epic-poem in prose' ([1742] 1964: 2) and *Tom Jones* as a 'heroic, historical, prosaic poem' and a 'prosai-comi-epic' ([1749] 1969: 152, 199). The two novels include mock heroic parodies, such as the 'Battle sung by the Muse in the Homerican Stile, ... which none but the classical reader can taste' ([1749] 1969: 172) in *Tom Jones*, an episode in which, reversing gender stereotypes and deploying the high style of epic in a rustic context, Fielding has the pregnant Molly Seagrim assume the mantle of a classical hero in a churchyard brawl with a mocking mob of hostile women. However, Fielding's direct forays into what he presented as his self-conceived genre of the comic epic in prose are not the main substance of his work and both *Joseph Andrews* and *Tom Jones* owe more to the Cervantean framework of the picaresque journey. Without demonstrating Cervantes' proclivity for satirizing the foolishness of romance (though Parson Adams in *Joseph Andrews* has more than a whiff of Don Quixote about him), Fielding offers his readers broad surveys of English life in which road trips occupy a central position. *Tom Jones* in particular offers a panorama of English society in the 1740s and in its way, although Fielding's brushstrokes are more laden with comic paint than Balzac's would be just under a century later, *Tom Jones* is also a *Comédie humaine*. As Irvin Ehrenpreis has pointed out, the novel divides into three 'extremely well-defined parts: six "books" for the country, six for the road, and six for the city' (1964: 16). Collectively, these three sections offer a portrait of the Condition of England at the time of the Jacobite Rebellion, which incorporates a critique of the vices and hypocrisy that Fielding saw as manifest in all areas of English social life, but particularly prevalent in the high society of London. In short, comic realism is the vehicle for an anatomy of social *mores*, in which satire plays a major part, fulfilling what Dryden saw as its 'true end ..., the amendment of Vices by correction' ([1681] 1962: 189). *Tom Jones* can, then, be seen as a blueprint for much subsequent English comic fiction. The novel is frequently scurrilous and down-to-earth – Fielding explicitly champions the 'low' on several occasions – but Tom's vices *are* amended by correction, and the trajectory of the novel enforces a particular moral code born out of Fielding's Latitudinarian Anglican beliefs: the view that good-hearted altruism is preferable to pious declarations of faith. His successors in this type of comic fictional realism – among them Smollett, Thackeray and Dickens, and twentieth-century novelists such as Evelyn Waugh and Kingsley Amis – vary considerably in the tone and reach of their fiction, but they can all be seen as Fielding's heirs, because they employ comedy as a mode for transferring the illusion of a lived reality onto the page, and because their novels invariably involve some form of social critique. So how does Ian McEwan's *Solar* fit into this tradition? How does it employ comic realism? And how effective is its use of the mode with regard to its treatment of the climate crisis?

Like *Flight Behaviour* and *The Overstory*, *Solar* includes a considerable amount of researched specialist information about climate change. Along with contemporaries such as Julian Barnes and Martin Amis, who like him came to the fore in the 1980s, McEwan is from a generation of British novelists whose interest in the natural sciences has helped to erode the two cultures split that C. P. Snow (1959) had seen as impeding development in the modern world. In *Solar*, as in much of his earlier fiction, he demonstrates a high level of scientific literacy, so much so that it can be seen as what Rachel Holland (2019) terms a 'third culture novel', a fiction that bridges the divide between science and the humanities. Consequently, *Solar* promises to rise to the challenge of engaging with climate change by communicating hard facts about its physical causes through the reader friendly medium of the comic realist novel. And, in one sense, it does precisely this. The protagonist, Michael Beard, an expert on quantum physics, who earlier in his career has received a Nobel Prize for his extension of Einstein's work on the photoelectric effect, is involved in projects devoted to countering climate change, and in a section of the novel set in 2005, he delivers a convincing speech on the issue to a group of institutional investors and pension fund managers at the Savoy Hotel in London. In this speech he adumbrates the history of how people came to understand the greenhouse effect, highlighting Darwin's contemporary John Tyndall's seminal work on the subject and the gradual growth of awareness that industrial civilization was sending carbon dioxide into the atmosphere, along with the fact that scientists had warned the US government of anthropogenic climate change more than a quarter of a century earlier, after which he goes on to advocate the benefits of artificial photosynthesis as a means of producing solar energy to help solve the crisis (McEwan [2010] 2016: 148–56).[1] Global warming takes second place to other concerns in the novel as a whole, but this passage is far from isolated. Elsewhere, Beard is a conduit for conveying further pieces of information about the consequences of climate change, such as the facts that a Great Extinction is under way and that the Arctic is likely to be devoid of summer ice by 2045 (184) and, when he rehearses a familiar litany of climate disasters, among them drought in the Amazon rainforest and methane pouring out of the Siberian permafrost, it is to make the point that 'The future has arrived' (216).

So at first glance, *Solar*'s credentials as a realist work that engages with the *present-day* realities of climate change would seem to be impeccable. However, from its first appearance, the novel attracted hostile responses. *The Independent*'s reviewer, James Urquhart, wrote:

> Although the overarching context of *Solar* is the search for clean energy, which is presented with McEwan's usual liberal salting of plausible research, it serves as little more than a proscenium for the turgid drama of sex, compromised integrity and serial irresponsibility played out by Beard's shambling figure. As a weak sybarite in thrall to his appetites and overly fond of his own voice, Beard could have been the richly flawed character that would carry *Solar*. However, despite the many ponderous ruminations on his own sensual and moral weaknesses, his smug lack of any humility or self-reproach gives the reader little purchase for any enduring interest. (Urquhart 2010)

The Guardian's reviewer, Jason Cowley, took a similar view, describing Beard as:

> A short, fat, balding, much-married man of immense bodily appetites and scant self-discipline. He rapaciously consumes food, women and drink, with little regard for the consequences. He's a resolute short-termist, fearful of commitment and of becoming a father, living for the here and now. His behaviour is a local example of the more general problem of human over-consumption: just as Beard devours everything around him, so we are devouring our world, with its finite resources and fragile ecosystems. (Cowley 2010)

and going on to identify the central problem that emerges from the use of such a protagonist:

> What is absent from *Solar*, ultimately, are other minds, the sense that people other than Beard are present, equally alive, with something to contribute. Without them, after a while, it feels as if you are locked inside an echo chamber, listening only to the reverberations of the one same sound – the groan of a fat, selfish man in late middle age eating himself. (Cowley 2010)[2]

The central conceit of the novel revolves, then, around an extended analogy between Beard's lifestyle and the future of the planet, with over-consumption, as Cowley points out, being the thread that links the personal and the planetary, and Beard's overeating and promiscuity functioning as metonyms for Anthropocene excess. This is also manifest in his short-termism. Richard Kerridge points out,

'Formidably good at adapting to his immediate short-term environment, [Beard] is catastrophically poor at adapting to long-term considerations' (2019: 162). Despite his prowess as a Nobel laureate, Beard is now something of a has-been, an egotistical, gluttonous, five-times married philanderer, whose personal shortcomings are paralleled by his opportunistic professional exploitation of the climate crisis: the ideas that inform his photosynthesis project have been stolen from a postdoc who worked under him.

The novel opens with an epigraph taken from John Updike's *Rabbit is Rich* (1981), which prefigures the text's linking of the personal and the planetary: 'It gives him great pleasure, makes Rabbit feel rich, to contemplate the world's wasting, to know the earth is mortal too' (qtd. McEwan [2010] 2016: v). In Updike's hands, this seems expressive of the mood of entropy that characterized much American literary fiction of the 1960s;[3] in McEwan's, 'the world's wasting' takes on a more specific significance since its descent into terminal decline is being caused by climate change. What is common to both novels, though, is the focus on an egotistical protagonist, and the Updike epigraph also sets the tone for the jaundiced mood that pervades *Solar*. Although McEwan's novel serves up a large helping of climate science information, this is undermined by its often less-than-funny comedy, which catalogues Beard's cynical transgressions. Putting it simply, *Solar* plays climate change for laughs and the way McEwan uses Beard, who is variously the butt of jokes *and* a consciousness employed to satirize the beliefs of others, has the effect of trivializing the subject.

The comedy of the novel operates in various ways, sometimes mocking Beard's physical ineptitude, as in a slapstick episode of schoolboy humour, which finds him struggling with a frozen penis, when, on a junket to the Arctic island of Spitsbergen, he has to urinate outdoors, and sometimes using his sardonic angle of vision to satirize progressive aspects of contemporary thought, including social constructivism and feminism. Satire is ubiquitous in *Solar*, but it lacks any clear centre of gravity. When Beard is invited to Spitsbergen, it is to join a party of twenty artists and scientists working with climate change on a ship, and his initial self-centred reaction is that there are only 'three hardships' involved: 'the size of his cabin, limited email opportunities, and a wine list confined to a North African *vin de pays*' (45–6). Meanwhile, the satire moves outwards to encompass the organizers of this gathering: 'the guilty discharge of carbon dioxide from twenty return flights and snowmobile rides and sixty hot meals a day served in polar conditions would be offset by planting three thousand trees in Venezuela as soon as a site could be identified and local officials bribed' (46). More generally in this section, in a passage that, at least in theory, directly relates to McEwan's own situation as a novelist, Beard's hostility to idealism leaves him speechless in the face of his companions' contention that art has the power to 'lift climate change as a subject, gild it, palpate it, reveal all the horror and lost beauty and awesome threat, and inspire the public to take thought, take action, or demand it of others' (77). Beard's satirical standpoint may or may not hit home with particular readers, but there is no foil to it, no attempt to suggest how art may be relevant to the climate crisis. Subsequently other self-referential passages engage with the role of fiction in representing climate change, but again without stressing any positive potential it may contain for raising consciousness or effecting change, and beyond this Beard views narrative itself with distrust. When he encounters a lecturer in urban studies and folklore, who declares himself 'interested in the forms of narrative that climate science has generated', he is said to be suspicious of 'people who kept on about narrative …, believing all versions of it to be of equal value' (147). It may be that this is McEwan poking fun at himself, but it leaves the novel unpositioned, seemingly employing satire for satire's sake. Beard satirizes; Beard gets satirized. No one escapes. Even Beatrix Potter is grist to McEwan's satirical mill: when Beard reads to his sleepy daughter at bedtime, the novel has to tell its readers that 'Beard was not the man for Potter's dystopia of hedgehogs with ironing boards and rabbits in breeches' (223).

This lack of satirical direction points towards nihilism, nihilism that operates as a twenty-first century equivalent of the centrifugal, amoral satire of Martin Amis's novel *Money* (1984), a novel that typifies the movement away from the classic view of the purpose of satire, expressed in the Dryden comment ('the amendment of vices by correction') quoted above. Of course, though, satire in the last century has seldom subscribed to such a morally earnest view. As P. R. Elkin, writing in the decade before *Money* was published, puts it:

> The twentieth-century satirist sees himself as completely alienated from society and for this and other reasons, he [*sic*] is fundamentally unsure of himself and his standards – less reasonable and judicial than Dryden or Johnson, more pessimistic than Juvenal or Swift. His tone may be cynical, or hysterical, but it is unlikely to be hortatory, and for *saeva indignatio* he may substitute a desperate nihilism. (Elkin 1973: 198)

If this was true then, it seems all the more so now and, sweeping though Elkin's assessment is, it seems relevant to *Solar*. Certainly, there is no sense of amending any vices and there is no escape from Beard's character, no moral touchstone to counterbalance his transgressions. Love him or hate him, Beard remains the third-person focalizer of the entire novel and *Solar*'s total immersion in his persona distances it from the hortatory role that one finds in much climate change fiction, a stance that would suggest satire should be impelled by ethical considerations. Beard's excesses are central to the plot throughout, and although *Solar* ends with his comeuppance imminent, the story is too riveted on his grotesque character to devote serious attention to other characters and other issues – among them climate change. Yet, even though his original contribution to the field is next to nil, Beard's scientific expertise enables him to demolish the arguments of vested interests that attempt to deny climate change with ease. In his Savoy speech, he dismisses the idea that 'there are two sides to this, that scientists are divided' (152), and, while much of this speech is plagiarized, he alludes to the overwhelming body of evidence that confirms the greenhouse effect. Yet he remains incapable of applying his awareness of overconsumption to his own diseased body. In the third part of the novel, set in 2009, he is described as sixty-five pounds overweight, in danger of osteoarthritis, heart failure, diabetes mellitus, prostate and kidney cancer and thrombosis, and his more immediate complaints include a blotch, which he views as 'a map of unknown territory, on his wrist' (238). So, again, there is a correlation between his body and the situation of the planet. The doctor he has consulted has told him the blotch is a melanoma and has advised immediate removal, but he has procrastinated, leading the doctor to link his deferral with climate change denial: ' "Don't be a denier," Doctor Parks had said, appearing to refer back to their climate-change chats. "This won't go away just because you don't want it or are not thinking about it" ' (238). It seems, though, that he will be spared from confronting *this* condition, because the novel ends with two lovers he has been two-timing bearing down on him, and his experiencing 'an unfamiliar, swelling sensation' (279) in his heart. If we continue to see his body as a barometer for the future of the planet, then it would seem that the end is nigh.

So, as a manifesto for climate action, *Solar* is arguably the least successful of the novels discussed in this book. Any possibility of viewing Beard's grotesqueness as a cautionary tale is torpedoed by the not-so-funny comedy, which itself lacks a clear focus. It would be easy to itemize more instances of his misdemeanours to further demonstrate this point, but these would be more of the same and it seems better to end here, rather than run the risk of mirroring Beard's overconsumption and *Solar*'s apparent relish for cataloguing his excesses.

7

'I used to be human once': Testimonial realism in Indra Sinha's *Animal's People*

Like Helon Habila's *Oil on Water*, Indra Sinha's *Animal's People* (2007) does not immediately appear to deal with the worldwide climate crisis, but rather with the disastrous impact of the activities of a multinational company on a local climate. In *Oil on Water*, ongoing oil exploitation is ruining the regional climate of the Niger Delta; in *Animal's People*, a cataclysmic single event, based on the Bhopal chemical disaster of 1984, has caused a more sudden catastrophe in a fictional equivalent of Bhopal. However, in both cases the climate-changing environmental damage that has occurred can be seen as more than local. It operates as a metonym of the consequences of neo-colonial economies that threaten the future of the planet generally and the global South in particular. Sinha has said that his novel is neither about the Bhopal disaster, one of the worst industrial accidents in history, which occurred when a leak at the Indian subsidiary of an American-owned pesticide firm killed thousands of people[1] and left a legacy that contaminated the local environment for decades afterwards, nor is it about Khaufpur, the fictional town onto which he displaces Bhopal. Instead, in line with the view that it deals with a broader critique of the exploitation of the global South, he has said that it is 'about people struggling to lead ordinary lives in the shadow of catastrophe' (Sinha 2007b). For him, 'Khaufpur is every place in which people have been poisoned and then abandoned' and, before eventually settling on India, because the voice of the protagonist 'was talking to [him] incessantly, and with a strong Khaufpuri accent', he had 'toy[ed] with the idea of setting the novel in a Brazilian favela, or a contaminated city in West Africa' (Sinha 2007b). Again, then, as in *Oil on Water*, although the particular setting is precisely realized, the local expands outwards to encompass issues that have a global reach and, in Pablo Mukherjee's words, the Bhopal disaster can be read as 'an appropriate, if somewhat extreme, synecdoche of the everyday condition of postcolonial existence' (Mukherjee 2011: 217).

Additionally, beyond its indictment of multinational companies' exploitation of the world's poorer communities, the novel mounts a powerful attack on the Anthropocene by using a nineteen-year-old narrator/protagonist, Animal ('Jaanvar'), who, as his name suggests, repudiates the human, as its focalizer. Animal is a survivor of the toxic chemical disaster in Khaufpur. Born just before what he always refers to as 'that night', he has been crippled by the tragedy, which from the age of six began to twist his spine, leaving him unable to stand upright. He has subsequently learnt to walk on all fours and has come to espouse disability and animality as positives, asserting that he does not wish to be human. So his assumption of a therianthropic identity provides a focus for the novel's critique of the human exclusivism embodied in the corporate criminality that has led to the tragedy.

'I used to be human once' (Sinha [2007] 2008: 1):[2] Animal's posthuman identity is made clear in the novel's opening words. He has first acquired the name 'Animal', when he was taunted by a fellow-boy with being a 'jungli Jaanvar' (15), a wild animal, but he turns this jibe on its head by affiliating himself with animality and, although he privately wants to be able to walk upright, particularly because it will enable him to fulfil his strong sexual urges, the mantra he recites to the external world is that he does not want to be human. His condition provides the focus for the novel's exploration of the boundary between the human and the non-human and, as in other novels discussed in this study, particularly *The Overstory* and *The Man with the Compound Eyes*, therianthropy emerges as a trope that interrogates the notion of human exceptionalism. Others tell Animal that he is really human, but he rejects this on the grounds that to accept himself as such would be to see himself as an aberration, as a 'wrong-shaped and abnormal' version of a man, whereas as an animal he can be 'whole, [his] own proper shape, just a different kind of animal from say Jara [his dog], or a cow, or a camel' (208). So his identification with animals involves far more than making a virtue out of necessity and it gives him a claim to uniqueness. On another occasion, he has looked through a book that depicts all the animals of India, and has found none that resemble him, but shortly afterwards he channels this sense of uniqueness by categorizing himself as 'the bat-eared ape that climbs only in the dark of night' (223), because of the ease with which he can scale a mango tree, an act he has accomplished to gaze voyeuristically at an American doctor, Elli Barber, who has come to Khaufpur to open a clinic.[3]

Physiologically, Animal is closer to the human end of the therianthropic continuum, but he affiliates himself with the animal pole. He particularly sees himself as existing outside the parameters of the human because he has no religious or communal affiliations, doubts whether he is trustworthy (25), and in any case, feels that as an animal he is not 'subject to the laws of men' (284).[4] His physical condition provides him with a scatological vision that is a correlative of his more general cynicism about *Homo sapiens* and from the outset, his colourful and highly distinctive idiolect is linked with the view of people's lower regions, to which he is consigned by his stature:

> The world of humans is meant to be viewed from eye level. Your eyes. Lift my head I'm staring into someone's crotch. Whole nother world it's, below the waist. Believe me, I know which one hasn't washed his balls. I can smell pissy gussets and shitty backsides whose faint stenches don't carry to your nose, farts smell extra bad. (2)

His choice of animality enables him, then, to exempt himself from the ethical standards expected of humans: he sees himself as a posthuman, and therefore post-ethical, product of the catastrophe that the American Kampani's (Company's) factory has inflicted on his people – Animal's people. For them, the night of the disaster represents the end of the world as they have known it. Quite apart from the destruction it has caused, it means that the name of their city, like that of Bhopal itself and places such as Chernobyl and Three Mile Island, becomes synonymous with the tragedy it has suffered, and the legacy of the disaster is ongoing because the Kampani has left Khaufpur without cleaning up, resulting in many more cases of sickness and death. Apart from Animal, the novel offers several vignettes of people who have been casualties of the disaster. Among them are Somraj, a nationally acclaimed singer, known as 'the Voice of Khaufpur', who has lost his vocation and, since his lungs have been infected, 'his life, because breath is the life of a singer' (33), and Pyaré Bai, who has been widowed when her husband was fatally poisoned on the night of the disaster and has had to turn to loan sharks, incurring a debt she is unable to repay. Animal says to his imagined auditor, 'Eyes you should hear it, because the story of this one woman contains the tale of thousands' (83) and so, as with Somraj, her story operates metonymically to convey the horror of the disaster by dramatizing it on an individual level that humanizes its consequences.

The catastrophe also has an ongoing psychological impact on the survivors, which Sinha particularly personifies in the character of an elderly French nun, Ma Franci. On 'that night', she has lost her sanity and her ability to speak or understand languages other than French, but she subsequently becomes a voice of reason in madness. She likens what she calls the 'Apokalis' to the Last Judgement of the Book of Revelation and, when news of the destruction of the World Trade Centre reaches Khaufpur, sees this as a manifestation of the Armageddon that the world is facing, predicting that the Apokalis will end, as in her view it has begun, in Khaufpur. There are, however, also non-Christian provenances for the notion of Apokalis in the text: Animal points out that Ma Franci's version of the word contains letters that spell out Kali and the land on which the Kampani's factory stands has formerly been known as 'Kali's ground' (32); and after the accident, the derelict remains of the site are plagued with cobras, snakes associated with Siva, whose dance betokens the end of the world. So Christian and Hindu versions of the end of the world are fused, with both holding out the possibility that there may be some kind of rebirth after this cataclysm: Siva is, of course, a god of procreation as well as destruction; the Christian account of apocalypse is linked with the second coming. Ma Franci predicts this is imminent and her prophecy is in one respect at least fulfilled, when, towards the end of the novel, a riot against the neocolonial Kampani brings a second night of terror, which, extending the frame of reference to Islam, she says is 'Qayamat, the [Islamic] end of all things' (328).

So, although Animal's narrative may appear to be a highly individual one – he refers to it as a tale 'sung by an ulcer' (12) – it also encompasses the stories of an ensemble cast of the victims-cum-survivors of the disaster and, without seeing himself as an activist, he becomes a spokesman for a subaltern community that he understands from the inside. He says as much, when he tells Elli Barber, who is puzzled by the local population's boycott of her clinic, that he understands the reason why, 'because these are my people' (183). His narrative is primarily about his interaction with the small group of humans with whom he associates, but, recorded on a series of tapes, it comes to constitute a body of testimony that bears witness to the more general sufferings of Khaufpur's people at the hands of the Kampani, which, acting like latter-day absentee imperialist landlords, refuses for most of the action to send representatives to India to face the charges levelled against it. Sinha, who has actively supported Bhopali causes, says he does not feel it is incumbent upon writers to try to bring about change, but *Animal* does see the need for this (Sinha 2007a). In the novel, Animal is represented as sceptical about activism, personified in the character of Zafar, a scholar who has given up his studies and come to Khaufpur to organize the struggle against the Kampani. Animal distances himself from Zafar's campaigning zeal, but through the testimony he records on his tapes – the substance of the novel itself – he provides his own critique of the Kampani's actions on 'that night' and its aftermath. On the night itself, the people of Khaufpur were choked by poison. Now, Animal says, 'it's words that are choking us' (3) and the novel is centrally concerned with the discursive construction of the disaster and its consequences, with Animal's narrative providing an oral grass-roots alternative to official versions of events that are controlled by the multinational corporation, in collusion with local politicians.

The issue of *how* to communicate the story is foregrounded in the opening pages, where the idea of telling it to a tape recorder is given to Animal by an Australian journalist, whose overtures to turn it into a book he rejects – he views journalists as 'vultures' (5) – but whose suggestion of recording it on tape he adopts, while claiming ownership of the story by using his own tape machine and imagining himself speaking his narrative to a single interlocutor, the figure whom he christens 'Eyes'. His rejection of the journalist's mediation enables Sinha to highlight the problem of the external commodification of subaltern experience for global consumption, but of course leaves him open to the charge of acting as just such an outside intermediary himself. Arguably he avoids complicity in this kind of appropriation through his ventriloquization of the original and compelling voice of Animal, though not all readers agree with such a view.[5] Most importantly for the present study, the testimonial mode of *Animal's People* employs a persuasive type of formal realism that creates the illusion of its being an authentic account of an external reality. The novel is prefaced by an 'Editor's Note' (v) which informs readers of the circumstances under which Animal has told his tale and claims that it is a verbatim transcription of his testimony, mediated only by having been translated from Hindi. In fact, the narrative voice is more complex than this, since, as Pablo Mukherjee points out, Animal's language is 'a polyglot mixture of Hindi, Urdu, Bhojpuri, English and French' (Mukherjee 2011: 225). Like his body and his self-categorization of himself as a singular animal, Animal's idiolect is unique, but personal though it is, it provides a highly effective way of conveying the predicament of already impoverished people whose lives have been further diminished by the disaster. He has evolved an argot filled with invective and obscenities[6] that is the vehicle for his testimony, and it comes across as an appropriate response to the suffering and terror – Khaufpur means 'city of terror' in Urdu (Walonen 2016: 97) – wreaked upon his people by the catastrophe.

Animal's assumption of agency as a response to the devastation caused by the accident and his desire to provide an unvarnished account from the viewpoint of the dispossessed are clear from the outset, where he expresses his unwillingness to have his story appropriated by the Australian journalist. Talking to the local shopkeeper who has introduced him to the journalist, he says:

> Does he think he's the first outsider ever to visit this fucking city? ... For his sort we are not really people. We don't have names. We flit in crowds at the corner of his eye. Extras we're, in his movie. Well bollocks to that. Tell mister cunt big shot that this is my movie he's in and in my movie there is only one star and it's me. (9)

The issue of what voice is appropriate for his story also arises with regard to his relationship with his interlocutor, 'Eyes', a constructed reader figure within the text, whose name suggests Animal's self-conscious awareness of the extent to which his words and deeds are subject to an external gaze. Defending himself against the potential charge that his language is salacious, he says:

> Eyes, I don't know if you are a man or a woman. I'm thinking the things I am telling are not suited to a woman's ears, but if a person leaves things unsaid so as to avoid looking bad, it's a lie. I have sworn not to lie to you. If you feel embarrassed throw down the book in which these words are printed. Carry on reading it's your lookout, there's worse to come, don't go crying later 'Animal's a horrible person full of filth', think I don't know it already? (79)

Such passages also, of course, have the effect of foregrounding Sinha's own position and, as it were validating the authenticity of the particular form of testimonial realism that he is employing to tell Animal's story: a warts-and-all, Rabelaisian form, which, in the name of truth, spares no blushes and is well-suited to the crotch-high view of the world, to which Animal has been confined. As with all forms of realism, such authenticity is a constructed illusion, but it is an illusion that vividly captures the daily suffering of Animal's life. Again, Sinha appears to be using his protagonist as a proxy for his own views. In an interview comment, he made it clear that Animal's 'foul language' was intended to 'help the Bhopalis' long struggle for justice' by triggering a response in his readers: 'Animal is sick of books about Khaufpur that achieve nothing. He's angry and cynical. He goads, provokes. As you read him, he's reading you' (2007a). Further playful validation of the narrative's authenticity is provided in the opening Editor's Note, where readers are directed to a website, khaufpur.com (readily available in February 2021, but only partly so in May 2022,)[7] about the city of Khaufpur. Among other things, this website featured a 'Matrimonials' section (no longer available at the time of writing) that included a nineteen-year-old 'private eye', Jaanvar (Animal), who identified himself as a 'sincere young guy' looking for a girlfriend. Sadly, the 'click to connect' invitation that accompanied this did not yield results in 2021, when the website was still fully accessible.

The novel's down-to-earth realism complements Animal's approach to his condition. His name Jaanvar means not just animal, but also 'one who lives' (35) and despite his sense of trauma, he is an embodiment of pragmatic survival. Other inhabitants of Khaufpur, as indicated above, have not been so lucky and an extreme of their fate is exemplified by a foetus, Khã-in-the-Jar, a dicephalic parapagus (two-headed conjoined twin), who has been preserved in liquid in a jar and who begs Animal to free him. Like such figures in late colonial writing, Khã can be seen as a trope for human potential denied life by oppressive external forces. For example, in the plays of African and Caribbean dramatists of the independence generation, there is the recurrent figure of the half-born subject that seems to relate to the stifling of consciousness in the colonial era: Wole Soyinka introduces the character of a 'half-child', based on the traditional Yoruba figure of the *abiku*,[8] into his play *A Dance of the Forests* ([1963] 1984), first performed at the time of Nigerian Independence in 1960, in a manner that suggests the earlier suppression of an embryonic independent consciousness. Prior to this, Derek Walcott had concluded his play *Ti-Jean and His Brothers* ([1957] 1970), which has attracted interpretation as an allegory of the development of a postcolonial sensibility,[9] with the coming into life of a *bolom*, or unborn foetus. Both figures are drawn from folk myths and are open to multiple allegorical interpretations, but they particularly lend themselves to being read as tropes for the emergence of a postcolonial consciousness at the time of Independence. There is no such hope for Sinha's Khã-in-the-Jar, a more deformed version of life aborted before birth. He is described as 'a half-rotted relic of that night' (337) and ultimately, when Animal endeavours to save him from a marauding mob, he drops Khã's jar and his remains spill out. The suggestion is that the consequences of a neocolonial ecological disaster, such as that which Khaufpur has suffered, are irreversible. The after-effects of the Kampani's actions continue and, although the novel itself can be read as a postcolonial protest against such environmental destruction and lack of accountability, its main voice of dissent is a character who rejects the human in its entirety.

This comes to a head towards the end of the novel, in an episode in which Animal moves beyond Khaufpur and the compromised human world it represents. He takes a large amount of the poisonous intoxicant datura, a plant used in small amounts in rituals and prayers to Siva. Under its influence, he retreats from society into the seemingly extra-social space of a forest, where he experiences a series of nightmarish hallucinations before appropriately being found and brought back to society by an animal, the dog Jara that has been his companion throughout most of the novel. Animal's time in the forest brings the novel's dialogue about what constitutes humanity and what comprises animality to a climax. As before, he sees himself as a unique one-creature species, claiming he's 'not just any animal', but 'THE ANIMAL' (345) and in his hallucinatory trance, he hears a voice asking him, 'WHAT IS A MAN?' (347). He enters the forest, saying he will discover his 'true state, die or live, animal returning to its truly home' (342), but initially he finds it devoid of other animals, an environment of parched earth and little vegetation. So, supposedly extra-social Nature is not immune to the ecologically destructive impact of human behaviour. There *seems* to be no possibility of entirely escaping from the dystopian human world, but then in the middle of his delirious personal apocalypse, Animal envisages himself dying and being reborn into a new life in a holistic paradise populated by 'animals of every kind [along with] small figures on two legs, except some have horns and some have tails they are neither men nor animals, or else they are both' (352). So this vision of paradise turns out to be therianthropic. The confluence of the human and the animal in a space where there is no separation between species offers the visionary possibility of a transformative response to the trauma and suffering brought about by the ecological disaster that the Kampani has caused. This ideal is, though, a temporary hallucination.

The end of the novel sees Animal, returned to society, being told that a possibility that has been mooted for much of the narrative – that he may be able to go to America for an operation that will cure his condition – is now a real prospect. However, he appears to be on the point of rejecting this opportunity, preferring to retain his uniqueness and to remain closer to the animal end of the therianthropic continuum. He says that as an upright human, he 'would be one of millions, not even a healthy one at that. Stay four-foot' (366). But this four-legs-good, two-legs-bad conclusion is ambivalent, because he sees the plight of his people, the poor. as ongoing. His final words are, 'All things pass, but the poor remain. We are the people of the Apokalis. Tomorrow there will be more of us' (366). The novel rejects the Anthropocene callousness of corporate capitalism and envisions the promise of a less ethically compromised way of perceiving experience through the therianthropic imagination, but it remains far from sanguine about attempts to counter the hegemony of the Anthropocene. The fabulist style of the visionary interlude in the forest gives way to realism. The wretched of the earth will remain wretched, and their numbers will continue to multiply.

8

Nordic noir: Urban realism in Antti Tuomainen's *The Healer*

Over recent decades, Nordic noir, a term that has more currency abroad than within the Scandinavian countries to which it is applied, has become an international byword, not just for superior crime fiction, television and film, but also for work that uses noir to foreground social issues, particularly issues that unsettle stereotypes of northern European life as calm, stable and highly organized. Writers such as Henning Mankell, Stieg Larsson and Arne Dahl, each of whose novels have been adapted for highly successful screen productions, have given the lie to any lingering illusions that Scandinavia has somehow managed to insulate itself from the harsher aspects of contemporary social change and, in addition to dealing with actual crime, they also suggest that lawbreaking is an index of a more general social malaise. As with American hard-boiled detective fiction and Hollywood film noir, both of which are significant influences on Nordic noir, the genre exposes the criminal underbelly of society, and frequently suggests that the merest scratch on apparently settled surfaces can plunge the detectives tasked with solving the crimes under investigation into a morass of uncertainties that disrupt the veneer of social stability.

Finnish crime writer Antti Tuomainen's *The Healer* (2010) uses noir for just such social and political purposes, particularly engaging with climate change issues. Like two Scandinavian television programmes that succeeded it, the second series of the Swedish/Danish co-production *The Bridge* (2013) and the Finnish *Tellus* (2014), *The Healer* expands the conventions of formulaic procedurals by making the crime under investigation eco-terrorism and in so doing raises questions about both macro-political and individual responses to the climate crisis. The novel is set in the meaner-than-mean streets of a near-future Helsinki, a city overrun by the effects of global warming, in which energy is in short supply, disease is rife, law and order have broken down and mercenary private security firms are replacing the police. Like Liz Jenner's *The*

Rapture, *The Healer* projects a future world that is recognizably close to the present. Tuomainen has referred to his Helsinki as 'the city of today' made 'very realistic' and insists that, despite dystopian elements, *The Healer* is not science fiction (Tuomainen 2013). Again, as with *The Rapture*, there is a strong sense of apocalypse in the here-and-now.

From the outset, the style of *The Healer* injects present-tense immediacy into its representation of climate change issues. The novel opens with the poet narrator, Tapani Lehtinen, asking, 'Which was worse – complete certainty that the worst had happened, or this fear, building up moment by moment? Sudden collapse, or slow, crumbling disintegration.' (Tuomainen [2010] 2013: 3).[1] The question could be seen to be related to a central climate change debate, a debate encapsulated in the twinned, but opposed, positions of two influential literary commentators. As discussed in the introduction to this book, Amitav Ghosh argues that beliefs about climate that rely on 'the calculus of probability', the view that meteorological changes occur gradually, have become unsustainable, since the growing proliferation of extreme weather-related events has made the hitherto improbable the new norm (2016: 23–4). This is not quite the same as saying 'the worst has happened', but it points to the likelihood of a sudden collapse amid obliviousness to the omnipresent threat of major disaster. In contrast, in a different context, the environmentalism of the poor of the global South, Rob Nixon speaks of the perils posed by 'slow violence', the kind of 'violence that occurs gradually and out of sight, a violence of delayed destruction that is dispersed across time and space, an attritional violence that is typically not viewed as violence at all' (2011: 2).

As he asks 'which was worse', Tapani, is on a bus and his posing of the question most obviously refers to the scenes he is witnessing from the bus's window. Collectively they may suggest 'slow, crumbling disintegration', since no single catastrophe has caused them, but the society is experiencing accelerating collapse and so the answer to the question remains open. The scenes Tapani is viewing include an abandoned burning truck, a subway tunnel that has been flooded by rains that have been falling for months, and mouldy, waterfront apartments, which, having been abandoned as uninhabitable by their owners, have been taken over by newly arrived refugees, willing to live in part-flooded accommodation without power. Tapani is also watching news items on a screen attached to the bus driver's bulletproof glass compartment. These form a litany of disasters, several of which relate to climate change and which provide a global complement to the picture of local social breakdown. They include warnings of possible pandemics – for H_3N_3, malaria, tuberculosis, ebola and plague – and reports of Bangladesh sinking into the sea, unextinguishable forest fires in Amazonas, a dispute between India and China that is driving the two countries to war and an estimate of 650 to 800 million 'climate refugees planet-wide' (4). Meanwhile, Tapani is trying unsuccessfully to contact his wife, Johanna, who has gone missing, and his feeling that the 'worst' may have happened could also refer to her situation. Like Rufus, the protagonist of Helon Habila's *Oil on Water* (see Chapter 2), Johanna, is an investigative journalist. She has been working on a story about an ecoterrorist and supposed serial killer, the eponymous Healer, who sees himself as 'the last voice of truth in a world headed towards destruction, a healer for a sick planet' (12) and appears to have been murdering politicians, executives and their families, along with anyone else whom he views as having 'contributed to the acceleration of climate change' (12). At the same time, again as in *Oil on Water*, with Tapani looking for Johanna, the plot pivots on the protagonist's quest to find a missing woman, and Tapani is tacitly enlisted as a detective by a police inspector, Harri Jaatinen, who candidly admits that the police lack the resources to investigate the majority of the city's rapidly escalating crimes, another index of the social breakdown occasioned by climate change.

The appropriateness of genre fiction for dealing with the realities of climate change may be questionable for some, but Tuomainen points out that crime fiction is perfect 'for putting people in extreme situations' (Tuomainen 2013) and the climate crisis unquestionably finds humankind living *in extremis*. So, from this point of view, in the hands of a deft practitioner of the genre like Tuomainen, who sets his action against the backcloth of the effects of the crisis on Helsinki and demonstrates how it is impacting on the lives of his characters, the crime novel becomes a highly effective medium for depicting the consequences of global warming. One commentator makes this point particularly trenchantly, albeit in general terms, by drawing an analogy between the *modus operandi* of the two genres, and saying, 'as the crime genre can provide the dirty thrill of, say, reading about a gruesome fictional murder set on a street the reader recognises, the best cli-fi novels allow us to be briefly but intensely frightened: climate chaos is closer, more immediate, hovering over our shoulder like that murderer wielding his knife' (Glass 2013).

This is certainly the case with *The Healer*, where, after the opening has juxtaposed what Tapani is seeing on the streets with the information about disasters around the world that is being relayed to him through the medium of the television screen, virtually every aspect of the action unfolds against a backdrop of disaster and decay. Roofs have been torn off buildings with designs that have proved inadequate to withstand the new norm of continuous high winds and rain. Thousands of people are living in the park. Armed daytime robberies have become commonplace in the city centre. Newspapers have abandoned serious news coverage in favour of salacious stories about celebrities engaging in activities such as shoplifting and bestiality. Many of the security firms that have taken over from the police are corrupt and extortionate. Soldiers guard the hospital, which resembles a prison: Tapani comments, 'There were rumours that the guards were there for two reasons: to keep the public out, and to keep the patients in' (70). He also speaks of a mass exodus from the city to the imagined safety of Northern Canada or Lapland and when, towards the end of the novel, he goes to the city's train station, the scene that confronts him there suggests that climate-induced migration is affecting everyone:

> All around there were shouts, arguments, pleas, entreaties and threats. There were trains going north every hour, but even that wasn't enough to lessen the flood of people. More and more people were coming from the east, the south and the west. There was a black market on the plaza for ticket touts, purchasers of valuables, hundreds of thieves and swindlers with hundreds of tricks and scams, and of course ordinary people, each one more desperate than the last. Every other person walking by seemed to be a policeman, a soldier or a security guard. (227)

This, then, is a partial summary of the circumstances that are engulfing the Finnish capital and they are narrated in a laconic form of realism which pulls no punches, but stops short of sensationalism. Historically, realism, whether in the novels of Balzac and Zola, or in hard-boiled American detective fiction, has, of course, more often been associated with the rough-and-tumble of city life than the supposed peace of the countryside, and the heightened realism of *The Healer* is in much the same vein as the urban realism of Raymond Chandler, whose influence looms large in the novel. In an interview, Tuomainen has said:

> One book that made a huge impression when I was a young aspiring writer was Raymond Chandler's *The Long Goodbye*. I realized then that you can make the crime novel into anything, even a literary novel, and you can write as beautifully as you like, even make it almost poetry, and still call it a crime novel. (Hay n.d.)

and the style of *The Healer* embodies Chandler's conviction that crime novels can be much more than genre fiction.[2] Its taut, clipped sentences ('They didn't say anything. I didn't say anything. Only the sea and the wind spoke, overlapping murmurs' [47–8]) sometimes expand into Chandleresque similes: 'A tram stood dark at the corner of Mannerheimintie and Nordenskiöldinkatu like a great, green forgotten thing, as if someone had simply walked away and left it there' (71). Additionally, Tapani bears several of the hallmarks of the Chandler hero, a figure that Chandler himself characterized memorably in his essay 'The Simple Art of Murder', when he wrote:

> down these mean streets a man must go who is not himself mean, who is neither tarnished nor afraid. ... He must be a complete man and a common man and yet an unusual man. He must be, to use a rather weathered phrase, a man of honor – by instinct, by inevitability, without thought of it, and certainly without saying it. (Chandler 1950)

Tapani is both an Anyman figure, a principled common man who proves to be something of an ingénu, as he uncovers secrets of which he was unaware from the pasts of Johanna and his friends, but also arguably 'unusual' in both his Chandler-like chivalric quest for Johanna and his poetic sensibility. His vocation as a poet, albeit a poet who has not had any work published for four years (another index of the social and cultural downturn?) helps Tuomainen to challenge the division between genre fiction and serious literature and in sentences such as the following, to adapt his own words from the interview cited above, he follows Chandler in 'mak[ing] it almost poetry': 'A fiery-red Christmas star shone in the third-floor window, exactly in the middle of the darkened house. The building around it seemed to guard it like a flame within' (223). And, given that the 'almost poetry' of *The Healer* conflates crime fiction and climate fiction, its artistic seriousness suggests that it deserves a place within the growing canon of cli-fi novelists that Amitav Ghosh sees as exempt from his contention that creative writers who have campaigned against global warming have generally avoided the form of novel (2016: 124–5).[3]

Tuomainen's urban realism is firmly embedded in the specifics of Helsinki's geography, and the novel's extensive invocation of the names of the city's streets and districts, a practice which is likely to conjure up an aura of mysterious alterity (doubly strange, because the names are non-Indo-European) for outsiders, involves, as Lieven Ameel has argued, 'a complex commentary to [sic] the twenty-first century urban planning projects for the Finnish capital' (2019: 167). Ameel explains that the novel depicts the failure, under the impact of climate change, of developments that were only in the planning stage at the time of its publication. Aspects, which are inaccessible to its international readership, suggest a *roman à clef*. In the Finnish original, in a passage omitted from the English translation, a description of the Healer, Pasi Tarkiainen, has him resembling the centre-right politician, Alexander Stubb, who would become

Finland's Prime Minister in 2014 (Ameel 2019: 166–7). Such overlaps with external 'realities' may be very localized, but they open up a window on larger issues. An innovative development of sustainable 'Lilliput' houses that have been rendered obsolete by the speed of environmental change provides a cautionary tale about inadequately thought-out initiatives to combat the climate crisis that has worldwide resonance and, when at the end, Tapani finally catches up with Tarkiainen, the ecoterrorist mounts a vigorous attack on the neoliberal belief that everyone has the right to choose, arguing that this has led to humanity's present impasse. Elsewhere in the novel, the effects of climate change are to be seen everywhere, but there is comparatively little discussion of its causes. An exception occurs when Tapani visits Laura Vuola, a woman whom he says was 'the love of my life – twenty years ago' (130). Laura is now a literature professor, but in the past, at a time when knowledge about climate change was coming to the fore, along with Pasi Tarkiainen and Johanna, she has been involved in groups that protested against the *status quo*. In the account she now gives to Tapani, she outlines how their idealism was co-opted by big business, which oversaw a return to 'old ways' that 'sped up the cycle of destruction exponentially' (139) by playing on people's desires for ever more consumer goods at ever cheaper prices. Extrapolating this into terms used by climate activists such as Bill McKibben,[4] the line of thinking being adumbrated here might seem to be that social policy predicated on endless growth-driven expansion dooms humanity, and of course all the planet's other species, to extinction, if it involves the unsustainable Anthropocene exploitation of finite natural resources.

This, though, is not the scenario that Tapani envisages overtaking humanity. In the chapter following his meeting with Laura, he adds a coda to what she has said by commenting on the situation with regard to oil supplies, which, he says, will still be abundant when 'the world ends one day':

> The oil hadn't run out yet, although they'd been predicting it would for decades. The problem was, in fact, the opposite. There was enough oil to do everything that accelerated the rise of the sea levels, enough to destroy the air, land and water for good, enough to pollute all the lakes, rivers and seas, enough to continue to manufacture all the same useless junk. (144)

So, as in novels such as Habila's *Oil on Water*, oil remains the villain of the piece, but Tapani sees it enduring until the end of the world, underpinning and perpetuating the Anthropocene cycle of destruction.

In his excellent short essay on *The Healer*, Lieven Ameel says, 'Quite disturbingly, it is the Healer himself, a cold-blooded killer, who appears as the only character with a long-standing ecological interest and with the concomitant desire to act according to his convictions' (2019: 168). Given that the stress is on *longstanding* activism, this is largely true – Laura and Johanna, who have been involved with ecological causes in the past have not sustained their interest; Tapani is a chronicler of what he sees rather than an activist, though his narrative could be said to constitute a manifesto for action. However, referring to the Healer as a 'cold-blooded killer' is reductive, because it ignores the ambivalence in Tuomainen's representation of Pasi Tarkiainen. The murders, which he is believed to have committed, have actually been carried out by Max Väntinen, his partner in a rogue security firm, A-Secure, and Väntinen's motives have been anything but altruistic. The firm has operated by murdering homeowners and tenants in particular neighbourhoods of the city and then, in the wake of the killings, as Johanna has discovered, securing 'a heap of contracts for surveillance, security guards, alarm systems, all kinds of services' (188). Pasi Tarkiainen is clearly culpable, but, while the novel's other criminals, including Väntinen, receive their comeuppance, and in so doing allow the text to dispense its own brand of justice, Tarkiainen's fate is left uncertain. At the end, in a confrontation with Tapani on the railway tracks just outside the city's main station, he still claims to be 'on the side of good', adding 'Maybe justice isn't winning, but it's not completely gone' (237). At this point, a train approaches and, once it has passed, it is unclear whether it has struck him or provided him with an opportunity to escape. The latter seems more likely since subsequently Tapani cannot see any trace of him, and his survival will be more or less confirmed in the final chapter. If indeed he has escaped, and *if* one reads this as evidence of the novel's verdict on him, then allowing him to survive, as a transgressor whose ecologically right-minded beliefs mitigate his criminality, suggests that any sentence he merits has, at the very least, been commuted.

The Healer is, though, most convincing, not in its use of the kind of action that reaches its climax in Tapani's encounter with Pasi Tarkiainen, action of the kind that is routine in screen thrillers, but in its depiction of the impact that the current social situation, in which climate change is playing a major role, has had on personal relationships. This comes out strongly, when Tapani visits his friends, Ahti and Elina, to see if they can shed any light on Johanna's disappearance. They tell him that they are among the Helsinki residents about to leave the crumbling city and move to the imagined safety of the North though their plans have been thwarted by their inability to sell their apartment, because of the collapse of the city's infrastructure: in addition to suffering from cuts to the power and water supplies, it is ridden with mould, holes in the roof, water in the basement and rats and cockroaches. To help them, Tapani buys a pistol from them, but, friends though they are, it is clear that they are hiding something from him, and as he leaves, Elina says cryptically, 'tell her [Johanna] we never meant any harm' (41).

Subsequently their plan to go north appears to have been frustrated, when Ahti is taken ill, after being bitten by a rat, but more is involved. Their apartment is far from unsaleable and they have been hoping to leave in a hurry because Ahti has been working as a lawyer for the criminal A-Secure firm. Johanna has discovered this, and she has disappeared. The details of Ahti's activities are sketchy and he appears not to have been aware of the full extent of A-Secure's activities, until Johanna tells him about three murders that have occurred in areas for which he has been handling the contracts. Nevertheless he is implicated and only comes clean and tells Tapani what has happened, after Tapani discovers his involvement by looking through Johanna's e-mails. For Tapani, their duplicity represents a total breakdown of trust and his comment, as he walks away from them is 'Friendship doesn't end with a bang but with a flop, a let-down' (198).

This is the novel's most striking illustration of the way relationships have been compromised, but there are several others and the learning curve which Tapani undergoes involves finding out that in the past Johanna, Elina and Laura, were all involved with Pasi Tarkiainen before he turned to 'radical, militant environmentalism' and a course of 'direct action' (139). Virtually all the characters in the novel – among them Johanna's editor, Lassi Uutela, and Vassili Gromov, the photographer who has worked with her, Ahti and Elina, Pasi Tarkiainen, who has faked his own death and assumed a new name, and Max Väntinen – are covering up secrets in their pasts and, while these vary in nature, climate issues are an important determinant of their present situations in the majority of cases. Tapani and Johanna apart, just two other characters represent uncompromised pragmatic realism in the struggle to deal with the declining situation. One is the North African cab driver Hamid, who takes Tapani from place to place during the course of the action and who saves his life at one point. Tuomainen's attitude towards immigrants is positive, and Hamid personifies the optimism that Europe holds for migrants who have come to Finland. This is evident when, in a similar situation to that in which he found himself on the bus at the opening of the novel, Tapani watches a catalogue of disasters on a restaurant television screen, and Hamid, expressing a view that is at odds with virtually every other character in *The Healer*, comments, 'I'm sure things will get better' (57). The other character who remains uncompromised is the world-weary, but dedicated police inspector, Harri Jaatinen, who, at a time when most of his colleagues are deserting the police force to work for private security companies, continues to believe in the work he does, telling Tapani, 'There's still a chance to do more good than harm here' (67), And interestingly, at the end of the novel, when he visits Tapani to let him know that the investigation is complete, he tells him that they now share a similar view of the world, since they see it 'realistically, without baseless expectations, without looking backwards' (244). Again, one has the sense of a Philip Marlowe-like character, who unsentimentally continues to pursue criminals with dogged everyday pragmatism, and in some ways Jaatinen fits the bill even better than Tapani in this respect, since Tapani has a sentimental side to his character.

The novel ends with Tapani being reunited with Johanna, who has been a shadowy figure throughout, despite the important part she has played in uncovering the activities of A-Secure. Until now, her appearances have all been in chapters in which Tapani revisits the past nostalgically. Now, at the end, she is with Tapani and he thinks of them as 'as happy as two people can be in this world', adding 'Whatever happens, I will love Johanna' (246). Tuomainen has spoken of *The Healer* as a love story (2013) and this ending suggests that love can be a palliative in a world of climate-induced entropy, but *The Healer* offers no solutions to the disaster that is sweeping the planet. The question asked at the very beginning of the novel, 'which was worse: complete certainty that the worst has happened, or fear, building up moment by moment? A sudden collapse, or slow, crumbling disintegration' is repeated almost verbatim, with Tapani adding, 'Maybe I should be satisfied now that I know the answer' (245). Again, this could refer to the situation at large or to the anxiety he has felt concerning Johanna, who has now been rescued, but the primary focus seems to be on their relationship. In one of the flashbacks to the earlier days of their marriage, Johanna, obviously aware that the investigation she is following is putting her in danger, has suggested that the world may not always be the same for them. Tapani's response has been, 'The world keeps on turning. We love each other' (195). In the final chapter his words are similar, but the novel stops short of a happy-ever-after romantic ending.

The short concluding scene takes place on Good Friday, and this would seem to have overtones. The earlier action has been concentrated into the three days before Christmas, but the traditionally unifying site of the festive season carries little of its usual celebratory connotations. Along with a general sense that it has lost most of its allure, personified Christmas lights convey a mood of elegy: 'Downtown Helsinki was doing its best to remind us that tomorrow was Christmas Eve. Here and there a lone string of Christmas lights twinkled desperately, looking in their feeble glimmer like they missed not just their finer days but also their lost comrades' (127), and when Christmas Eve actually arrives, the ambience is equally lacklustre: 'It was Christmas Eve, but there was nothing there to indicate it' (229). So the run-up to Christmas underscores the bleakness of life in the city of the climate-damaged near future. In contrast, the advance to Easter in the closing chapter may suggest the possibility of renewal. Lieven Ameel suggests this, saying that 'The plot thus moves from darkness to light, and from despair to redemption' (2019: 168). This is certainly a possible reading, but, given that the day in question is Good Friday, not Easter Sunday, the emphasis would seem to be on crucifixion rather than resurrection and, while Tapani remains an incurable romantic, it is difficult to square the view that the plot has moved from despair to redemption with the future that seems to await Tapani and Johanna, a future which *he* imagines, but about which *she* is given no say. This is in keeping with the way she has been represented throughout the novel: she is never a realized figure in its present. In the dénouement where Tapani rescues her from Pasi Tarkiainen, she has been drugged and in the last chapter she is represented as sleeping, with her faithful husband watching over her. Denied agency in the events described at first hand, she is, then, effectively a Sleeping Beauty, and in the final sentence, as she wakes up, Tapani tells her why he is mounting guard with a gun in his hand. He has received an 'unnerving' message with the heading 'THE BATTLE FOR GOOD CONTINUES' (245). So Pasi Tarkiainen appears to be alive and well. Beyond this, Sleeping Beauty is awakening to a world in which climate change and social decline appear to be irreversible and Tapani, who does not feel the world is 'going to fall apart' (194), seems, like the novel, to be more intent on recording the effects of climate change than trying to counter them. *The Healer* introduces climate issues in the form of Nordic noir very effectively, but, ultimately, it lacks its own environmental agenda.

9

'Boiling the frog'? Gradualist realism in James Bradley's *Clade*

Asked, in an interview about his 2015 novel *Clade*, what work of climate fiction he would most recommend, James Bradley chose Annie Proulx's *Barkskins*. At first sight, this choice may seem surprising, since it is hard to imagine two more formally different novels: *Barkskins* (discussed in Chapter 4) is a sprawling, loose and baggy monster; *Clade* is a spare, elliptical work. Bradley refers to *Barkskins* as 'a deep history of environmental change that ends in the dislocation and wrenching grief of today' (Brady 2017), while his own novel, far from trawling through the past to provide a genealogy for the contemporary situation, begins at a moment very close to the present and moves forwards into the late twenty-first century, employing a series of loosely connected chapters, which, unlike *Barkskins*, seem dislocated from the outset. Where *Barkskins* is expansive, albeit while often dealing with details in a very perfunctory way, *Clade* challenges its readers to fill in the hiatuses that loom large between, and sometimes within, its sections, and Bradley has spoken of the way 'it lets so much of the story happen in the gaps between the sections, and relies upon association rather than plot' (Brady 2017). As such, its method seems to chime with the attitude that Ellie, one of the novel's main characters, takes towards new projects. She is an artist and photographer working on subjects such as biodiversity and dementia, and she embarks on fresh undertakings tentatively, 'feeling the ideas coalescing in her mind ..., the shape of a project coming before she has the detail, as if the idea were already present, inchoate; she has learned to trust this feeling, to give the connections time to form' (Bradley [2015] 2017: 146).[1] The structure of *Clade* invites a similar response on the part of its readers, who have to piece together the novel's numerous apparent fresh starts and discrete episodes to form connections.

Such an approach is, then, a world away from the circumstantial, linear realism of *Barkskins*. Nevertheless there are commonalities between the two novels, particularly in their shared emphasis on genealogies. *Barkskins* covers more than three centuries of two family-histories. *Clade*, again, is altogether more restrained, but through the prism of depicting sporadic events from its characters' life-stories, it provides a fragmentary account of a family's relationships. Again, the parentage trope that recurs frequently in climate fiction[2] is central and on one level *Clade* can be read as a family saga gone wrong, possibly, at least in part, as a consequence of the disruptions between generations, caused by climate change. Ultimately, though, *Clade*'s approach leaves such an assumption unconfirmed, since it expands outwards from chapters in which the primary emphasis is on climate change to suggest that this is just part of a complex of phenomena that have come together to create 'the dislocation and wrenching grief' of the twenty-first century predicament. These include virtual reality, pandemics, the loss of biodiversity, a range of altered mental states and the quest for evidence of extraterrestrial intelligence. None of the works discussed in this book, and one might add, no climate change novel at all, is ultimately a single-issue text, but *Clade*'s technique of probing multiple areas of twenty-first century transitions and hinting at how they may be interacting with one another makes it a much broader environmental novel than most. A chapter-by-chapter analysis helps to show how it is both a text that is centrally about climate change and a work that insists that it is part of a larger congeries of Anthropocene transitions that have come together to shape the evolving twenty-first century predicament. The effects of climate change are most clearly to the fore in the early chapters and so in what follows I devote more attention to these than to the closing chapters, where they continue to underlie the action, but are less obviously prominent.

Clade begins in a moment very close to the present and through the course of its ten chapters progresses forwards, sometimes with very short gaps between the actions of its chapters and sometimes with hiatuses of a decade or more, to a time late in the twenty-first century. So, while *Barkskins* belongs to the long present, because it travels from the historic past of the seventeenth century to arrive in the present, *Clade*'s trajectory takes it in an opposite long-present direction, from a time close to that of the novel's publication to a moment some sixty or seventy years in the future.[3] Its time-scheme allows it to document the evolving consequences of climate change, focusing on the fortunes of a small group of characters, the 'clade' of the title, as well as providing a plausible account of how global society may be affected. As such, it offers its readers a form of gradualist realism, which provides a staggered series of snapshots of how the planet and its microcosm of characters are progressively being changed. One of the chapters is entitled 'Boiling the Frog', and this title alludes to the allegorical fable which maintains that if a frog is put into boiling water suddenly, it will jump out, whereas if it is placed in lukewarm water, it will be unaware and will slowly cook to death. The analogy is, of course, to climate change, and it has much in common with Amitav Ghosh's contention in *The Great Derangement* (discussed in the introduction) that human beings rely on 'the calculus of probability', the view that meteorological changes occur gradually, a view which, he argues, is no longer tenable, given the increasing proliferation of extreme weather-related events. Implying the two positions are mutually exclusive is, though, unfortunate, since gradual change and catastrophes occur alongside one another; the warming of the planet and the multiple tell-tale signs that Eaarth has replaced Earth (McKibben 2010) continue in a steady, unrelenting way, while sometimes, and now all too frequently, erupting with catastrophic consequences. In the 'Boiling the Frog' chapter, through the consciousness of his initial protagonist, Adam Leith, Bradley alludes to the fable to enforce the case for taking action to combat climate change:

> There was a time when people talked about boiling the frog, arguing that the warming of the planet was too gradual to galvanise effective action, and although in recent years that has changed, delay having been replaced by panic, resistance by calls for more effective solutions, Adam still suspects that at some level people do not understand the scale of the transformation that is overtaking them. Even if it hasn't happened yet, the reality is that this place is already lost, that some time soon the ocean will have it back, the planet will overwhelm it. (Bradley [2015] 2017: 102)

Adam's view has resonance throughout the novel, but it is particularly pertinent at this point. He is in England, in East Anglia, and about to be caught up in a storm which floods London, devastates much of Eastern England and is reported to have killed thousands. Yet, apocalyptic though this is, the main characters survive and the novel moves on, inching its way into the future, to provide further vignettes of everyday life, which suggest that the frog is continuing to boil slowly. This, then, is engrained in *Clade*'s gradualist structure, which makes it clear that the frog is dying a slow death, though this does not pre-empt occurrences such as the devastating hurricane-force storm.

The title, a word which also provides the heading for one of the chapters, is never explained in the novel,[4] though it is likely to be unfamiliar to many of its readers. Once clarified, it immediately signals the direction of travel. Coined by Julian Huxley in 1957,[5] 'clade' is a term that connotes a monophyletic group of organisms, that is to say a group of organisms believed to comprise all the descendants of a common ancestor, and the most obvious way in which this manifests itself in the novel is in Adam Leith's immediate family. The novel opens with Adam and he is present, often in the background, until the final chapter, in which he dies. And, of course, his being called Adam means that, along with his partner Ellie, he offers himself up as an originary ancestor for the three generations of his family that appear in the novel, notably his daughter Summer and his grandson Noah, as well as various people who extend the notion of family beyond biological bloodlines. Yet Bradley does not leave the matter there. In a Penguin release on the title of the novel, he explains how he came to choose it and what it meant to him:

> Technically speaking 'clade' is a biological term, describing a group of organisms that share a common ancestor, so in a very simple sense it captured the novel's focus on one couple and their descendants. But it also seemed to me to speak to the book's interest in the transmission of memory and meaning through time in a larger sense, and, perhaps just as importantly, its interest in extinction and loss and the ebb and flow of life more generally. (Bradley 2015a)

Deserting the primarily scientific bent of his approach, he followed this up by invoking a more poetic connotation of 'clade', in linking it with 'the word "glade", a word that came replete with associations of beauty and mystery and, perhaps most importantly, the sacred, associations that were only deepened by the fact biologists sometimes describe a clade as a single branch on the tree of life (the word itself comes from the Ancient Greek word, *klados*, which means branch)' (2015a). Clearly, 'clade' is equally, if not more, associated with the notion of branch – the branches of a family tree – than 'glade', but Bradley's conflation of the two is interesting, since it is typical of his practice in the novel, which not only seems to pride itself on researched scientific accuracy, but also displays a contrary poetic tendency that leans towards the mystical. In what follows, I consider the effect of this admixture of elements and how it impacts on the novel's effectiveness as climate fiction. First, though, it needs to be said, that in addition to reflecting Bradley's extension of the biological meaning of 'clade' to encompass 'extinction and loss and the ebb and flow of life more generally', the novel invites another interpretation of the notion of descent from a common ancestor. Read from a broad environmental point of view, *Clade* also suggests the confluence of a range of forces that have a shared departure-point as outcrops of the Anthropocene. Climate change is at the epicentre of these, but, as mentioned above, it is entwined with numerous other modalities that are altering the nature of life on earth.

The opening chapter, 'Solstice', juxtaposes two narrative strands that immediately raise issues about generational continuity. It begins with Adam in Antarctica as part of an expedition that is examining fossilized plants and pollen traces in an attempt to learn more about the transitions that the continent has undergone over the millennia, as its landscape has been transformed from rainforest and tundra to its present condition. This bears the inescapable marks of Anthropocene intervention, which is epitomized on the very first page by a headland, where 'tracks of human activity scar the snow like rust, turning it grey and red and dirty' (3). For Adam's fellow members on the expedition, the summer solstice is a time of celebration, but the text, with Adam as its focalizer, highlights the ambivalence of the moment. This high point in the annual calendar also marks the end of summer and the beginning of a descent into darkness, and by the end of the chapter, Adam senses that his companions share his 'awareness that they are at the end of something' (21). This sets the tone for a primarily realistic novel that effectively begins in the present, and is haunted by a recurrent, often elegiac, sense of entropy. The festivities surrounding the solstice leave Adam asking himself whether they contain 'symbols of loss, of the running down of things?' (4). This is a progression that moves through the ensuing years covered by the novel, charting the ways in which 'human activity' is despoiling landscapes and threatening the future of the planet, but which also suggests there may be another more abiding order: Antarctica is seen as 'a place of the infinite, a place that exists without reference to the human' (20).

The second action of 'Solstice' takes Adam back into his past, giving an account of his first meeting with Ellie six years before, the beginnings of their relationship and the problems they have had in conceiving a child. Now, in Antarctica, he pictures Ellie, alone in the waiting room of a Sydney fertility clinic, which they have been attending for two years for IVF treatment that has so far proved unsuccessful. Their personal situation is set against news of disasters that are engulfing the planet. Adam reads a study about methane being released from the ocean floor, a scenario reminiscent of the main cause of the apocalyptic catastrophe in Liz Jensen's *The Rapture* (see Chapter 3), a novel with which *Clade* will turn out to have other affinities as it continues. The report on the methane release is followed by a listing of disasters around the world – floods in the United States and India; intense heat in Africa and Europe; burning forests in Brazil, Indonesia and Malaysia – and these lead Adam to think, 'It wasn't simply that they needed to consume less, to bring humanity's impact on the biosphere under control, it was that there were just too many people' (18). So it will be impossible for technological advances and economic restructuring to avert disaster. This, then, forges the link between the two narrative strands of 'Solstice'. Adam and Ellie's attempts to have a baby raise ethical questions about bringing children into the world, and Adam asks himself, 'What sort of world would that child inherit? Were they really doing the right thing by bringing another life into it?' (18). The chapter ends with no answers to these questions, though, like Antti Tuomainen's protagonist Tapani in *The Healer*, Adam believes that the world, diminished though it may be, as it passes beyond the moment of solstice, 'will go on' (22).[6] In the next chapter, readers learn that Adam and Ellie now have a daughter, and since she is named Summer, it seems reasonable to associate her with the trope of the solstice and to see her as a character, whose actions and experiences relate to the ethical questions Adam has asked himself in Antarctica.

The succeeding chapters continue the pattern of juxtaposing the familial and worldwide consequences of climate change, with a particular focus on Summer's growth and development, which is far from untroubled. In the second chapter, Adam's research group has now been attached to a project that is trying to model changes in South Asian monsoon activity. Floods caused by torrential rains coming at the wrong time of year have occasioned a million deaths on the subcontinent, with as many more left homeless, and a subsequent collapse in the economy has led to riots in Mumbai and Kolkata. Adam listens to television reports of stalled climate talks in Bangkok[7] and the unprecedented deaths of fish and birds, and becomes incensed as he watches a climate change denial columnist promoting his book, a book that argues that the world is entering a period of rapid cooling. Again, these macrocosmic manifestations of the climate crisis are complemented by details of how it is affecting Adam and Ellie's domestic microcosm, where power blackouts and brownouts, caused by fires damaging lines and an increased demand for air conditioning, are disrupting the former norms of daily life. This, of course, is the world that Summer is inheriting and the main action of the chapter has her suffering an asthma attack and being rushed to a hospital, which is also suffering from a loss of power, for emergency treatment. Bradley stops short of directly attributing her condition to climate change, but he opens up the possibility and leaves readers to join up these particular dots, if they so choose. Similarly, the novel does not take sides on the issue of whether it is right to bring another human being into a declining world, but the question remains on its slow back burner.

By the third chapter, the chapter actually entitled 'Clade', Summer is a thirteen-year-old, visiting the beachside house of her step-grandmother, Maddie, the woman whom Ellie's late father has remarried. Here, the human action is played out against a backdrop of coastal erosion, dying birds, crop failures, increased coffee prices and a red haze in the sky that is the 'legacy of the eruptions in the Philippines and Indonesia and the fires in Borneo and Sumatra' (46). Even the local fish and chip shop has gone, because it depended on the catch from the nearby wharf and the depletion of fish stocks pushed the prices prohibitively high. Maddie is the focalizer for this chapter and this initially disjunctive switch of perspective has the effect of disturbing any sense of linear generational continuity that readers may have been expecting, or, to put it another way, the shift of point of view expands the notion of what constitutes a clade, to encompass a broader, albeit troubled, sense of kinship. All three characters – Maddie, Ellie and Summer – are nervy and uneasy, but to Maddie, who has lost her own son to cancer, Summer, as she moves into adolescence, seems to exhibit a particular rage and vulnerability. She 'cannot help but feel there is an edge to Summer's manner, a sharpness to her judgements that is unsettling. There has always been a ferocity in Summer, a ferocity Maddie knows Ellie feels might turn inward' (62) and, as she talks to Ellie about Summer's condition, this is related to the precarious state of the world and the prospects it holds for Summer's generation, with Ellie saying they 'seem so closed off' and wondering 'what kind of future there is for her …. For any of them' (63).

The next chapter, 'Breaking and Entering', opens with another disjunctive shift. Initially, its action appears to be completely removed from the concerns of the novel so far, but it goes some way to answering Adam's questions about the inheritance of the next generation and it follows on from Ellie's comment that they are 'closed off'. The chapter is seen from Summer's perspective and it depicts her, along with two other disaffected teenagers, compulsively invading people's houses and taking liberties with their personal possessions for no immediately obvious reason. Summer has become involved with her two companions, Dan and Meera, after having previously been drawn to political causes, including raising money for refugees and joining a coalmine blockade. Now, though, she is influenced by Meera, the dominant figure in the group, who 'goes out of her way to show her contempt for people who make the mistake of caring' (91), a response which Summer feels may be particularly directed at her. She is discomforted by Meera and Dan's behaviour and appears uneasy about her role in society and her sexuality. When she is alone, she asks herself why they are engaging in their housebreaking activities. Part of the reason seems to be the thrill that comes with the risk of getting caught, but she feels more is involved, and for Meera, 'it's as if their intrusions are less about the risk than about transgression, power' (82). This is as close as the chapter comes to providing a rationale for their behaviour, and Summer herself still seems caught between anger and vulnerability, but the lack of a clear motive is itself revealing, because it reflects the sense of disempowerment that is consuming her generation, for whom the foundations that underpinned their parents' existences no longer exist. Whether or not they are consciously aware of it, it provides an explanation for their temporarily asserting themselves through their transgressive acts. Climate change is less explicitly to the fore, but it can be seen as a partial determinant of the teenagers' behaviour and it is physically manifest in the form of fires that are burning on Sydney's fringes. The chapter ends with Summer looking towards the fires and inhaling their smoky air, as if embracing destruction.

The opening of the next chapter, the 'Boiling the Frog' chapter, returns to using Adam as the focalizer, but it is discontinuous in other ways, since it opens with him arriving in England, hoping to re-establish contact with Summer, who has moved there close to a decade before. What has happened in the interim is unclear. As Adam travels east towards the address where he hopes to find her, he is journeying through an East Anglian landscape he has known previously and had once thought of as 'a reminder of another age, unaltered by the passage of time' (99). Now, though, it has taken on aspects of the tropics – it is about to be hit by a massive hurricane and has drug-resistant malaria – and, although the imagined England he still wants to look back to elegiacally is at best a pastoral fantasy, there is very real evidence of change. So the setting is an appropriate milieu for the discontinuity in his own clade. As the storm approaches, the roads are cluttered with evacuees. A flood seems inevitable and the fields of the Fens look as though they are about to be reclaimed by the sea. Genetically engineered trees, designed to consume carbon dioxide, but opposed by environmental groups, have, in a gesture towards John Wyndham's 1951 sci-fi classic, spawned 'triffids', which the protesters regard as a catastrophic displacement. Adam, however, sees them as consistent with the view he has taken of the Antarctic environment in the opening chapter, as just 'one more factor in the ongoing transformation of the world's ecosystems' (100) and wonders 'if they are not simply the latest stage in a process that goes back millennia' (101). This, then, is the context in which he finds himself as he goes in search of Summer, who has herself undergone a transformation. He finds her squatting in a flood-damaged house on a farm and at the same time discovers he is a grandfather. Summer has a seven-year-old son,[8] Noah, who is 'on the spectrum' (111) and who, she says, is part of the reason why she has not returned to Australia. The remainder of 'Boiling the Frog' is mainly concerned with the three characters' attempt to escape from the devastating storm and, again as in *The Rapture*, this section of the narrative is action-driven.

However, the chapter ends abruptly with Summer, who has said she has found Noah's behaviour challenging, disappearing unexpectedly and leaving Adam to look after his grandson. So the issue of whether the three characters escape from the storm is left unresolved at this point – later the text will return to this episode – but narrative closure is a side issue in a novel, which suggests climate change and the phenomena accompanying it demand a different structure. This becomes even more marked in its second half.

In an interview, Bradley has aligned himself with what he refers to as Amitav Ghosh's observation that 'social realism seeks to smooth out and regularize the world by moving the extreme and the uncanny into the background, meaning novels that include the sorts of disasters that are an integral part of climate change are likely to end up looking cheap and trashy' (Brady 2017). This interpretation of what Ghosh says in *The Great Derangement* sheds light on his representation of the storm in 'Boiling the Frog'. He does not shy away from depicting the disaster, but it takes second place to the personal situations it engenders. More generally, in the same interview, Bradley talks about how the structure of *Clade* evolved as a response to the difficulties of writing about climate change:

> Stories demand we break reality up into manageable chunks by selecting particular sequences of events and identifying beginnings, middles and ends. But climate change resists that process by demanding we recognize how interconnected everything is, meaning any attempt to parcel reality up making [*sic*] us uncomfortably aware of the artificiality of the process, and of narrative more generally. (Brady 2017)

This, he says, is what led to his employing a structure that sought to hold such closure at bay. Paradoxically, then, he suggests that interconnectedness needs to be achieved through disconnectedness and the novel, as he sees it, operates in the way that musical leitmotifs function, with an exponential expansion of the timescale towards the end. One might add that the quest for interconnectedness also leads to an expansion of the range of intersecting issues that particularly come to the fore in the second half of the novel. Elsewhere, in a piece of writing that wrestles with the usefulness of the term 'cli-fi' and suggests that it can be delimiting, he recycles a comment that 'all fiction is anthropocene fiction' and goes on to enumerate the factors that can come together with climate change in 'a larger process of transformation, one that embraces, amongst other things, genetic engineering, virtuality, over-population, species loss, habitat destruction and the broader disruption of natural and social systems by environmental change and capitalism' (Bradley 2015b). It is a listing that approximates to a summary of the themes that inform the second half of *Clade*.

Climate change remains implicit in *Clade* when it is not foregrounded, but the novel's field of vision funnels outwards to encompass several of the elements that Bradley cites here as coming together in the 'larger process of transformation'. As mentioned above, these include the influence of virtual reality, migration, pandemics, and the quest for extraterrestrial intelligence. So the novel becomes both more and less than a climate change novel. The first of the chapters in the second half, 'The Keeper of Bees', is very obviously linked with global warming, since it focuses on an endangered bee colony and, complementing this in the human sphere, its eponymous keeper, Amir, a former doctor, but now a climate change refugee, who has fled from a disintegrating Bangladesh and been interned in a camp in Australia. His wife and daughter have died and, as an illegal, his own situation, like that of the bees, is imperilled. Ellie is the focalizer for this chapter. She shares Amir's sense of wonder at what she sees as the strangeness of bees, and this prompts her to embark on a project that will represent their uniqueness. For her, bees blur 'the boundaries between insect and mammal' (146) and are 'a reminder of the presence of otherness in the world, and of the loss of its passing' (182–3). This is the closest *Clade* gets to challenging anthropocentrism by suggesting the interdependence of humans and other species on the planet, though throughout the novel, from the moment when Adam thinks of Antarctica as 'a place of the infinite, a place that exists without reference to the human' (20) in the first chapter, there is an appeal to an extra-human order.

Bees have become a threatened species, because of the spread of ACCD (accelerated colony collapse disorder), which has killed off colonies in Europe, America and Asia and is now having an impact in Australia. Climate change may be a cause, but this is left unstated. Insecticides seem to have been a factor, since the collapses slowed down when they were banned in the 2020s, but now the disease is spreading faster than ever. Genetically engineered plants may be responsible, but it has not been possible to establish a direct correlation between their introduction and the decline in bee populations. Meanwhile, impressed by the way honey changes with the seasons, Ellie sees bees as a repository of 'a time when the planet still moved to its own cycles' (151). For her, they are a stimulus to artistic activity and this is typical of the way in which the novel looks back to the past, with a quasi-poetic eye. Her nostalgia is similar to Adam's view of the entropic, Antarctic world and his imagined version of an earlier East Anglian landscape, and this is an aspect of Bradley's approach throughout. Where bees are concerned, it is interesting to compare *Clade* with another Australian novel, published in the same year, where they also figure prominently: Mireille Juchau's *The World without Us* (2015), which is also centred on a particular clade, spells out the consequences of the loss of bees altogether more explicitly. For example, it recycles a quote often attributed to Einstein, when one of the characters says, 'If the bee disappears from the earth, man would have no more than four years to live' (Juchau [2015] 2016: 130), and more generally, it embeds itself in apiological discourse through extensive intertextual references to Maurice Maeterlinck's classic work, *The Life of the Bee* (1901). *Clade*, as indicated above, represents bees as endangered and as a source of wonder, because they are a species that attests to the vanishing presence of 'otherness' in the world, but, as is the case with most of the issues it addresses, it stops short of offering a conclusive connection with climate change or any other aspects of 'the larger process of transformation', with which it is centrally concerned. That said, one can argue that the situation of bee colonies in *Clade* is, both literally and analogically, related to that of Amir and, just as the migration of the Mexican characters in Barbara Kingsolver's *Flight Behaviour* parallels that of the monarch butterflies, his displacement from his homeland has been brought about by a radical alteration in an ecosystem.

In 'The Keeper of the Bees', Ellie is looking after Noah, a role which, in Summer's continuing absence, she shares with Adam, who will become a major figure in the chapters that follow. Similarly, the plight of the bees leads naturally into the next chapter, 'A Journal of the Plague Year'. Again, the dots have to be joined up, but in this case, since the two chapters have been placed side by side, it seems reasonable to expect readers to connect the disorder that is decimating bee colonies with the plague that afflicts humans. Although no clear causal connection is spelt out, the juxtaposition raises the possibility that the two are linked in some way, as part of a common collapsing ecosystem. As Susan Lever puts it in a more general comment on the novel's disparate strands, '*Clade* doesn't explicitly connect the changing environment with infertility, asthma, childhood cancer or autism but those conditions form a clear pattern in the story' (2015).

'A Journal of the Plague Year' takes the form of diary entries written by a sixteen-year-old Chinese girl, Li Lijuan, who comes into Adam and Noah's lives, when she deputizes for her mother, who has been looking after Noah, now also sixteen, but has had to go back to China, because her sister is sick. So Noah and Adam are seen from an oblique angle of vision and again the change of focalizer is potentially disorienting. It serves, however, to provide a particularly pertinent perspective on the 'plague', a respiratory illness that has originated in China and is now spreading worldwide. Writing about a global respiratory virus in a novel published four years before Covid-19 was detected in Wuhan is clearly prescient, and several of the details in the chapter, such as the suggestion that it may have started in a laboratory (in this case in Taiwan) and the apparent attempt by the Chinese authorities to stifle media coverage, also verge on the uncanny in foreseeing what would subsequently transpire. The plague is, though, just one more element in the congeries of transitions that Bradley envisages as effecting a major sea change in existence. Nothing in the chapter is implausible, but now the elliptical technique leaves an increasing amount open to speculation, on the personal as well as the global level, and details that are included run the risk of appearing irrelevant. For example, Li Lijuan tells her journal that Noah is 'Indian, or part-Indian' and, when she adds, 'how Mum managed not to mention that I don't know' (189), the reader is left asking much the same question of the text, and wondering what, if anything, is the point of bringing this detail in now. It has not been mentioned when Noah was first introduced and appears to have no bearing on his identity, assuming, that is, that Bradley is not associating it with his being 'super-bright' (189) when it comes to technology! Similarly, one might ask what relationship is implicit in the fairly direct allusion to the title of Defoe's *A Journal of the Plague Year* (1722), a novel which offers an eyewitness account of the bubonic plague that devastated London in 1665. Characterized by a level of verisimilitude that led some critics to view it as fact rather than as a work of historical fiction, Defoe's plague tale is very different from *Clade*, where, although there is a first-person narrator, the effects of the virus are not seen at first hand. As the virus spreads, Adam takes Noah and Li Lijuan away from society to a house in the bush, where they will be safer, both from its impact and from the breakdown that is occurring in the cities, and this provides Lijuan with an opportunity to wonder, as Adam has, at the beauty of the depleted natural world. Anticipating the novel's final conclusion, the chapter ends with Li Lijuan marvelling at the moon's shimmering on the waters of the ocean.

By this point in the novel, then, it is clear that the climate crisis has become part of a larger agenda, and this is markedly so in the remaining three chapters, which extend the remit further and in so doing, without suggesting it is no longer urgent, deflect attention away from it. In the next chapter, 'Echo', another new character, Dylan (who will subsequently turn out to be Lijuan's husband) creates sims (a.k.a. 'echoes'), virtual reconstructions of people who have died, in order to console their loved ones. In the penultimate chapter, '1420 MHz', Noah's high-functioning autistic intelligence has borne fruit: he is now an astronomer, working on a project to detect signs of extraterrestrial intelligence and the chapter centres on attempts to identify an intermittent signal from outer space.[9] This is paralleled in the human action by a scene in which Noah is persuaded to visit his dying mother. Summer is now seemingly unconscious, but, the novel suggests, may be able to hear voices. So he talks to her about the signal, thinking to himself that 'what is said is less important than the act of speaking, letting people know they are there' (283). This comment on the signal maps onto the way he is talking to his mother at this point in a fairly obvious way, and so again the personal is linked with the planetary (and in this case very possibly intra-planetary) issues that *Clade* is exploring.

The novel concludes with a chapter entitled 'The Shimmer', in which a group of young revellers go to a party on an offshore island. Towards the end, the central figure in the chapter, Izzy, Li Lijuan's daughter, receives a call from her mother to tell her Adam has died. So, if one has read the novel as the story of his immediate clade, this provides a neat completion of the cycle, especially because the party is for the summer solstice. The wheel has come full circle, but the experience of the partygoers is very different from that of the members of the Antarctic expedition in the opening chapter. They experience virtually rendered phenomena, such as temple walls and Chinese lanterns, through lenses and aural receptors, and assume new identities through their overlays. What is one to make of such late twenty-first-century psychedelia? Fairly clearly, new virtual realities are crowding into the space of physical reality and seemingly replacing some of the losses in the natural order that have been documented throughout *Clade*, but given that the context is carnivalesque partygoing, does this suggest taking refuge in escapist hedonism? Arguably not. Clearly in one sense, the gradualist progression of *Clade* has moved beyond realism, but the inference is that virtual reality and older notions of reality have coalesced into a transcendent vision of the present and future that holds out hope for the generation to which Izzie belongs. The novel ends with her looking up at the so-called Shimmer in the sky, a 'flickering dance' of lights with 'a constantly changing hue' (296). Their cause is unknown, though it is suggested that they may be 'related to a new instability in the Earth's magnetic fields, an instability that may presage the poles flipping from north to south, as they have occasionally in the distant past' (296). This is closely related to earlier passages that involve a critique of the Anthropocene. In the previous chapter, Noah reflects that if global warming is to destroy the planet as we know it, there will come a time in the future, when 'the world will change once more, the turmoil and destruction of the past century being little more than a spasm, an interregnum in the great cycle of the planet's existence' (281) and, if there are still humans, they will be radically different from those that people the earth today and, linking this with his astronomical research project, he muses that perhaps they will be travelling out to the stars.

Izzie's concluding vision of the Shimmer echoes this, as she envisages satellites moving through the aurora and imagines 'a future that may be wonderful or terrible or a thousand things in between', but which will certainly constitute 'not an end but a beginning' (297). So the novel's ending rekindles the visions of wonder that at various points in the text have informed the responses that Adam, Ellie and Noah have had towards their transitional environment. Collectively, these suggest a posthuman humanism, in which new perceptions of the natural world enable a quasi-mystical movement beyond the Anthropocene, but this remains something of a leap of faith, given that it is envisaged against the background of both sudden climate disasters and gradualist climate decay. Perhaps most tellingly, while earlier chapters, most notably 'The Keeper of Bees', have suggested the need for humans to interact with other species, at the end this kind of ecological responsibility is left aside in favour of the poetic light show that may or may not presage a brighter future. At this point, then, the gradualist realism that makes most of the novel very effective has been replaced by an appeal to look towards an indeterminate luminary future, in which extraterrestrial forms of intelligence may play a part.

10

'Everything change': Speculative realism in Margaret Atwood's *MaddAddam* trilogy

In an interview, in which she discussed 'hope, science and writing about the future', Margaret Atwood talked about the inadequacy of the term 'climate change', saying that she would 'rather call it everything change', because the effects of climate change affect all areas of life, including crop sustainability, human habitation and the survival of species:

> I think calling it climate change is rather limiting ... because when people think climate change, they think maybe it's going to rain more or something like that. It's much more extensive a change than that because when you change patterns of where it rains and how much and where it doesn't rain, you're also affecting just about everything. You're affecting what you can grow in those places. You're affecting whether you can live there. You're affecting all of the species that are currently there because we are very water dependent. We're water dependent and oxygen dependent. (Atwood 2015)

Her *MaddAddam* trilogy (2003–13) embodies just such a view, and in this chapter I consider the role that climate change plays in the trilogy's representation of the complex of actions and events that lead to a cataclysmic disaster for *Homo sapiens*, along with actions such as small-scale organic gardening that are undertaken to combat it. The chapter particularly focuses on the first and most assured part of the trilogy, *Oryx and Crake* (2003), a stand-alone work when it initially appeared and the novel in the trilogy that most obviously explains the causes of the disaster, but it also includes discussion of aspects of the two subsequent parts, *The Year of the Flood* (2009) and *MaddAddam* (2013).

At first sight, the trilogy may appear to be futuristic science fiction, but Atwood, who is a self-confessed 'lifelong' devotee of the genre, 'both as reader and writer' ([2011] 2012: 1), has always claimed that her work is not sci-fi, but 'speculative fiction' ([2011] 2012: 6).[1] She has made this point in several comments on *Oryx and Crake*² and her acknowledgements to both *The Year of the Flood* and *MaddAddam* emphasize the closeness of her future worlds to present-day actualities. At the end of *The Year of the Flood,* she writes that the work 'is fiction, but the general tendencies and many of the details in it are alarmingly close to fact' ([2009] 2010: 517). At the end of *MaddAddam*, she says that, although the novel 'is a work of fiction, it does not include any technologies or biobeings that do not already exist, are not under construction, or are not possible in theory' ([2013] 2014: 475) and when, for example, she writes about a new type of superpig developed by corporate culture to provide organs for spare part surgery for humans ([2003] 2004: 25), she is developing a present-day reality. The first heart transplant from a genetically modified pig took place in January 2022, with the patient surviving two months.³

Atwood introduces *Oryx and Crake* with a highly pertinent epigraph from the final chapter of *Gulliver's Travels*, which sets the tone for what will follow in her trilogy: 'I could perhaps like others have astonished you with strange improbable tales; but I rather chose to relate plain matter of fact in the simplest manner and style, because my principal design was to inform you, and not to amuse you' (Atwood [2003] 2004: v; Swift [1726] 1976: 234).⁴ Gulliver has just returned from the land of the Houyhnhnms, where he has been transformed from being the epitome of Augustan Middle England and a lover of *Homo sapiens* into a misanthrope, who aligns himself with the supposedly utopian horses who are the ruling beings in the country that bears their name and where he has been revolted by the bestial humanoid Yahoos.⁵ Swift's straight-faced association of his mode of narration with the style of a writer like Defoe, who initially claimed that *Robinson Crusoe* was 'a just history of fact' ([1719] 1965: 25) is, of course, highly ironic, but, as with Atwood, the 'improbable tales' Gulliver has told, have their foundation in contemporary realities: Swift based his satire of the 'mad' scientists of the Grand Academy of Lagado, visited by Gulliver on his third voyage, on actual experiments performed at the Royal Society in London.⁶ Similarly, Atwood's accounts of bioengineering and computer gaming are very close to contemporary developments in these spheres and her representation of fundamentalist cults, a target of her fiction from *The Handmaid's Tale* (1985) onwards, is modelled on actual North American sects. All of this is very close to reality. As Atwood says herself, although 'there are some of what Huckleberry Finn would call "stretchers", there is nothing that's entirely without foundation' ([2011] 2012: 94). And, along with this, as with the tongue-in-cheek claim to veracity that Swift puts in the mouth of his gullible protagonist, she narrates her 'speculative' material in a style that creates its own reality through its succinct use of minutely realized, darkly comic detail. This informs the whole trilogy, and is at its most inventive in passages such as the following, where she gives free rein to her flair for neologisms: 'Jimmy and Crake played a few games of Three-Dimensional Waco in the arcade and had a couple of SoyOBoyburgers – no beef that month, said the chalkboard menu – and an iced Happicuppuchino, and half a Joltbar each to top up their energy and mainline a few steroids' ([2003] 2004: 84–5).

Oryx and Crake opens with its protagonist, Snowman (formerly Jimmy), living an isolated existence amid flotsam on a North American seashore. He appears to be the last man in the world, the sole human survivor of a so-called 'Flood', a deadly pandemic that has swept the planet. This opening, in a post-cataclysmic future in the middle of the twenty-first century, may seem to distinguish *Oryx and Crake* from the other novels I have been discussing in this book, but, along with the two subsequent parts of the trilogy, it moves backwards and forwards between this moment and a slightly earlier pre-Flood time, and this alternation underscores the causal link between contemporary ecological irresponsibility and apocalyptic disaster. The pre-Flood backstory is set in a world, recognizably close to that of the first half of the twenty-first century, in which society is divided into a technological upper-class who live in insulated compounds, reminiscent of the gated communities of contemporary America, and a subordinate population who live in the 'pleeblands' outside. The connection between the two actions has, then, the effect of placing the novel in a particular long present. It moves between a familiar near-present world – solar cars are now the norm, but petrol vehicles are still in use (([2003] 2004: 145) – in which corporate interests, personified by the crazed technocrat, Crake, who unleashes the virus that causes the pandemic, dominate the global economy and the middle-distance future of the post-Flood action, which opens with Snowman beached on his seashore.

Snowman's situation has clear affinities with the figure of the shipwrecked mariner – he calls himself 'a castaway of sorts' (([2003] 2004: 45) – and this is a motif that Atwood develops throughout *Oryx and Crake*, concluding the novel with a chapter entitled 'Footprint', which evokes Robinson Crusoe's discovery of a footprint on his supposedly uninhabited island. One of the effects of using the castaway analogy is that, while Crusoe can envisage himself as an Adamic figure, the first man in the world, invested, as in Genesis (2: 19–20), with the task of naming the earth's creatures, Snowman appears to be the last man in a post-catastrophe world, sentenced to live among a group of childlike transgenic humanoids, the Crakers, with whom meaningful dialogue is impossible.

However, countering this, as the trilogy progresses, there is an emphasis on the possibility of latter-day Adamic naming practices bringing new forms of being into existence. In *The Year of the Flood*, Adam One, the leader of a pre-Flood New Age religious group, the God's Gardeners, insists that 'The time of the Naming is not over' ([2009] 2010: 15) and the group strives to continue the work of Creation, despite the threat of imminent catastrophe. The Gardeners live in the pleeblands and espouse values that are diametrically opposed to those of the corporate world of the compounds. Atwood has described their cult as 'a utopia embedded within a dystopia' ([2011] 2012: 93) and summarizing their beliefs in the résumé of the first two parts of the trilogy that she provides at the beginning of *MaddAddam*, the third part, she writes that they stand for 'the convergence of Nature and Scripture, the love of all creatures, the dangers of technology, the wickedness of the Corps, the avoidance of violence, and the tending of vegetables and bees on pleebland slum rooftops' ([2013] 2014: 3). That said, her representation of their sustainable lifestyle is not uncomplicatedly sympathetic and passages such as the following, where the ethics of eating stolen pigeon eggs are debated, abound with satire:

> Adam One said that eggs were potential Creatures, but they weren't Creatures yet: a nut was not a Tree. Did Eggs have souls? No, but they had potential souls. So not a lot of gardeners did egg-eating, but they didn't condemn it either. You didn't apologise to an egg before joining its protein to yours, though you had to apologize to the mother pigeon, and thank her for her gift. ([2009] 2010: 161)

Similar reservations about the cult have been anticipated in *Oryx and Crake*, where Jimmy has shared a dormitory suite with one of their members, 'a fundamentalist vegan called Bernice, who … wore a succession of God's Gardeners T-shirts, which – due to her aversion to chemical compounds such as underarm deodorants – stank even when freshly laundered' ([2003] 2004: 221). Their utopianism is, then, subject to the kind of mockery that is often directed at 'tree huggers', but Atwood's irony is mainly sympathetic, and their own discourse incorporates elements of light-hearted merriment. Thus, when Adam One addresses the Gardeners on one of the many special religious days they commemorate, 'fun-filled April Fish Day', his sermon is on the 'Foolishness within all Religions' ([2009] 2010: 233) and, along with enjoining his followers to humbly accept their kinship with fishes, he challenges human exclusiveness by identifying mischievous non-human animals as God's subjects: 'As God contains all things good, He must also contain a sense of playfulness – a gift he has shared with Creatures other than ourselves, as witness the tricks Crows play, and the sportiveness of Squirrels, and the frolicking of Kittens' ([2009] 2010: 233–4). At the same time, his April fish day oration continues by urging his listeners to meditate on the environmental damage done to the planet's oceans, seas and lakes 'through the warming of the Sea' and he itemizes the 'Great Dead Zone[s]' of the Gulf of Mexico, Lake Erie, the Black Sea, the Grand Banks of Newfoundland and the Great Barrier Reef' ([2009] 2010: 235). In short, the Gardeners' green credo is clearly preferable to the wanton damage being inflicted by the corporate culture. As one of the characters in *The Year of the Flood* puts it, 'the Gardeners might be fanatical and amusingly bizarre, but at least they were ethical' ([2009] 2010: 170) and their emphasis on renaming and recreating is in line with Atwood's own playful praxis, as an Eve who appropriates the supposedly male act of naming. The whole trilogy is peppered with neologisms. Along with words such as 'biofreak' ([2003] 2004: 92) and 'bimplants' ([2009] 2010: 66), Atwood includes an extensive bestiary of genetically engineered animal splices such as 'wolvogs' (wolf-dogs) and 'rakunks' (raccoon-skunks), which first appear in the early pages of *Oryx and Crake* and figure prominently throughout. Towards the end of the pre-Flood action of the same novel, Jimmy feels that 'language itself had lost its solidity; it had become thin, contingent, slippery, a viscid film on which he was sliding around like an eyeball on a plate' ([2003] 2004: 305–6) and, along with the way characters change names – Jimmy becomes Snowman; Crake has previously been known as Glenn – Atwood's neologisms are an obvious reflection of this slippage, a formal correlative of the 'Everything change' message of the trilogy. She foregrounds the extent to which narrative can create worlds by presenting much of the action as a series of metafictive stories and, at one point in the third part, *MaddAddam*, she writes, 'There's the story, then there's the real story, then there's the story of how the story came to be told. Then there's what you leave out of the story. Which is part of the story too' ([2013] 2014: 70). Earlier the enigmatic Oryx has been presented as a composite of alternative fictions – seven possible authors of versions of her are mentioned – that Jimmy has to try to piece together ([2003] 2004: 132–3). And Oryx's name also involves a rechristening. It derives from 'ORYX BEISA …, a gentle water-conserving East African herbivore' ([2003] 2004: 365), and she has chosen it from a list provided by Crake, only to be less than pleased when she discovers that the species is extinct. So satire, playful neologisms and metafiction rub shoulders with meticulously documented contingent detail in Atwood's persuasively realistic projection of a future catastrophe that develops from the all-pervasive transformations that are taking place in contemporary society.

'Everything change': amid the many transformations that have occurred, climate change may seem incidental, but it figures as an omnipresent subtext in both the pre- and post-Flood sections of the novels and, talking about the origins of *Oryx and Crake* and *The Year of the Flood*, Atwood has referred to worries about climate change that she had had, since '1972, when the Club of Rome accurately predicted what now appears to be happening' (Atwood [2011] 2012: 94). In *Oryx and Crake* seasons are no longer recognizable: October is 'one of those months that used to be called *autumn*' ([2003] 2004: 81; emphasis in original); June is 'now the wet season' ([2003] 2004: 203). And even a detail such as the gentle, water-conserving Oryx Beisa having become extinct contributes to the general picture of a planet undergoing a seismic transformation. In the pre-Flood sections, environmental disasters are ubiquitous: cities and beaches on the East Coast of America have been washed away by a tsunami that follows the eruption of a Canary Islands volcano ([2003] 2004: 71), Florida's Lake Okeechobee and the Everglades have been stricken by a disastrous drought ([2003] 2004: 72) and the southern shores of the Mediterranean are desertified ([2009] 2010: 109). Again, at the very least, Atwood is writing about events that are 'possible in theory' and in several cases they have occurred since the three volumes of the trilogy were published. An eruption at the Cumbre Vieja volcanic ridge, in the southern half of the island of La Palma in the Canary Islands, lasted for three months in 2021 and, while this devastating event did not generate a tsunami, scientists have continued to warn that the collapse of the volcano *could* cause one (O'Shea 2017; Channon 2017). In 2017 the Everglades, now half their former size, experienced their driest spring on record (Erdman 2017). A 2016 study, using the Palmer Drought Severity Index, which involves tree-ring dating, concluded parts of the Mediterranean were experiencing their worst droughts in 900 years (Cook et al. 2016).

In the post-Flood sections, the chickens have come home to roost, and the endgame of human life on earth seems closer. At the beginning of *Oryx and Crake*, the beach on which Snowman is living is said to be white from 'ground-up coral and broken bones' ([2003] 2004: 6), not sand, and a remorseless sun has 'evil rays' ([2003] 2004: 41). Later in the novel, he has to contend with an exceptionally strong tornado with a howling wind that creates 'an unearthly noise like a huge animal unchained and raging' ([2003] 2004: 278). Elsewhere, global warming and related environmental changes are less explicitly to the fore, but the damage caused by anthropogenic action underlies the action throughout the trilogy. The events that bring Oryx to North America, the perverted logic behind the projects that Crake devises to combat population growth and to perfect a form of humanoid life, and sections that engage with the carbon economy, in the form of a petrol-based religion and oil excavation in the Canadian north, are three instances of ways in which climate issues inform the 'Everything change' argument of the trilogy.

The chain of events that brings Oryx to North America is most obviously a story of poverty, sexploitation and people trafficking, but it is climate change that sets it in motion. Oryx grows up in a deprived village in an unspecified country in Southeast Asia. Crops are failing, because of 'strange' weather that can 'no longer be predicted' and, when her father dies, she finds herself favoured with better food and clothes, because she is a potential asset that can be sold to a 'rich uncle' ([2003] 2004: 136), who visits the village and selects some of its children to take to the city. He is the first of several men through whose hands Oryx passes. When Jimmy later hears of this, he is outraged, but Crake contextualizes it as part of the current world order, telling him, 'You can't couple a minimum access to food with an expanding population indefinitely' ([2003] 2004: 138–9). Unlike other species, *Homo sapiens* continues to procreate. Ergo, it seems logical, in Crake's view, that human trafficking will occur. The economic imperatives that lead to displacement are broadly similar to those depicted in Ghosh's *Gun Island* (see Chapter 11), but while Ghosh's migrants are exploited by traffickers, they retain a degree of agency. Oryx, acquiescent though she is in her fate, is a victim of child slavery.

As Crake explains the causal chain that has brought Oryx to North America to Jimmy, his argument about overpopulation is logical enough from one point of view, but he represents the darker side of Malthusianism. Earlier in the novel, Jimmy has shared a condominium with two artists, who have told him that 'it had been game over once agriculture was invented, six or seven thousand years ago. After that, the human experiment was doomed, first to gigantism due to a maxed-out food supply, and then extinction' ([2003] 2004: 285) and now, when Crake takes up the subject, he talks in very similar terms. He, too, predicts disaster for the whole planet, because population growth is outstripping the supply of food and other resources, but he relates this more specifically to the impact of climate change: 'As a species we're in deep trouble, worse than anyone's saying. … Demand for resources has exceeded supply for decades in marginal geopolitical areas, hence the famines and droughts; but very soon, demand is going to exceed supply *for everyone*' ([2003] 2004: 347; emphasis in original). So, what has so far mainly affected the poorer regions of the earth, glibly dismissed as 'marginal', is going to impact on the hitherto insulated worlds of the elite and, along with his unit, Paradice (does the switch from 's' to 'c' in the spelling of the name suggest gambling – a throw of the *dice*?), Crake takes active steps to remedy this situation, by developing the BlyssPluss Pill, a multipurpose medication reminiscent of Viagra. Designed to combat the aggression that leads to war, contagious diseases and overpopulation, BlyssPluss ostensibly has three functions: to provide protection against sexually transmitted diseases, to offer unlimited libido and to prolong youth. It also has a secret fourth property: it operates as a birth-control pill, which without those who take it being aware of it, will sterilize them after a single dose. Jimmy's response when Crake tells him this sums up what is involved: 'So basically you're going to sterilize people without them knowing it under the guise of giving them the ultra in orgies?' (347).

In tandem with the BlyssPluss Pill, Crake's unit is also working on a second project, the creation of the Crakers, a species whose genes are being edited to eradicate perceived weaknesses in human DNA. The implied critique of eugenics as a solution to the problem of overpopulation echoes Aldous Huxley's *Brave New World* (1932), a novel published just before the Nazis came to power, and an important influence on Atwood's speculative fiction. In an introduction (Atwood 2007) that she wrote for an edition of Huxley's novel that came out in the years between the publication of *Oryx and Crake* and *The Year of the Flood*, Atwood discusses what she views as *Brave New World*'s soft form of totalitarianism, commenting on its emphasis on genetic engineering, officially sanctioned promiscuity and a drug, soma, which 'confers instant bliss with no side effects' (Atwood [2011] 2012: 184). Each of these recurs in *Oryx and Crake*. Her equivalent of soma, the BlyssPluss Pill will wipe out most of the human species, but the eugenics side of Crake's project, which attempts the supposedly utopian task of remedying the imperfections in *Homo sapiens*, lives on, after Jimmy kills him, in the shape of the Crakers. Initially, they are developed as designer babies whose particular attributes can be tailored to suit the wishes of prospective parents, but beyond this, Crake is developing a prototype that alters 'the ancient primate brain' (Atwood [2003] 2004: 358) to eliminate its destructive features, among them racism, notions of hierarchy, territoriality and sexual competitiveness. Earlier *Oryx and Crake* has included details of animal hybrids that have been 'improved' by genetic engineering: in a restaurant Crake has a dish that is playing its part in limiting global warming: 'kanga-lamb', an Australian splice that combines the docile characteristics and protein richness of sheep with a kangaroo's 'absence of methane-producing ozone-destroying flatulence' ([2003] 2004: 344). Now the process is taken further, with the production of a humanoid species, stripped of the characteristics that distinguish humans from other animals. Thus, where sexuality is concerned, the Crakers are designed to come into heat, like other mammals, at particular intervals, freeing them from the hormonal urges that plague humans at all times. Crake has programmed them so that matings of females only occur once every three years, with the woman in heat being distinguished by the baboon-like bright-blue colour of her buttocks and abdomen, which attract four men, who take turns copulating with her over a period of hours. So, Snowman thinks, 'Maybe Crake was right', since the 'free-spirited romp' (195) the quintets enjoy signals an end to prostitution, the abuse of children, rape and the torment of sexual competition that engenders disappointment. However, he finds their women unattractive, when they appear to him on his beach: 'No body hair, no bushiness. They look like retouched fashion photos, or ads for a high-priced workout program'. And he reflects that it was 'the thumbprints of human imperfection that used to move him, the flaws in the design' (115).

So, like other novels discussed in this book, particularly *Animal's People* and *The Man with the Compound Eyes*, Atwood interrogates Anthropocene exceptionalism, through the use of the trope of the therianthrope. The Crakers have been 'perfected' by eradicating human attributes such as competitiveness from their make-up and instilling them with traits that make them akin to non-human mammals, but their ersatz manufactured homogeneity and their limited communication skills give them a robotic quality that reflects their genetically engineered origins. They *are* Crake's children, a creation of perverted corporate thinking, and Snowman finds he has little in common with them, when they appear to be his sole companions in the post-Flood world. Earlier when, as Jimmy, he has travelled by train through the wasteland of the pleeblands, their geography has seemed to him 'so boundless, so porous, so penetrable, so wide-open. So subject to chance' (231) and this contingency is the antithesis of what the Crakers represent. Nothing has been left to chance in their composition. So, when Jimmy has actually visited the pleeblands with Crake, he is fascinated by their crowded diversity and the sight of 'Asymmetries, deformities: the faces here were a far cry from the regularity of the Compounds' (339) and also, one might add, from the perfected bodies of the Crakers.

The Crakers' lack of randomness comes, then, with a loss of individuality, and just as *Brave New World* exhibits a double-edged view of utopias that aim to perfect human beings by denying them the capacity for choice, Atwood displays an ambivalent attitude in her depiction of the mindless innocence of the Crakers. In a non-fiction essay, she uses the term 'ustopia', her own coinage, to cover both utopias and dystopias, because in her view 'each contains a latent version of the other' ([2011] 2012: 66), and she cites a long line of texts, from Plato's *Republic* and More's *Utopia* to *The Stepford Wives*,[7] and including *The Tempest*, *Gulliver's Travels*, Book 4, and *Brave New World* ([2011] 2012: 66–96) to support this contention. In the same essay, she describes the Crakers as 'a group of quasi-humans who have been genetically engineered so that they will never suffer from the ills that plague *Homo sapiens sapiens*' and, again with a degree of flippancy, she lists some of the advantages the Crakers have, among them inbuilt insect repellent and sunblock, while also posing the question 'How far can humans go in the alteration department before those altered cease to be human?' ([2011] 2012: 91). The Crakers are a living embodiment of this dilemma.

In *MaddAddam*, the third part of the trilogy, Atwood engages with the carbon economy, particularly foregrounding its role as a cornerstone of American capitalism, and issues surrounding the excavation of oil in the Canadian north. One of a number of fundamentalist cults that appear in the novel is a so-called Church of PetrOleum, a group said to be affiliated with a more mainstream sect of Petrobaptists. The Church has oil at the heart of its theology, and its contribution to the carbon economy is explicitly linked with corrupt corporate American practices and right-wing political movements. Like the society of Gilead in *The Handmaid's Tale*, Atwood's best-known dystopian novel, and its sequel *The Testaments* (2019), it claims a biblical provenance for its central tenets, saying that 'a vision of the Age of Oil' (Atwood [2013] 2014: 138) has been foretold in the New Testament. Matthew (16:18), where Christ says that he will found his church upon the 'rock' of Peter ('Petros' in Greek), is invoked as scriptural authority for a petrol-based vision of the future, while the 'Oleum' half of PetrOleum is taken to refer to the Latin word for oil (137–8). The Church is a profit-oriented, 'high-tech enabled' organization, with sites devoted to 'skimming the cash from the faithful 24/7' (144) and its rhetoric demonizes environmentalists as 'Satanic minion[s] of darkness, hell-bent on sabotaging the American Way and God's Holy Oil, which were one and the same' (223). Atwood's fiction has often proved prescient[8] and here, of course, climate change denial and the rhetoric deployed to this end resonate with populist American political beliefs that would become even more widespread in the succeeding years, as evidenced by the election of Donald Trump to the Presidency in 2017. And speciesism goes hand in glove with hostility to environmentalists in the Church's propaganda:

> The Rev, and the whole Church ... were all death on ecofreaks. Their ads featured stuff like a cute little blond girl next to some particularly repellent threatened species, such as the Surinam toad or the great white shark, with

a slogan saying: *This?* or *This?* Implying that all cute little blond girls were in danger of having their throats slit so the Surinam toads might prosper. (223; emphasis in original)

Again, then, what might initially seem to be futuristic bears out Atwood's comment 'that the general tendencies and many of the details ... are alarmingly close to fact'. With the accelerated growth of right-wing populism in the second decade of the twentieth century, the action of the novel belongs in a very recognizable long present.

Amitav Ghosh's comments on 'petrofiction' suggest that 'for the arts, oil is inscrutable in a way that coal never was: the energy that petrol generates is easy to aestheticize – as in images and narratives of roads and cars – but the substance itself is not. Its sources are mainly hidden from sight, veiled by technology, and its workers are hard to mythologize, being largely invisible' (Ghosh 2016: 74–5). In the activities of the Church of PetrOleum, oil is far from 'inscrutable', but elsewhere in *MaddAddam*, it does figure in a covert way. In the pre-Flood action, Adam One's brother Zeb has worked for an organization called Bearlift, whose purpose is to feed 'biotrash' (Atwood [2013] 2014: 82) to bears that are threatened by melting ice in the Canadian north. In reality, Bearlift's conservationist policies are a scam to placate liberal consciences, since many of the bears are adapting by moving south and interbreeding: polar bears and grizzlies are coming together and producing further hybrid species: 'grolars' and 'pizzlies' ([2013] 2014: 75). Zeb narrowly escapes being killed by a mysterious infiltrator into Bearlift and subsequently comes to the conclusion that this man must be a member of the Church of PetrOleum. He decides this both because of the Church's anti-environmentalism, and because Bearlift is operating in a remote area where oil may well be discovered. After escaping and finding himself alone in the wilderness, he kills and eats a bear. At this point, like the protagonist of Atwood's second novel, *Surfacing* (1972), and like characters in *Animal's People* and *The Man with the Compound Eyes*, he experiences a oneness with animal life, and there is a further erosion of the gap between the human and the animal, when, paralleling Snowman's identification with Bigfoot (the former Jimmy has named himself after the *Abominable* Snowman), he is mistaken for the sasquatch.

So climate change and oil exploration come together in this part of the novel, with the erosion of the boundary between species (the hybrid bears and Zeb's ursine identity) offering a more positive challenge to the Anthropocene than some of the other therianthropic splices of the trilogy, such as the pigoons. These episodes take *MaddAddam* into territory beyond the normal confines of realist fiction, and again this is prompted by human interventions that have disturbed the balance of nature. But supposedly speculative fiction *becomes* realist fiction, when external geopolitical realities change – as is again the case here, as a consequence of human activity disturbing hitherto self-sustaining ecosystems – and Atwood's prescient sampling of future probabilities operates in exactly this way. Probability itself is a moveable feast and, after all, fiction has always evolved in response to the changing parameters of the probable.

11

'Outside the range of the probable'? Picaresque realism in Amitav Ghosh's *Gun Island*

In the introduction to this book, I discussed Amitav Ghosh's indictment of anthropogenic interventions that have contributed to global warming in his 2016 monograph *The Great Derangement: Climate Change and the Unthinkable*. I put particular emphasis on two of Ghosh's contentions: his argument that beliefs about climate that assume meteorological change is a gradualist process are no longer sustainable, given the increasing incidence of extreme weather-related events, and his view that the 'scaffolding' of the realist novel prevents it from being able to 'confront the centrality of the improbable' (Ghosh 2016: 23). Ghosh reaffirmed the second of these contentions by republishing the first part of *The Great Derangement*, the section in which he made the claim, as *Uncanny and Improbable Events* (2021c). He did, however, take a step back from this view in a 2019 interview, in which, while he spoke about his dislike of the term 'cli-fi' and the difficulty of writing fiction about climate change, he suggested that Richard Powers' *The Overstory* (discussed in Chapter 5) had signalled a sea change in the novel's capacity to deal with environmental issues (Ghosh 2019b). He did not indicate exactly what he had in mind when he singled *The Overstory* out in this way on this occasion, but in his novel *Gun Island* ([2019] 2020) like Powers, he interrogates the distinction between humans and other forms of sentient life, and at the Delhi book launch of the novel he spoke about Powers' challenge to anthropocentrism (Ghosh 2019c).

In this chapter, I offer a close reading of *Gun Island*, locating it in the context of Ghosh's comments on the problematics of representing climate change in the genre of the novel and in relation to other work he has published since *The Great Derangement* appeared. After it came out, Ghosh published four further books, each of which, in one way or another, engaged with climate change, in fairly quick succession. Of these only *Gun Island* presents itself as a novel, but climate issues and, explicitly or implicitly, the problematics of finding discursively appropriate forms for the representation of the ecological crisis are to the fore in all four. *Uncanny and Improbable Events* is the simplest of these to summarize, since it is a reprint of the first of the three sections of *The Great Derangement*, 'Stories'. *The Nutmeg's Curse* (2021) is altogether different. Subtitled *Parables for a Planet in Crisis*, it is a non-fiction historical work that moves from an account of the predatory Dutch colonial exploitation of the Banda Islands (a small archipelago in Maluku), fabled for their once being the world's sole source of nutmeg and mace, to a wide-ranging indictment of the Anthropocene mindset that informs the contemporary neocolonial exploitation of the earth, its resources, its animals and its people. As such it finds the origins of the contemporary ecological omnicide that has generated the climate crisis, and along with it the loss of biodiversity and all the other injurious consequences of global warming, in the epistemology that legitimized a 'new economy based on extracting resources from a desacralized, inanimate Earth' and 'the subjugation of human "brutes and savages"', along with 'an entire range of nonhuman beings – trees, animals, and landscapes' (Ghosh 2021b: 38). In comparison, *Jungle Nama: A Story of the Sundarban* (2021) may seem a slight work. Generically it is a world away from the persuasive non-fictional prose of *The Nutmeg's Curse* and *Uncanny and Improbable Events*, and the particular mode of fictional realism that informs *Gun Island*. It is a verse retelling of a traditional Bengali legend, set in the mangrove forest of the Sundarbans:[1] the story of Bob Bibi, the tutelary goddess of the region and her adversary Dokkhin Rai, a tale that figures prominently in Ghosh's novel *The Hungry Tide* (2004), which is also set in the Sundarbans, and which shares characters with *Gun Island*. The story of Bon Bibi and Dokkhin Rai is generically similar to a legend that is central to the plot of *Gun Island*, the legend of the Merchant, Chand Sadagar, and his struggles with Manasa Devi the goddess of snakes and other venomous creatures, such as spiders.[2] So, although the mode in which *Jungle Nama* is written – verse fabulation – may seem distant from both the style and subject of *Gun Island*, there is an affinity between the two works, and comments that Ghosh makes in his Afterword to *Jungle Nama* serve to indicate their interconnectedness:

> The planetary crisis has upturned a vast range of accustomed beliefs and expectations, among them many that pertain to literature and literary forms. In the Before Times, stories like this one would have been considered child-like, and thus fare for children. But today, it is increasingly clear that such stories

are founded on a better understanding of the human predicament than many narratives that are considered serious and adult. (Ghosh 2021a: 77)

This too, then, ministers to the belief that changed times demand changed narrative forms, and in this case Ghosh takes a backward journey into non-Western, pre-Enlightenment storytelling, suggesting that fabulation is a mode that continues to resonate in the present. So, like *The Nutmeg's Curse*, *Jungle Nama* deserves to be read alongside *Gun Island* because there are commonalities in their self-conscious approach to narrative and to the 'planetary crisis'.

At first, *Gun Island* appears to be a conventional enough novel, conforming to realistic iterations of the genre and set, in a range of locations, in the present. Its first-person narrator, Dinanath (Deen) Datta is an all-too-credible character: a nervous antiquarian book dealer, who informs the reader at the outset that his therapist has told him he is 'in a peculiarly vulnerable state' (Ghosh [2019] 2020: 21).[3] He exhibits signs of awkwardness and inhibition throughout the novel, but initially, he seems a reliable enough narrator, despite moments when his character displays an accident-prone quality that verges on the comic. Thus, he becomes agitated when he accidentally sets off the portable Bluetooth speaker that he has stowed in the overhead luggage bin of a Los Angeles-bound plane, causing concern because of his Asian appearance, and subsequently on the same flight, he panics further when he sees two raptors fighting over a snake they have foraged from the ashes of a wildfire, with the result that he is apprehended by a security agent. Later he experiences a similar fate in Venice's Querini Stampalia library, when his total immersion in a rare incunabulum, the *Hypnerotomachia Polyphili*, leads him to try to prise open the cabinet in which it is being displayed. Overall, though, despite his bookishness and these momentary aberrations, he appears to be a trustworthy reporter of events, not least because he sees himself as 'a rational, secular, scientifically minded person' (36). In his youth, he has written a PhD on the dating of an early Bangla verse epic, and from the first page of the novel he demonstrates a near-pathological interest in etymological detective work, which makes him an ideal participant in the decoding of cryptic elements in the legend of Bonduki (Chand) Sadagar. His pride in his scientific outlook makes him distrust anything that smacks of the supernatural. So, in short, the novel establishes him as a focalizer who can be trusted not to get carried away by flights of fancy. Or so it would seem. In fact, his rationalist mindset, and with it the realism of the novel, are challenged by events that appear to be paranormal, coincidences that stretch the bounds of credulity and an accretion of events, each plausible enough in isolation, that cumulatively speak to the abnormality of the climate emergency.

A brief inventory of some of the events occasioned by climate change helps to demonstrate their omnipresence in *Gun Island*. Dinanath is an eyewitness at several disasters that attest to global upheaval, a Kilroy who just happens to be on the spot when they occur. In the first part of the novel, he experiences the changes that the Sundarbans have undergone at first hand: the cetologist, Pia, who has previously been a protagonist in *The Hungry Tide*, explains to him that the particular species of dolphin she has been studying for years is behaving in increasingly erratic ways. As a consequence of rising sea levels, salt water has intruded into what was previously fresh water and the salinity has made the dolphins seek new habitats upriver, where they have become more vulnerable to human interference and their numbers have decreased. This is just the most specific instance of the widespread loss of biodiversity in a region that has an 'an astonishing proliferation of life, in myriad forms' (104).[4] Piya also informs Dinanath about the rapidly expanding incidence of oceanic 'dead zones' (104), which have now extended into the estuaries of rivers such as the Mississippi and the Pearl. In the recent past, the Sundarbans have been struck by two devastating cyclones and now, Piya says, they are particularly suffering from a 'fish kill' (106), a worldwide phenomenon that has recently struck the region, in this case, she suggests, because a refinery has been dumping effluents into the waters.

Subsequently, when Dinanath attends a conference in California, the venue has to be evacuated because of raging wildfires. The opening address at the conference is on 'Climate and Apocalypse in the Seventeenth Century', when the Little Ice Age devastated large portions of the globe, and the scene that the delegates have been watching prior to entering the auditorium has a similarly apocalyptic air: 'A dark cloud had reared up above the horizon, taking the shape of an immense wave, complete with a frothing white top. From where we stood it looked as though a gigantic tsunami were advancing upon the distant outskirts of the city' (134). This, too, is contextualized as a local manifestation of a worldwide phenomenon, and other characters in the novel have also had first-hand experience of such fires: there are specific references to a Sicilian wildfire that a character has witnessed personally and to an Oregon fire, which has been brought on by a town council's failure to listen to an entomologist's warning that bark beetles are eating trees up from the inside, leaving them like tinder, likely to catch fire in a dry period.

Locations change in *Gun Island*, but the effects of climate change are ubiquitous, and Ghosh sees parallels across continents. The first half of the novel ends with Dinanath reflecting that 'it was possible to mistake the Venetian lagoon for the Sundarbans' (162) and in the second half, which is set in the sinking city, his encounters with climate disturbance intensify. In a chapter entitled 'High Water',[5] Dinanath and his friend Professor Giacinta (Cinta) Schiavon experience the kind of flooding that has beset the city in recent decades, and when Cinta tells him that shipworms are hollowing away at the wooden pilings on which Venice is built, 'literally eating the foundations of the city' (251), it evokes the earlier reference to bark beetles eating up Oregon trees from the inside. Again, global warming is causing a species to migrate and this is upsetting a finely balanced ecosystem. However, not all the changes that Dinanath experiences in Venice and subsequently on the Mediterranean, are occurring in such a gradual and superficially imperceptible way and as the novel builds towards its action-filled climax, the city is assaulted by extreme winds and hailstones, followed by a 'shimmering, mirage-like fog' (268). The conclusion, where a series of freak tornadoes descend on the Venetian lagoon and the whole of Italy is said to be affected by various kinds of strange weather, takes this to another level, which has interesting implications for what Ghosh says in *The Great Derangement*. I will return to this in a moment. For now, though, what is most striking is that the 'scaffolding' of *Gun Island* challenges notions of probability, less because of the suddenness and widespread nature of some of the catastrophes that the novel depicts than because so many climate disasters occur to one man in multiple locations in a comparatively short period of time. This upsets 'the calculus of probability' (Ghosh 2016: 23) and conventional notions of 'realism' are also disturbed by apparently paranormal elements. Yet most of the novel is built on a realist scaffolding, which is underpinned by the fussy, bookish Dinanath's attention to detail.

Gun Island is filled with minutiae that endorse Dinanath's credibility as a narrator. He provides brief insider information on parts of central Kolkata and, in the Venetian chapters, in more extended passages that benefit from Cinta's expertise, there are several very readable passages that breathe life into the geography and history of particular parts of the city, among them accounts of the origins of the Ghetto and the iconic church of Santa Maria della Salute. There is also, in passages such as the following, a sense of the reader being given a privileged glimpse of a quasi-authentic off-the-beaten-track Venice:

> Cinta's apartment was a ten-minute walk from the Ghetto: they were both in the same *sestiere* – Cannaregio. ... She liked to boast that only in Cannaregio was it possible any more to think of Venice as a proper city. where ordinary people lived: this was the one district that still had a substantial number of residents as opposed to tourists and transients. (179)

This appeal to authenticity suggests, then, that on one level, through Dinanath's particular pair of eyes, the novel is providing a realistic transcription of an observed reality. However, other aspects of Dinanath's narrative move in a different direction. He repeatedly encounters extraordinary coincidences and has to ask whether these can simply be attributed to chance or whether they move into the realm of the uncanny. He tells himself that chance offers an explanation for what would otherwise be inexplicable, adding that 'to cease to believe in it was to cross over into the territory of fate and destiny, devils and demons, spells and miracles – or, more prosaically, into the conspiratorial universe of the paranoiac, where hidden forces decide everything' (202).

Much of *Gun Island* is predicated on this tension. On one level, it is a realistic narrative that emanates from Dinanath's 'rational, secular' mind, but it can also, since Dinanath is torn between the competing claims of contingent reality and the uncanny, be read self-referentially as a work that wrestles with the problematics of writing climate change in the form of the novel or, to put this another way, a text that confronts the problem that Ghosh expounds on in *The Great Derangement*. Two particular elements in his narrative particularly suggest this, and they relate very closely to passages in *The Great Derangement* (repeated in *Uncanny and Improbable Events*), in which he talks about events that he suggests would seem implausible in the pages of a novel. In the first part of the earlier work, he recounts a personal experience he had while he was a student in Delhi. Returning to his room by a route he had seldom taken before, he narrowly escaped injury from a tornado, a phenomenon so unprecedented in the area that it has initially left the press at a loss for a word to describe it. It was, he says, the first tornado to hit the region in recorded meteorological history, and it has had a major impact on his psyche: 'in that instant of contact something was planted deep in my mind, something irreducibly mysterious, something quite apart from the danger that I had been in and the destruction that I had witnessed; something that was not a property of the thing itself but of the manner in which it had intersected with my life' (Ghosh 2016: 14–15). Subsequently, though, despite attempts to draw on this experience in a novel, he has found it impossible to do so. This, then, is adduced as evidence of the difficulty of introducing meteorologically improbable events into a novel: 'Surely only a writer whose imaginative resources were utterly depleted would fall back on a situation of such extreme improbability' (Ghosh 2016: 16). Yet in *Gun Island* he does exactly this. In the closing pages, a tornado threatens the central characters as they drive along a road in the Veneto and subsequently, when they are on board a ship in the Venetian lagoon, they see a plethora of tornadoes on and above the water. For the rational Dinanath, what he is witnessing seems to belong to an alternative world that lies outside the bounds of realism and he relates this to the pre-Enlightenment text he has seen in the Querini Stampalia library: 'The sight was like nothing I had ever seen before; it seemed to belong not on the earth of human experience but in the pages of some unworldly fantasy, like the *Hypnerotomachia Polyphili* [sic]' ([2019] 2020: 276).⁶ So at this point, *Gun Island* is incorporating just the kind of material that Ghosh has previously said he has found himself unable to render in fiction, because of its implausibility, but at the same time he has Dinanath suggest that the events involved belong to another kind of discourse. *The Great Derangement* passage continues by linking probability and the modern novel, saying that prior to its emergence, 'wherever stories were told, fiction delighted in the unheard-of and the unlikely', and pointing out that narratives such as '*The Arabian Nights*, *The Journey to the West*, and *The Decameron* proceeded by leaping blithely from one exceptional event to another' (Ghosh 2016: 16). However, *Gun Island*, which presents itself as a novel, demonstrates a similar fascination with the unlikely, not least in its having the globetrotting Dinanath happen to be on hand when extreme climate events occur.

The second area where *Gun Island* is markedly at odds with Ghosh's *Great Derangement* view that the 'scaffolding' of the realist novel prevents it from being able to 'confront the centrality of the improbable' (Ghosh 2016: 23) is in the proliferation of unlikely coincidences that accumulate during the course of the novel. In the earlier work, the contention that 'the calculus of probability that is deployed within the imaginary world of a novel is not the same as that which obtains outside it' (23) is particularly exemplified by his remark that, 'Within the pages of a novel an event that is only slightly improbable in real life – say, an unexpected encounter with a long-lost childhood friend – may seem wildly unlikely: the writer will have to work hard to make it appear persuasive' (24). Just such an unlikely encounter occurs, though a childhood friend is not involved, when, in Venice, Dinanath runs into Rafi, the grandson of the last keeper of a shrine to Manasa Devi that he has visited in the Sundarbans, a visit which provides the catalyst for the quest to decipher the mystery of the legend on which he subsequently embarks. As I have said in the introduction to this book, it seems tendentious to argue that such events are 'wildly unlikely' in realist fiction, while they would only seem 'slightly improbable' in real life. It is, after all, a staple of one of the earliest forms of European fictional realism, the picaresque, that 'long-lost' characters turn up. So much so that by the time Voltaire came to write *Candide*, he was able to satirize the motif in his own picaresque by having his wonderfully naïve hero remark, 'I find that a man often meets people that he never expected to see again' ([1759] 1968: 117). Be this as it may, meeting Rafi so unexpectedly leads Dinanath to ponder whether 'such an encounter, in such a place, was outside the range of the probable' (Ghosh [2019] 2020: 201). Struggling to ward off any suggestion of the extraordinary, he tells himself that this is pure chance: 'To lose sight of that was to risk becoming untethered from reality; chance was the very foundation of reality, of normalcy … any number of inexplicable things could happen without disproving the possibility of their being connected by chance' (201).

In both these instances, then, Ghosh deploys the very kind of action that he has previously seen as beyond the sphere of what is plausible in serious fiction. They are, however, only the tip of the proverbial iceberg, just one aspect of the coincidences that abound in *Gun Island*, and others stretch the imagination further by venturing into the paranormal that Dinanath tries to hold at bay. The novel is awash with uncanny incidents, many of which involve precognition of events that have yet to happen. Cinta, who has had preternatural foreknowledge of her husband and daughter's death in a car crash just before it happened and who throughout the novel recurrently senses her deceased daughter Lucia's presence, is a firm believer in this manifestation of the paranormal and, trying to convince the sceptical Dinanath, cites the historical evidence of the Aztecs having predicted the coming of the Spanish invaders with an uncanny degree of detail. Other instances of precognition are particularly associated with the character Tipu, a protégé of Piya, who, feverish after being bitten by a snake at the shrine to Manasa Devi, foresees the imperilled situation of the dolphin pod she has followed over the years, and later in the novel, though now far away in Egypt, appears to have similar foreknowledge of imminent dolphin beachings.

Tipu also appears to be an intercessor between worlds when he messages Dinanath in Brooklyn to ask him the meaning of the word *bhuta* and, in the Internet conversation that follows, elicits a complicated reply that opens up a portal on issues that are central to the novel. Dinanath explains that *bhuta* comes from a Sanskrit word that 'simply means "a being" or "an existing presence"' (114), but when Tipu pushes him further, he concedes that animals, snakes and dolphins can also be included as 'beings' and that the word can carry the sense of 'ghost', because it can refer to '"a past state of being"' (115). It becomes a seminal word in the decoding of the mystery of the ancient Bengali legend, because it breaks down the distinction between human and non-human animals – threatening though snakes may seem, this renders them co-equal planetary inhabitants – and it also collapses the distance between the past and present. Dinanath is exasperated when Tipu asks him if he believes in ghosts, but agrees that it suggests that the present is haunted by the past. At this point in the novel their conversation may seem to be incidental, but it underlies much of the action, which increasingly suggests that the present is permeated by the past, particularly in the sense that Dinanath is following in the Merchant's footsteps in travelling to Venice.

Dinanath has the growing conviction that the 'unlikely encounters, … improbable intersections between the past and the present' (201), which he is experiencing, are part of a pattern in which his own life has been determined by forces from the mythical past. In short, the novel stages a debate as to whether contingent 'chance' lies behind the action or whether 'hidden forces' are controlling what happens to Dinanath. The latter possibility is lent credence by revelations that emerge in the course of his quest to decode the meaning of the legend in which the Merchant has travelled to the Gun Island of the title. On a formal level, this blurs distinctions between fabulation and realism and the challenge to formal realism is further foregrounded by the novel's use of thriller elements, which, as one reviewer very reasonably pointed out, 'call to mind a Bengali Da Vinci code' (Thomas-Corr 2019), since cryptography plays an important role in solving the mystery.

Dinanath's predilection for etymological research, evident from the opening page of the novel, takes him on a picaresque cross-cultural journey that attempts to decipher the series of linguistic and semiotic clues that promise to cast light on the legend of Bonduki Sadagar, the Gun Merchant, and his combative relationship with Manasa Devi. The welter of clues offered in the first part of the novel begins to coalesce around three issues: the identity of the eponymous Gun Island, the route that the Merchant has taken to reach it and the nature of his relationship with the snake-goddess. The island has initially been represented as two concentric circles. After a while it is revealed that this indicates an 'island within an island' (81) and eventually it turns out that this is not a mysterious site in the Indian Ocean, but Venice's Ghetto, itself an island within an island. Cinta, knowledgeable in Arabic, explains that in Persia and parts of India 'to this day guns are known as *bundook* – which is, of course, none other than "Venice" or "Venetian"!' (151). So the term 'Bonduki Sadagar' connotes not the Gun Merchant, but the Merchant who went to Venice. And, piecing together various other pieces of evidence that Dinanath supplies, Cinta is able to date the Merchant's travels in the seventeenth century and reconstruct the route by which he has come to Venice – via the Maldives, Egypt and Turkey. Later it becomes clear that Tipu is following a similar route. So two levels of discourse are conflated. Both Dinanath's own current experience and Tipu's are intricately intertwined with the supposedly mythical journey of the Merchant. When Dinanath has earlier returned to Brooklyn, after visiting the shrine to Manasa Devi in the Sundarbans, he has felt that he has emerged from 'some submerged aspect of time' (113), but there is no escape from what he has tried to pass off as 'an extended hallucination' (110). The two worlds and the states of mind that he believes they engender are not discrete and the suggestion, which comes first from Tipu and subsequently from Cinta, is that his body is possessed. The very idea of possession is anathema to him, and he rebuffs Tipu by telling him, 'Possession is when someone is taken over by a demon', which is 'just a metaphor for greed. An imaginary thing', to which the rejoinder is 'I got news for you: greed's real, it's big. You got greed, I got greed, we all got greed. ... If that's what a demon is then there's no way it's imaginary. Shit no! We're all demons' (121). Later, when he confesses to Cinta that he feels he is losing his will, a feeling that has been brought on by his encountering a venomous species of spider, a brown recluse, in Venice, a phenomenon which the rational side of his mind recognizes as a product of its habitat having changed as a result of global warming, she responds by telling him that, like it or not, he is connected to the spider. In the days of the Inquisition, people could believe they had been possessed by spirits because they were no longer able to assert their presence on the land, animals and people who were close to them. Today, Cinta says, there is a loss of presence, attributable to other causes, specifically dependence on 'impersonal systems' (236), such as cash machines and cellphones, which do not require any self-assertion on the part of the humans who use them. The nature of possession has changed, leaving people possessed by inertia and, *inter alia*, this has implications for passivity in the face of climate change. However, Cinta continues, Dinanath is not a victim of possession in any negative sense, but rather someone who is experiencing a kind of awakening.

It gradually becomes clear that the crux of this awakening involves a movement away from the Anthropocene to an animist view of the world, a view in which he comes to reverse his initial understanding of the legend of the Merchant.[7] This has begun earlier when, in Venice's Ghetto, he has an epiphany that leads him to realize he is looking at the Merchant's predicament from the viewpoint of Manasa Devi, whom he now views in a new light, no longer as a maleficent deity intent on inflicting harm on humanity, but as 'a negotiator, a translator', mediating between animals and humans and counterbalancing the Merchant's relentless 'quest for profit' (167). Prior to this, the snakes that Dinanath has encountered – at the Sundarbans shrine, above the wildfire flames that Dinanath sees from the plane, and on Venice Beach in California, where a sea snake kills a Labrador – have simply seemed hostile to humanity. But Dinanath's about-face casts a completely different light on the legend and on his own related situation. He comes to see Manasa Devi as a protector, so much so that when, along with Cinta, he is directly threatened by the flooding in Venice, and is moved to pray, he finds himself praying to the image of a cobra's hood. The awakening he undergoes is, then, an initiation into a reverence for all creatures. Shortly before this, he has visited the Salute with Cinta and she has drawn his attention to the fact that the Byzantine Black Madonna, to whom the church was dedicated after the Virgin's supposed intervention to deliver the city from the plague, is a mediator as well as an earth goddess figure, related to the Minoan goddess of snakes, Asasarame.

All of this, then, ushers Dinanath into a new vision of experience and, bibliophile that he is, his awakening is also played out in terms of his response to the various books he encounters during the course of his travels. The Los Angeles conference has been held to celebrate a museum's[8] acquisition of a rare seventeenth-century edition of *The Merchant of Venice* and the opening address on the Little Ice Age, which may initially appear to be an interesting set-piece that is slightly off at a tangent from *Gun Island*'s main concerns, will prove centrally important by the end, not just because it documents information about an earlier period of climate change and mentions that this was the time when dependence on fossil fuels began, but also because, the speaker suggests that Enlightenment thinkers such as Hobbes and Leibniz were completely unaware of the implications of the consequences of releasing the 'angry beast [coal], which had long lain dormant within the earth' (137).

In Venice, Dinanath initially feels he should be reading *The Aspern Papers*, a work that also deals with a literary quest, but he eventually abandons this idea on the grounds that James's novella does not resonate with either the Venice of the Gun Merchant or the Venice that he is currently encountering. The missing elements seem to be its lack of improbable connections and the capacity to envisage other worlds. Two other books take him in an opposite direction. Putting *The Aspern Papers* aside, he picks up a copy of Emilio Salgari's *I misteri della giungla nera* (*The Mystery of the Black Jungle*) (1895), an Italian children's classic that he has not known about until Cinta has mentioned to him. The cover depicts a tiger stalking some turbaned men, and he is surprised to find that it is set in the Sundarbans. So, like both the Merchant's travels and his own, Salgari's book links Bengal and Venice, and it takes its readers into terrain of a very different kind to *The Aspern Papers*. Inside the book, on the first page, he finds the name of Cinta's dead daughter Lucia, and since Lucia has been a presence, a *bhuta*, sensed by both her mother and others after her death, the effect is not only to bring different worlds together, but also to elide the difference between past and present, the normal and the paranormal.

The other book Dinanath encounters that contains a completely different world-view to *The Aspern Papers* is the rare incunabulum, *Hypnerotomachia Poliphili*, which he sees in the Querini Stampalia library. On a screen he is able to read a late sixteenth-century translation, *The Strife of Love in a Dreame*, a romance told by a man who goes in search of his absent beloved and is transported into a forest, where he finds himself 'surrounded by savage animals – wolves, bears and hissing serpents'. He loses himself in a dream-within-a-dream, where he finds himself assaulted by voices emanating 'from beings of all sorts – animals, trees, flowers, spirits …' (227; ellipsis in original). Again, the discourse involved is pre-Enlightenment and, like Salgari's *Mystery of the Black Jungle*, it belongs to the realms of fable. What is most uncanny in this instance, though, is Dinanath's feeling that he himself is lost in the dream and being dreamed by 'creatures whose very existence was fantastical to me – spiders, cobras, sea snakes – and yet they and I had somehow become a part of each other's dreams' (227). So dream supersedes reality in a vision, in which non-human species have equal agency with humans, and more generally the pre-Enlightenment, non-Western texts challenge the primacy of the Anthropocene, in a manner similar to the animist vision developed by Richard Powers in *The Overstory* and James Bradley in *Clade*, though, in one respect, Ghosh goes further, since he adds a pantheistic dimension to the sense of Dinanath's being possessed, which comes to a head when, threatened by the flooding, he imagines himself praying to the cobra's hood.

As mentioned above, Ghosh has distanced himself from the term 'cli-fi' (2019b) and he has also aligned himself with Margaret Atwood's comment that she would 'rather call it everything change' (2019c; see Chapter 10). Despite the focus on Dinanath's breathless journey from one climate disaster to another, *Gun Island*, again like *Clade* and like Atwood's *MaddAddam* trilogy, ranges across a complex of issues that are central to the problems confronting global society. These come together in the form of a small fishing vessel, the Blue Boat, which is carrying refugees across the Mediterranean. It is a boat which, according to another Bangladeshi migrant in Venice, Palash, 'has become a symbol of everything that's going wrong with the world – inequality, climate change, capitalism, corruption, the arms trade, the oil industry' (218) and, although it is not spelt out at this point, these are the forces that are generating mass migration from Asia and Africa into Europe. From early on in the novel, Ghosh has had Tipu spell out to Dinanath how new technology in the form of cellphones has given subalterns in what were once seen as remote regions of the earth access to information about the lifestyles enjoyed by people in the West. At the same time, it has facilitated the 'people-moving industry', which Tipu, himself involved in trafficking, describes as 'one of the world's biggest and still growing fast' (65). Subsequently, the novel charts the picaresque journeys to the West of Tipu and Rafi and, as an interpolated set-piece, Palash's account of how he has come to Venice.

Ghosh's agenda widens in the final chapter, where he makes a theme that has been implicit throughout explicit: chickens are coming home to roost, as the migrants enter European space and, in so doing, reverse the journey of indentured labourers, who, in the colonial era, were transported from the subcontinent to work on plantations, in situations that left them powerless, ignorant of their destinations and totally subject to the commercial requirements of their masters. Now, with their ready access to mobile networks, which facilitate their travels, as well as familiarizing them with the consumer goods that have become the *sine qua non* of everyday life in more affluent countries, a major change has taken place and they are no longer disempowered. Dinanath sees their aspirations as the culmination of a long historical process:

> They, like me, were completely conversant with the laws and regulations of the countries they were heading to. Instead, it was the countries of the West that now knew very little about the people who were flocking towards them. ...
>
> Beginning with the early days of chattel slavery, the European imperial powers had launched upon the greatest and most cruel experiment in planetary remaking that history has ever known: in the service of commerce they had transported people between continents on an almost unimaginable scale, ultimately changing the demographic profile of the entire planet. ...
>
> This entire project had now been upended. ...
>
> The world had changed too much, too fast; the systems that were in control now did not obey any human master; they followed their own imperatives, inscrutable as demons. (304–5)

The passage harks back to the moment earlier in the novel when Dinanath has told Tipu that 'possession is when someone is taken over by a demon', adding that this is 'Just a just a metaphor for greed', and Tipu has replied, 'If that's what a demon is then there's no way it's imaginary. Shit no! We're all demons' (121). So, while they have been displaced from their homeland by the impact of climate change, the Bengali migrants seeking to find a new life in Europe have also been taken over by the demons of the Internet, which promises to act as a great leveller between people of different countries and backgrounds. This emphasis on variant motives for migration alone makes *Gun Island* more than simply a climate change novel.[9]

Human migration is complemented by and influenced by the migration of many of the non-human species that appear in the novel. Dolphins, fish, yellow-bellied sea snakes, bark beetles and brown recluse spiders have all been displaced from their traditional habitats, to the point where the migration of species is a new norm, and several passages in the novel draw explicit analogies between human and non-human migration. Thus, when Tipu on his journey to the West is stranded in Turkey, Piya sees it as parallel to the stranding of the dolphins she has been studying in the Sundarbans, and underlying such parallels is the sense of therianthropic fusion that is most obvious when Dinanath in the Querini Stampalia library feels he is being dreamed by the creatures he has thought of as Manasa Devi's subjects and that they have somehow become part of one another's dreams. These issues come to a climax in the conclusion, in which Dinanath accompanies several of the novel's other main characters on a ship that sets out to rescue refugees, who include Tipu, from the Blue Boat. Amid the freak weather, they encounter abnormal sightings of marine life, which also appears to be an effect of changing weather patterns. When they see half the cetacean species of the Mediterranean in a single day, Piya sees it as 'a little bit unusual', but, staying true to the empirical scientific approach that has characterized her throughout, rebuts Cinta's suggestion that it is 'miraculous' (293). This, though, is only a prelude to what will follow. Dinanath's sense that the tornadoes have taken them into the realms of fantasy is further compounded by events that are again redolent of the *Hypnerotomachia Poliphili*. Their ship is surrounded by cavorting dolphins and whales and a '*stormo*'[10] of millions of birds migrating northwards, and the waters around the Blue Boat are filled with an 'unearthly' glow of bioluminescence, caused by the extraordinary throng of cetaceans that are encircling it in a seemingly protective way. This again suggests both a harmonious conjunction of species and an event that defies normality. Cinta experiences it as a moment of extreme joy, saying, 'Time itself is in ecstasy' (306), and the novel ends with her dying and, as Dinanath sees it, finding 'release from the grief of her separation from her daughter' (312). He recalls words from a mosaic in the Salute church that she has told him to remember, '*Unde Origo Inde Salus* – "From the beginning salvation comes"',[11] and in the gnomic conclusion he interprets these words to mean that 'the possibility of our deliverance lies not in the future but in the past, in a mystery beyond memory' (312).[12] The effect is to collapse the distance between the two worlds that he has seen himself as straddling, as he has attempted to unravel the meaning of the Gun Merchant's story and the outcome seems to be that 'deliverance' can come from a non-Western, pre-Enlightenment world-view. Such a conclusion brings many of the earlier plot strands together and none more so than the inference that he has retraced the Merchant's steps. It also suggests that fabulation, whether it be in the form of the legend of the Merchant, the *Hypnerotomachia Poliphili* or Salgari's *Mystery of the Black Jungle*, offers more solutions to the problems that the novel has addressed than scientific rationalism, and this creates a degree of tension with regard to the issue of climate change.

The suggestion that present-day salvation is to be found in the past runs the risk of promoting a cross-cultural, atemporal universalism, a perspective that would be at odds with the view, central to both *The Great Derangement* and *Gun Island*, that climate change is an anthropocentric, post-industrial phenomenon. Arguably, though, the two positions are reconciled when Piya, who remains the voice of scientific empiricism to the end, says that, while she has never heard of anything like the bioluminescence they have just seen happening before, 'animal migrations are being hugely impacted by climate change so nothing is surprising now', and they can expect to 'see more of these intersecting events in the future' (309). In her view, then, the old norms no longer obtain in the new age of meteorological and geological change and perhaps this view can be extended to the stance Ghosh takes on the form of the novel. As he sees it, climate change challenges representation in realist fiction and yet in *Gun Island* he serves up a novel, which, whatever caveats he may advance, is centrally concerned with its impact. *Autre temps, autre moeurs*: a re-envisioned form of realism is needed to deal with the hitherto paranormal fact of climate change and *Gun Island* embodies this in its incorporation of several cases of apparent precognition of disasters and Cinta's preternatural sense of Lucia's presence as a *bhuta* who haunts the present in what ultimately proves to be a beneficent way, since it offers a form of 'salvation' through recourse to pre-Enlightenment thinking. Similarly, the story of the Merchant and Manasa Das haunts Dinanath, particularly in the Venetian second half of the novel, and he gradually comes to realize that, along with other fabulist narratives, it offers a blueprint for contemporary life, in which humans can live in harmony with non-human species for the good of the planet. The environmental message is clear.

How, though, does this finally affect Ghosh's view of the novel genre's unsuitability for representing climate issues? Unlike his other recent responses to climate change, *Gun Island* remains a novel written in an ostensibly realist mode. Fabulist storytelling and a concomitant series of events that defy probability are central to its *themes*, but it encapsulates these within the framework of Dinanath's primarily realistic narrative. When he ventures into material outside what would normally be seen as the calculus of probability, it is foregrounded as such: it exists in the pages of a dream-narrative or an oral fable, or it represents an expansion of conceptions of the probable, which is analogous to the fact that global warming is itself taking human beings into previously inconceivable territory. All of this, then, has an air of realism about it, since the novel travels from place to place with Dinanath, providing contingent details that are rooted in specifics, so that individually the episodes are plausible enough, provided one is prepared to see unexpected meetings, foreknowledge and extraordinary coincidences as within the bounds of *possibility*, even if they are 'outside the range of the probable'. As above, what remains hard to accept is Dinanath's being present at one climate emergency after another, but this remains within the realm of *possibility* and has ample precedent in the picaresque novel. At the same time as *Gun Island* pays its homage to Bengali fable by transposing motifs from the legend of the Merchant and Manasa Devi into the present, its Western analogues give it a place within the anti-romantic fictional tradition developed by writers such as Cervantes, Le Sage, Fielding and Voltaire, which were one important departure-point for realism in the West. *Gun Island* is not picaresque in the original Spanish sense, in which a rogue hero upends the conventions of romance, but with its peripatetic protagonist, it is picaresque in the looser sense of the term that came to the fore in episodic novels such as *Don Quixote*, *Gil Blas*, *Tom Jones* and *Candide*, novels which are quintessentially realistic in their panoramic social canvases and their engagement with contemporary issues and events. Thus, as mentioned above, the central sections of *Tom Jones* are played out against the background of the 1745 Jacobite Rebellion, and Candide happens to be in Lisbon at the time of the 1755 earthquake, which, *avant la lettre*, unleashed a tsunami on the city. In much the same way Dinanath is conveniently on hand when Venice is flooded, a first-hand observer of Californian wildfires and a witness of a stand-off over migrant boat crossings on the Mediterranean. So, while the overriding message of *Gun Island* involves an animist vision that challenges Enlightenment thinking, the novel mainly operates within the conventions of a picaresque realism that legitimizes the inclusion of the unexpected and allows the uncanny to claim a space within the quotidian.

12

'Innumerable ommatidia': Multi-realism in Wu Ming-Yi's *The Man with the Compound Eyes*

Without having the encyclopaedic breadth of a text like Richard Powers' *The Overstory*, Taiwanese[1] novelist Wu Ming-Yi's *The Man with the Compound Eyes* (2011) provides a fitting conclusion to the case-studies explored in this book, since its depiction of the dramatic impact of climate change on a Pacific Rim nation touches on almost all the climate issues that figure in the novels that I have been discussing. Additionally, Wu's novel employs a broad range of fictional modes that bring realism into dialogue with various forms of fantasy and metafiction, and the intricacies of the collage of techniques involved foreground the problematics of writing climate change. Like *The Overstory*, James Bradley's *Clade* and Amitav Ghosh's *Gun Island*, *The Man with the Compound Eyes* demonstrates that literary realism can be reworked to 'confront the centrality of the improbable' (Ghosh 2016: 23). My main focus in the chapter is on the formal complexity of Wu's novel, especially its shifting use of point of view, but before coming on to this, I would like to indicate some of the commonalities it shares with the other novels discussed in this book, particularly, but not exclusively, with regard to its engagement with the climate crisis.

Like the majority of the texts that I have been considering, *The Man with the Compound Eyes* critiques Anthropocene exceptionalism. It projects a hylozoist vision, in which the recurring trope of compound eyes, particularly associated with insects, represents an alternative way of looking at the world. Mountains and rivers are given voices; the sea has emotions; trees walk and speak; houses are living organisms, subtly attuned to the identities of their occupants. As in Barbara Kingsolver's *Flight Behaviour*, the behaviour of butterflies complements the human action. As in Indra Sinha's *Animal's People* and Margaret Atwood's *MaddAddam* trilogy, the supposed gap between the human and the non-human is undermined by therianthropic figures and, as in *The Overstory*, this challenge to human exclusivity is sometimes extended into *arbor*anthropic fusions. As in *Clade*, the dangers that human population growth, with its ever-increasing demands on ever-diminishing resources, poses to other forms of life on earth is identified as a threat to the planet's survival. The novel moves between representing the devastation caused by global climate change and environmental disasters that have more local repercussions. The former manifests itself in earthquakes, storms and tsunamis of the kind that figure in Liz Jensen's *The Rapture* and in *Gun Island*, and these are seen as becoming more frequent; the latter in the form of water pollution caused by petrochemicals discharged from factories, which, as in Helon Habila's *Oil on Water* and as in *Gun Island*, are ruining the natural beauty of a littoral environment. As in Antti Tuomainen's *The Healer*, waterfront properties are flooded and, as in *Clade*, coastal erosion is eating away at a shoreline. As in *Flight Behaviour*, unparalleled rains cause landslides. As in *The Rapture*, Ian McEwan's *Solar* and *Clade*, the dangers of methane released from the bed of the ocean are spelt out. As in Annie Proulx's *Barkskins*, traditional native wisdom about the natural world is juxtaposed with the expertise of specialists and, as in *Gun Island*, the experts involved include a marine biologist. In addition to associating compound sight with insects, the novel also links it with 'a technologically mediated vision of nature' (Sterk 2016: 188) and, while the idea is implicit rather than explicit here, as in *The Overstory* and *Clade*, there is the suggestion that artificial intelligence (AI) may provide a solution to the problems of climate change; the opposition to the Anthropocene destruction of the planet may involve a coalition between traditional, particularly aboriginal, responses to the environment and AI's development of strategies that are not constricted by human biases and limitations. As in *The Rapture* and *Gun Island*, realism is juxtaposed with the uncanny and, as in *The Overstory* and *The Rapture*, the novel offers a holistic vision, in which the earth is seen as a self-sustaining entity, a vision in line with James Lovelock's Gaia hypothesis, though Lovelock is not an intertext in *The Man with the Compound Eyes*, as he is in those novels. Bringing these various issues together, as in Atwood's trilogy, Wu suggests that climate change is part and parcel of a broader terrestrial transformation: 'Everything change'. And lastly, like *Solar*, *The Overstory*, *Oil on Water* and *Gun Island*, *The Man with the Compound Eyes* alerts its readers to the complexities surrounding the narrativization of climate change, making it clear that this is culturally mediated, by showing how it takes different forms in modern Taiwanese, aboriginal Taiwanese and Pacific island societies, groupings which themselves prove to be far from unitary.

The opening chapters introduce readers to two main characters and to two contrasting narrative modes. They employ a braided structure, in which the focalization alternates between Atile'i, an adolescent living on the fictional Pacific island of Wayo Wayo, which is isolated, both geographically and epistemologically, from the world at large, and Alice Shih, a Han Chinese writer and professor, who, at the opening of the novel, is contemplating suicide. Atile'i's story has an air of fable about it; Alice's story is told in a mode that does little to disturb the conventions of Western realism.[2] Ostensibly these two protagonists are worlds apart, but the action indicates commonalities between them from the outset, most obviously in their existential situations. Atile'i faces death, because he is a second son, and Wayo Wayo customs dictate that such sons must be sent away to sea 'on a mission of no return' (Wu Ming-Yi ([2011] 2014: 14).[3] Alice has lost the will to live, after the death of her husband Thom and the disappearance of her son Toto on a climbing expedition years earlier, and because of a more general disillusion with the daily grind of her profession and the damage being inflicted on the East Taiwan landscape where she lives. Told in parallel in the opening chapters, the two characters' stories are complementary in other ways, most obviously in their finding themselves detached from the certainties of their very different earlier lives, and the first two chapter headings, which both refer to the 'last nights' they are experiencing, make the link between them clear.

Having left Wayo Wayo, Atile'i finds himself on another island, a mysterious island that he calls '*gesi gesi*' (170), the term the Earth Sage of his people uses for things that cannot be understood. He is ignorant of Western consumer society and consequently unaware of the island's nature and, since it is seen through his ingenuous eyes, which generate ironies as everyday objects are defamiliarized, the island's composition is not initially clear to readers, though clues are evident from the moment when Atile'i emerges from 'dreamland' to realize that:

Apparently boundless, the island was made not of mud but of a multi-hued mishmash of strange stuff, and there was a weird smell hanging in the air. ...

Atile'i soon discovered that there were many sorts of coloured bags all over the island. They were different from the burlap bags of Wayo Wayo in that they could hold water, though with some of them the water whooshed out as soon as you picked them up, leaving mussels, sea stars and other odds and ends high and dry. There were bags like this on Wayo Wayo, too. The elders said the white man had left them behind, but the past few years you often found them floating in the sea as well. (31)

Alice's home on Taiwan's east coast is a seaside house, which she and her now-deceased Danish husband Thom have built, taking their inspiration from the modernist Swedish architect Erik Gunnar Asplund's Summer House at Stennäs. For Alice, the house is a 'living organism' (55), a sanctuary that is a world away from what she sees as the hideous architecture of the ironically named nearby Haven County.[4] However, without being physically displaced in the same way as Atile'i, she, too, finds herself on a strange island, when an earthquake hits the local shoreline and, although she is still within the house that is so special to her, she is left 'standing on a remote island in the midst of an immense ocean' (26). What she and Thom have called the 'Seaside House' comes to be known as the 'Sea House' and later she rechristens it 'Alice's Island' (178). Both characters are, then, islanded, literally and also figuratively, in the sense that they are isolated from their communities, and their interdependence is reflected in the headings of the two chapters in the middle of the novel where they first meet: Chapter 13, in which Alice is the focalizer, is entitled 'Atile'i'; Chapter 14, in which 'Atile'i' is the focalizer, is entitled 'Alice'. The affinities between them suggest that, despite the vast cultural differences that separate them, they are kindred spirits, not least because they are fellow-victims of climate change in the form of the Pacific Trash Vortex, which is, of course, the island on which Atile'i has found himself after leaving Wayo Wayo and which, in a second devastating storm, carries him ashore in Taiwan, where he is found by Alice. Their coming together is perhaps an unsurprising development in the narrative dynamic of a novel, which has begun by charting their parallel lives and in which a number of motifs have been linking them already. However, by the time the two narratives converge, the bifocalism of the braided structure has expanded to encompass the stories of a number of other characters and phenomena, and this suggests that the initial alternation between Western realism and non-Western fabulation is itself a delimiting straitjacket that fails to allow for the compound multi-optic vision, which the novel employs to undermine the exclusivism of human modes of perception.

From the third of the novel's eleven parts onwards, the initial bifurcation of the narrative between Atile'i and Alice is subverted by a series of shifts in time and focalization, which destabilizes any sense of straightforward linear progression or unitary perception. If one were trying to find a precedent in the Western canon, then the Conrad of *Lord Jim* or *Nostromo* might come close, since the technique of these novels works to subvert any sense of definitive authority, though finally it is less radically subversive. *The Man with the Compound Eyes* conveys a similar sense of being built on metaphorical as well as literal shifting sands by extending the range of characters who act as focalizers, by moving between different levels of reality, and ultimately, close to its end, by interrogating the reliability of the story it has been telling. The suggestion is that the fragmentation of contemporary experience is akin to the bricolage of the Trash Island and also that, while on one level the novel has provided a realistic account of the forces that are imperilling Taiwan's east coast, a metonym for life on earth, on another level this is inadequate and a completely different way of perceiving the world is needed.

When the novel moves beyond its initial alternation between Atile'i and Alice in the third part, it takes up the stories of two characters from aboriginal Taiwanese east-coast communities, Hafay and Dahu. These are narrated in a primarily realistic, albeit non-linear, mode and with references to aboriginal customs that sometimes parallel the traditions and practices of Wayo Wayo. Hafay is an independent Pangcah woman who runs a café, the Seventh Sisid, at which Alice is a regular, since it is just five minutes away from her house, though proximity is not the only reason why she frequents the café and again, there are links between the characters. The Seventh Sisid has a special significance for Hafay, because she has grown up, in Taiwan's capital Taipei, in a makeshift village with houses that were 'haphazard, more like shacks' and she comes from a people who 'think houses are for spirits to inhabit' (188). As with Alice, her home is an extension of herself and since their two houses were begun at the same time, she thinks of them as twins.

Dahu embodies a complex balance between modernity and traditional aboriginal ways. He is a Bunun with a degree in forest ecology from Taipei and, although his education has in one sense separated him from his community, his vocation is in keeping with the reverence for nature, particularly forests and mountains, that are central to his people's ancestral beliefs. He is introduced as 'many things: a taxi driver, a mountaineer, an amateur sculptor, a forest conservationist and a volunteer for some east-coast NGOs' (20). Just as Atile'i and Alice are twinned, Hafay and Dahu are linked, with both having had similar experiences in the past. Hafay has worked as a masseuse in Taipei; Dahu has visited a massage parlour in Haven, where he has fallen in love with and married one of the workers, Millet, who has subsequently abandoned him and their daughter Umav. And as the novel continues, it reveals a degree of overlap between Hafay and Millet. The parallels in their experiences are only loosely developed, and there is no suggestion that they are one and the same – they worked as masseuses in different towns – but Hafay's name actually means Millet in Pangcah (158). So there is a blurring of the lines between them, and when Hafay talks to Dahu about her past, she admits to feeling an affinity with Millet: 'Maybe I understand how Millet felt, more or less. Besides, maybe at the same time as I was working she was doing the rounds in a place with little rooms somewhere else' (188). This is typical of the novel's use of motifs that link characters and episodes, while leaving the connections tenuous. On one level this seems to suggest that subjectivity is not altogether unitary, and this could be read as a challenge to the post-Enlightenment Western privileging of individuality. At the same time, the novel's use of variations on a theme also serves to enforce its contention that experience is not singular, but rather a product of multiple optical perspectives. So both the use of diverse focalizers – others are added as the novel continues – and the overlap between characters and experiences are formal correlatives of the central argument, which is most persuasively conveyed through the figure of the eponymous man with the compound eyes.

This figure first appears in the story of her past that Hafay tells to Alice, when she relates an encounter that took place shortly after the makeshift Taipei village in which she and her mother Ina were living was destroyed by torrential rainfall. She sees Ina talking to a man, who seems both young and middle-aged, both big and small, and who, amid these perceived contradictions, when Hafay makes eye contact with him, appears to have eyes that are invested with an abundance of non-human features. Using similes that are typical of the whole novel, Hafay says, 'Those eyes were … how shall I put it? Ah, it's hard to say. It was like a tiger, a butterfly, a tree and a cloud looking at you all at once' (96; ellipsis in original). Ina has been searching for her elderly lover, who has gone missing in the flood, and the figure of the man, whom she identifies as a Pangcah ancestral spirit, directs her to the pool where he has drowned. So the figure appears to personify an animist wisdom that has preternatural powers. There is no further development of the man's identity at this point, but the chapter ends with Alice feeling she has been initiated into 'a new conception of life: that life doesn't allow you any preconceptions' (97), and Hafay's big toes, which Alice now sees for the first time, provide ocular proof of this. Alice realizes that these are split into two, so each foot has an extra toe. Embarrassed, she looks away, but an alternative view of reality remains with her, as she sees 'the window covered in moths, moths of all different colours, many of them with eyespots of different shapes and sizes on their wings … as if they were staring at something' (98). While the spots are not literally eyes, as Darryl Sterk has put it, they extend a sense of 'the ubiquity of the ecological gaze' (2016: 204) and further destabilize any sense of sovereign, authoritative vision.

The man has also appeared to Dahu at a moment when *he* has been confronted with the death of someone close to him. As a boy, he has been on a hunting expedition with his father, and when he is separated from the hunting party pursuing a wild boar, he falls in the forest and gets up to find himself confronted by a man whose eyes again seem to contain various aspects of non-human life forms. He describes them as follows:

> They were more like compound eyes composed of countless single eyes, the eyes of clouds, mountains, streams, meadowlarks and muntjacs, all arranged together. As I gazed, each little eye seemed to contain a different scene, and those scenes arranged to form a vast panorama the likes of which I had never see. (186)

When he is reunited with the group, he learns that they have been looking for him because his father has been accidentally shot – it will turn out to be fatal – in his right *eye*. A possible significance of this is that it represents the fate that awaits those who engage in hunting, an activity that is alien to Dahu. He is told by both the man and his father that he can never become a good hunter, and this is the beginning of his turning instead to forest ecology. After the man has spoken to him, the young Dahu finds himself on the edge of a sheer cliff, alienated as if he is 'standing on an *island*' (186; emphasis added) and each time he goes on subsequent hunting expeditions, he has a similar experience of feeling dazed on a cliff edge. The implication is that the encounter with the man is a primal experience that isolates (islands) him and places him on an ontological precipice. Providing another instance of Wu's hinting at analogies between characters, but leaving them suspended and unconsolidated, the island trope echoes the predicaments of Atile'i and Alice, without there being any direct correspondence between Dahu's experience and theirs; similarly, the cliff trope relates his experience to the issue of what happens to Thom and Toto on the climbing expedition from which they never return, and as an adult Dahu will be tasked with trying to find them.

The latter part of the novel offers a version of what befell the father and son in four chapters that each bear the heading 'The Man with the Compound Eyes', but leave Thom and Toto anonymized,[5] as it were stripping them of their social identity, a factor which will assume added significance when their very existence is cast into doubt shortly before the end. In the first of these four chapters, a father and son climb a cliff, but the purpose of their expedition seems to be as much concerned with finding insects as mountaineering. The 'boy' (Toto) has been fascinated by insects, and at the top of the cliff, they use a flashlight to try to find beetles. Unsuccessful in this, they only attract a few moths, but one of these is 'an erebus, a kind of butterfly with huge *eye spots* on its wings' (224; emphasis added). It is a discovery that leaves them feeling fully content, an emotion that seems to be a product of their being subject to the 'ecological gaze', in which they imagine themselves as perceived rather than perceivers. The man promises the boy that the next day they will descend the cliff to go looking for long-armed scarab beetles, but it is a promise that is never fulfilled, since the man goes missing in the night. Next day the boy waits for his return, while finding himself still subject to the gaze of non-human life forms, as 'trees, deer and goats all keep their eyes trained' (226) on him. At this point, the man with the compound eyes reappears and gestures to indicate that the man (Thom) has gone over the edge of the cliff, where the boy is now perilously poised. So again, the man is associated with death in the form of a cliff-edge predicament and, since the boy has been dreaming, he also seems to be hovering on the borderline between the imagined and the real. Appearing as he does immediately after the reference to the boy being the object of an animist gaze, the man with the compound eyes also seems to personify the natural forces of an ecosystem that unites the non-human organisms that make up life on earth. Like Powers in *The Overstory*, Wu does not eschew the sometimes frowned-upon practice of anthropomorphization as a way of dramatizing the agency of non-human life forms.

The second of the four chapters entitled 'The Man with the Compound Eyes' focuses on the man (Thom), but by this point discrete identities no longer obtain and the distinction between dream and reality is further blurred. The Thom figure has a dream in which he has tried to '*blind* climb' (252; emphasis added) his way down the mountain. Apparently having woken up from this, though he subsequently moves in and out of a dream-like state, he decides to go over the cliff and climb down the mountain in reality. On the way down, he senses someone else on the cliff and falls to the ground below, where he has a conversation with this second presence, who tells him he is more or less dead and who, when their eyes meet, gives him the feeling that 'it is less like he is looking at someone else and more like he is looking at himself' (254). It is significant that eye contact is as important a part of their interaction as words, since the man (Thom) is confounded by his doppelgänger's compound vision, in which 'innumerable ommatidia' (255) have converged. He asks him for help to save his boy at the top of the cliff, but is rebuffed by the man with the compound eyes, who tells him he has no power to help anyone. If one sees the figure as a personification of the insectile non-human order, this response could be seen to suggest that anthropocentric action has confined humankind to a solipsistic planetary existence. The man (Thom) is also told that he knows very well that there is no one at the top of the cliff, and this throws the boy's (Toto's) very existence into doubt, which could be seen to raise questions about the continued existence of the human species in the future. As mentioned in Chapter 3, Adeline Johns Putra emphasizes the significance of the figure of the child in environmentalist discourse: 'it is a synecdochic representation of future generations and readily conjures up an impulse toward protection, shelter, and guardianship. ... Moreover, the association of children with innocence and hence with the "natural" allows additional slippage between children and the nonhuman, especially between children and charismatic animals' (2017: 6). If there is no boy, then there is no such promise for the future.

In the third of the four chapters entitled 'The Man with the Compound Eyes', the vision of the eponymous man is again associated with that of insects, bringing to a climax one of the novel's central tropes: butterflies, prominent in the novel less because of their crucial ecological role as pollinators and more because of the alternative vision they represent, recur throughout and the autistic Toto is especially fascinated by beetles. Verbally challenged to the point where he has struggled to express himself until the age of three, he has 'amazing visual acuity' (75) and this is linked with insectile sight. When a rare stag beetle, which he has been taking care of, dies, he identifies with it and utters a complete sentence, 'I can't see what you can see any more' (75). Now, in this climactic chapter, where the Thom figure's dialogue with the man with the compound eyes at the moment of his supposed death, continues, each of the latter's eyes is said to contain 'at least tens of thousands of ommatidia' (278), and these 'seem to change from moment to moment in hallucinatory permutations and combinations. And the scene in each of the tiny ommatidia that compose every compound eye is completely different with each passing instant' (276). The Thom figure watches this ever-changing kaleidoscope mesmerized by the scenes it encompasses, each of which 'seems to be playing a kind of documentary' that draws on images from the natural world: 'an erupting undersea volcano', 'a falcon's-eye view of a landscape', 'a leaf about to fall' (276). At the same time, the scenes on display suggest a different kind of visual imagery, the imagery of video montage and Darryl Sterk has offered a persuasive discussion of the novel, which argues that 'each mini-eye, in the eyes of the man with the compound eyes could be produced on PC-based nonlinear editing software', though in the novel the myriad montages are integrated in the man's 'hypersubjectivity' into a 'composite image' (2016: 189). That said, the focus on compound vision is clearly predicated on the notion of humans assuming an insectile perception of the world. The two ways of seeing – entomological and computerized – may not be exclusive and the challenge to combat ecological disaster through technological means *is* certainly prominent in *The Man with the Compound Eyes*, as it is in *Clade* and *The Overstory*, but throughout the course of the novel, the emphasis on transcending anthropocentric exclusivism is more widely associated with a reconfigured approach to the natural world, in which insect vision becomes a key signifier of a holistic world-view. Sterk is rightly wary of any suggestion of unmediated access to 'nature'. He associates this with 'primitivism', and defends Wu from the possible charge that his primitivism is 'retrograde', by saying, 'Whatever premodern cultural inspirations one may cite for the man with the compound eyes, he is most importantly a symbol of the audiovisual technologies that mediate our relationship with nature' (Sterk 2016: 190). However, while such mediation may be playing an increasingly important role in humanity's relations with nature[6] – on the simplest level, natural history documentaries have gone a long way to replacing zoos as a site for learning about the animal world – more direct botanical and zoological, particularly entomological, encounters, mediated only by the novel's prose, recur throughout the novel and there are numerous passages in which the non-human is invested with agency that does not rely on audio-visual intercession. The opening sentence gives voice to a mountain: 'The trickling of water through the fissures in the subterranean rock was suddenly drowned out when the mountain made an immense but also somehow distant sound' (9). What is happening here will only be contextualized in the novel's latter stages, where it becomes clear that the episode refers to the digging of the Hsuehshan, or Snow Mountain, Tunnel, which links Taipei with Ilan County in north-eastern Taiwan,[7] but it is the first of numerous passages in which natural phenomena, particularly sea, forest and mountain, are seen in animist terms. Here, on the opening page, the sound made by the mountain is a curtain-raiser to what follows. It conjures up a sense of imminent catastrophe and, using an insect trope, it is a small-scale forerunner of the mounting ecological disasters that are central to the narrative: 'It obviously wasn't a verbal echo. It sounded more like when something bumps into a flawless glass vessel – from somewhere within the glass you hear a spider's web begin to spread before the cracks appear' (9). This chapter is detached from the stories of Atile'i and Alice, which follow in the first part of the novel, but it is the perfect prolegomenon to what will succeed it, since it anticipates the gradual accumulation of ecological catastrophes that the novel will document and also the method in which they are presented: spider-like, *The Man with the Compound Eyes* will spin an ever-widening web of stories that collectively attest to the need for a visual praxis that dismantles habitual human modes of perception.

The third of the chapters with the title 'The Man with the Compound Eyes' has a further revelation in store for the Thom figure, a revelation that explains the man's earlier comment that he knows perfectly well that the boy is not at the top of the cliff. The man tells him that his wife's writing kept his son alive, and the clear suggestion is that Toto died from a snakebite at a young age. Since then, he is told, 'at the opposite extremes of life and death, your wife and your son have enjoyed a kind of symbiotic coexistence' (280). Thus far in the narrative, Alice has been represented as accepting the reality of Thom's accidental death – his body has been found by Dahu – but, the implication is, she has been inventing a life for her dead son, who died long before the time when he is supposed to have gone on the fatal expedition with Thom. The significance becomes clearer when the man with the compound eyes continues his homily by saying that Toto 'didn't die by the regular definition, only he wasn't alive any more' (281). Uniquely, through writing, humans can reconstruct the world, as an 'organism', akin to '"the realm of nature"' (279). As the Thom figure 'dies', the man with the compound eyes again says that he has no power to intervene: he can only observe.

Following this, there is a brief fourth chapter with the title 'The Man with the Compound Eyes', in which the boy (Toto) overhears what has been said about his not being alive any longer, and from the moment when he hears this, the reality of most of the preceding narrative is thrown into doubt. The boy – the significance of his not being named takes on added resonance now – becomes a blurred image, 'as if he is transforming into a leaf, an insect, a birdcall, a drop of water, a pinch of lichen, or even a rock'; he becomes an incorporeal entity, 'received into one of the ommatidia, far smaller than pinpoints' (286), a being who now only exists in memory. Then, in the final chapter, Alice completes two fictions, a short story and a novel, both of which have the title 'The Man with the Compound Eyes'/*The Man with the Compound Eyes*[8] and this, of course, suggests that she may be the author of everything in the novel so far.

Where, one has to ask, does this leave the novel in terms of realism? Does the act of writing become the primary 'reality' of the novel with all the supposed lived experience that has previously been represented now relegated to a secondary level of meaning? Such a reading would be in line with the view of fiction advanced by formalist critics such as Viktor Shklovsky, who regarded *Tristram Shandy* as 'the most typical novel of world literature', because art forms cannot be explained 'in terms of their motivation to exhibit a mode of life' (Shklovsky ([1929] 1968: 89, 88) and, from first to last, Sterne's masterpiece is concerned with the problematics of writing fiction. Seen in this light, the 'mode of life' exhibited so far in *The Man with the Compound Eyes* turns out to be, wholly or mainly, a product of Alice's writerly imagination. She now appears to be a fantasist – after all, her namesake is Lewis Carroll's traveller in wonderland – and the unreliability of the main body of the narrative has been hinted at earlier: prior to completing her two works of fiction, Alice has told Atile'i that she plans to write about 'something that apparently happened, but maybe never actually did' (289). The novel continues after the moment when she is revealed as the author of two fictions that share its name and the Alice who has written the stories remains as a character – as an extradiegetic narrator who could be said to exist on a more 'realistic' plane – but by now the metafictive emphasis seems paramount.

However, while all fiction can be read as metafiction, even overtly self-reflexive novels include non-metafictive material, and *The Man with the Compound Eyes* is also centrally concerned with social issues that 'exhibit a mode of life', particularly the consequences of climate change and the exploitation of Taiwan's east coast. So self-conscious though its narrative mode may be, the novel is not simply, or only, metafictive. It also employs a highly effective use of strategic realism.[9] Considered in its entirety, it employs a range of discursive modes that stage dialogues between the different world views it depicts, and the effect is to initiate *readers* into compound vision. At first, the juxtaposition of different modes revolves around the alternation between Alice and Atile'i's very different world-views, but this expands outwards and when the reality of the episodes centred on Thom and Toto's expedition is undermined, readers have to contend with the constructed, seemingly self-begetting nature of the whole narrative, with just the closing pages appearing to exist outside the frame of Alice's account. At the point where Alice appears to be the author of most of the narrative so far, the stories of Hafay and Dahu, the account of how Alice and Thom first came together in Scandinavia, and episodes centred on a German engineer Detlef Boldt and his Norwegian marine biologist wife Sara, who come to Taiwan when Detlef is enlisted as an adviser for the work on the mountain tunnel, could be said to belong to the second internal level of narrative, as they too are, at least potentially, intradiegetic figures in Alice's narrative. Yet little or nothing in these sections steps outside the conventions of classic realism, and they embody a level of social commentary that is as important, in the critique of Anthropocene damage to the environment, as the less conventionally realized encounters with the man with the compound eyes.

The central trope of this critique is the Pacific Trash Vortex, which carries Atile'i to Taiwan, and the various ways in which it is represented typify the multiple realisms of the novel's compound vision. When Atile'i is first observed on it, it is the 'multi-hued mishmash of strange stuff', described in the passage quoted earlier in this chapter, and seen through his eyes, which defamiliarize everyday objects, its representation is in keeping with the fable-like quality of the Wayo Wayo sections. For Alice, the debris the Vortex brings into her flooded home makes it 'like the unknown organisms of an alien world', but she is able to place this detritus in realistic terms as an agglomeration of 'myriad plastic objects' (243). Journalists extend this optic, when they call the Vortex 'the Primeval Plastic Soup' (214). Acting as a kind of curator of trash, Dahu provides a further perspective, when he adopts a taxonomic approach and thinks of all the tales that the various pieces it comprises have to tell. He takes the view that one day it may be 'an important source for the study of the cultural history of globalisation' (182) and in so doing allows the novel to highlight the extent to which *it* is making a small fictional contribution to this. It extends the reality of the actual Pacific Vortex into speculative fictive territory by bringing it to shore on Taiwan's east coast, but it also includes a newspaper report that provides documentary information about the known reality of its location and composition. So, along with the surreal episodes where humans come into contact with the man with the compound eyes and amid sections that appear to be the product of Alice's fantasies, the text incorporates a factual account of how the oceanographer Charles J. Moore discovered what he thought was 'some kind of alternate dimension' (122), when he stumbled across the Trash Vortex in 1997. Moore himself subsequently founded an institute to contain its spread, which to him, the novel says, 'had the same symbolic significance as humanity's efforts to combat global warming' (122), but this, if anything, underestimates the extent of the Vortex's contribution to climate change, since the link is more than analogical: when the Vortex's plastics break down into methane and ethylene, in addition to causing massive damage to marine life, they also increase the rate of global warming.

These, then, are some of the varied ways in which the Trash Vortex is depicted and, as well as playing a major role in the novel's action, it is its central trope for the damage occasioned by Anthropocene exclusivism. It is, though, just one manifestation of this and, along with dramatizing the case for an alternative vision, *The Man with the Compound Eyes*, introduces numerous other details to convey the ubiquitous effects of climate change, as well as a plethora of related ecological issues. Some, such as the increased incidence of earthquakes and floods in the last decade (69), dust storms from China that have filled the skies of eastern Taiwan with a haze (73), the melting of polar ice, making the North West Passage navigable (233), the average sea temperature off Taiwan's east coast being 1.6°C higher than the previous record (289) and the unsustainable growth in the population of *Homo sapiens* (199), are mentioned almost incidentally; others such as coastal erosion and rising sea levels underpin the whole novel, coming to a climax when Wayo Wayo is completely destroyed by 'a tsunami of unprecedented power' (298). At this point Wu introduces lyrics from Bob Dylan's 1960's vision of apocalyptic disaster, 'A Hard Rain's a-Gonna Fall', as an intertext. It is a song which in retrospect seems to foresee the climate crisis, and its line about a wave that can drown the entire world has a particular resonance in the novel, since it anticipates the fate that awaits Wayo Wayo and the older ecosystems of which it is a repository.

The destruction of Wayo Wayo, a metonym for the dangers facing low-lying Pacific islands more generally, is followed by the movement of a pod of sperm whales, avatars of the second sons of the island, who like Atile'i have been exiled, to the coast of Chile, where they beach themselves and die. Their gruesome deaths, and the consequences for both human and non-human species of the extinction of this all-male therianthropic group, seem cataclysmic, and the prospects for Taiwan's east coast appear to be little better. The novel ends with Atile'i going back to sea as the unprecedentedly severe storm approaches. Yet the picture is not entirely pessimistic. As Alice walks along a forest path, Ohiyo, a cat – like Atile'i a refugee from the elements – that she has taken in earlier in the novel while it was still a kitten, brushes against her leg, and she resolves to care for her. The novel ends with the cat looking at her, with its differently coloured eyes – one blue, one brown. So amid actual disaster, the trope of alternative vision, associated with a non-human creature seems to serve as a fragment shored against the world's ruin. It is the culmination of numerous references to binary, not compound, vision that have appeared earlier in both the Taiwanese and Wayo Wayo sections of the novel. Fascinated by Ohiyo's eyes, Umav has asked Alice ingenuously, 'do different coloured eyes see the world the same way?' (71), and Atile'i tells a highly pertinent tale he has heard from his father about a pair of twins with different coloured eyes. He is, of course, from a society organized around primogeniture – the sending of second sons to sea to perish is a form of population control – but the twins of the tale, sons of the island's Sea Sage, come into the world side by side as co-equals. The story relates to an earlier era, when the two sages who are the guiding spirits of the islanders, the Earth Sage and the Sea Sage, were one, but since this time asymmetrical binaries have taken over and the kind of egalitarianism that both the twins and the unified sages represent has ceased to exist. The moral of the fable would seem to be that, as in more 'developed' societies, hierarchical divisions have destroyed social equilibrium, and most importantly, this is extended into the asymmetrical relationship between the human and the non-human.

Collectively, the novel's numerous references to different ways of seeing come to form part of a holistic vision in which the earth is seen as a self-sustaining system and, as suggested above, this is a view that has much in common with James Lovelock's Gaia hypothesis. However, in Wu's East Asian hands it more obviously draws on Daoist thinking, which, Justin Prystash has argued, underpins Wu's 'radical decentering of the human' that stresses 'aesthetics and hylozoism' to engage 'a speculative realist genealogy' (2018: 511). Wu, himself a lepidopterist, incorporates numerous references to butterflies into *The Man with the Compound Eyes* and has written, in *The Dao of Butterflies* (2003), that 'the aesthetics of nature is not situated at the top of the natural sciences, but at rock bottom. The first step is to change human-centered aesthetics. Then human-centered environmental aesthetics will change' (qtd. in Prystash 2018: 512).[10]

In conclusion, the novel offers an answer to Ghosh's reservations about literary fiction's ability to represent climate change, by developing a multi-optic mode that brings classic realism into dialogue with other realisms to respond to an unprecedented global situation. Its variety of styles has elicited critical responses that categorize it in very different ways: for Justin Prystash (2018) it is an expression of Daoist aesthetics; for Darryl Sterk its 'videomosaic gaze' is 'postmodern ecological sublime' (2016: 183–222). It clearly also operates on a local as well as a global level as a social critique of Taiwanese public policy (Byrnes 2014) and, arguably subsuming all such readings, it takes up a position in line with Margaret Atwood's view that 'Everything change' (2015): the climate crisis is seen as part of an all-encompassing challenge to what until recently were seen as the norms of life on earth. What is incontrovertible is that, like the majority of the novels considered in this study, it lays the blame for the crisis at the door of Anthropocene exceptionalism. It sees exclusivist *Homo sapiens* as a species that places itself outside the coalition of life forms that combine together to form mutually sustaining ecosystems. The man with the compound eyes looks on at the human race, offering advice but making it clear he is unable to intervene. Humanity needs to return his gaze and transform itself into an egalitarian organism that no longer arrogates to itself the right to adopt a predatory stance towards the flora, the fauna and the inorganic matter with which it shares the planet.

Conclusion: A new realism?

While all the novels discussed in this study are examples of realist climate fiction that challenges the Anthropocene order, some are more centrally focused on the climate crisis than others and, as I have been pointing out, none is a single-issue novel. Barbara Kingsolver's *Flight Behaviour* is as much a social novel about a particular Appalachian community as it is a novel about the climate implications of the changes in the seasonal migratory patterns of the monarch butterfly. Wu Ming-Yi's *The Man with the Compound Eyes* deals with divisions in Taiwanese society along with the anthropocentric exceptionalism that views non-human species as lower orders of being and the changing meteorological patterns that threaten the continuing existence of Pacific islands and the Ocean's littoral edges. The novels' responses to the crisis also vary considerably, with some, particularly those written at the beginning of the twenty-first century, demonstrating more concern with disseminating information to combat climate change scepticism and denial than is subsequently the case.

Similarly, while each of the novels represents the toxic effects of anthropogenic climate change, the ways in which they do so vary considerably. Helon Habila's *Oil on Water* and Indra Sinha's *Animal's People* are concerned with showing how corporate capitalism has devastated a particular ecosystem rather than with depicting the more general effects of global warming. However, in both these cases the focus on a local catastrophe can be read as a metonym for the planetary damage occasioned by neocolonial interventions, which is also to the fore elsewhere, and in Janet Fiskio's view, 'it is crucial to identify imperialism, not industrialization, as the driving force behind the onset of the Anthropocene. ... Anthropogenic climate change, whether the reduction or increase of greenhouse gases, and settler colonization are inseparable at every point along the timeline' (2021: 58–9). This may not always be immediately apparent in the novels discussed in this study, since for the most part they deal with contemporary situations rather than historical colonialism, but it is implicit in the long historical sweep of Annie Proulx's *Barkskins*, and exploitative neocolonialism is seen as responsible for the environmental disasters that underlie not just *Oil on Water* and *Animal's People*, but also Richard Powers's *The Overstory*, Liz Jensen's *The Rapture*, Margaret Atwood's *MaddAddam* trilogy, James Bradley's *Clade* and Wu Ming-Yi's *The Man with the Compound Eyes*. Two particular motifs recur in most of the novels. One is that climate change is part of a broader phenomenon. As Atwood says, 'Everything change' and much of the change can be laid at the door of corporate capitalism's subordination of environmental concerns to the pursuit of profit. The other is a stance which goes beyond showing the threat that climate change poses to *humanity*, by replacing Anthropocene exclusivism with an emphasis on the shared danger facing all the planet's species.

An attack on the limits of the Anthropocene is perhaps only to be expected in climate fiction, but it assumes an extra level of urgency in the realist novel, since interrogating Anthropocene exceptionalism strikes at the roots of the milieu in which the action of the genre is usually set, namely human society. As pointed out in my introduction, the traditional bedrock of most realist novels inheres in the shared assumption that the complications of the plot will be resolved and the stability of the social order reaffirmed in the dénouement. However, this consensus no longer obtains in the realist fiction of the age of climate change, since former epistemological certainties and the primacy of human society are no longer a donnée. Of the novels discussed here, only *The Man with the Compound Eyes*, with its use of the eponymous man as a personification of non-human Nature, its attribution of emotions to the sea and its giving voice to mountains and rivers, makes a significant movement beyond human focalization, but the centrality of butterflies in *Flight Behaviour*, and of trees, which sometimes speak, in *The Overstory*, and to a lesser extent in *Barkskins*, negates the tendency to see the climate crisis as a solely human problem. Similarly, Atwood unsettles notions of human exclusivism by according prominence to hybrid species, such as the transgenic humanoid Crakers and the various therianthropic splices that appear in her trilogy. Ghosh suggests something similar in *Gun Island*, through his use of the Bengali legend of Bonduki Sadagar, which, coupled with the European intertext of the late sixteenth-century translation of the *Hypnerotomachia Poliphili*, enables him to move beyond post-Enlightenment Western humanism, and break down the distinction between human and non-human animals, such as snakes, dolphins and spiders. And a similar distrust of post-Enlightenment notions of the human hovers just below the surface of *The Rapture* and *The Healer*, while *Clade* and *The Overstory* both introduce the possibility that artificial intelligence may step in to provide a posthuman solution to problems that appear to be defeating human brains. In various ways, then, the human is no longer accorded centrality. Only one of the novels I have considered, Ian McEwan's *Solar*, limits its focus to the human, doing so by riveting its attention on the grotesque body of the protagonist, Michael Beard. Here the playful use of the analogy between Beard's overconsumption and the wanton excesses of *Homo sapiens* more generally can still be read as a critique of anthropocentrism, but the novel remains locked in a world of speciesism.

Each of the twelve novels I have discussed represents a subset of realism and, taken together, they suggest that the mode needs to be reformulated to address the contemporary situation of change. As indicated in the introduction, what constitutes realism has been subject to numerous reinterpretations since it emerged as the lynchpin of a certain kind of European fiction some 300 years ago, reaching its apogee in nineteenth-century France. In this incarnation, it was primarily concerned with a form of verisimilitude, which purported to represent a social world and was hesitant to include anything that might stretch the bounds of credulity. As Guy de Maupassant, whose aesthetic developed Flaubert's emphasis on representing banality, put it:

> The artist, having chosen his theme, will select from such a life cluttered with random and trivial events only those characteristic details useful to his subject, and will reject all the rest as superfluous.
>
> Here is one example out of thousands: a considerable number of people in the world die every day as a result of accidents. Yet can we drop a roof tile on the main character's head, or throw him under the wheels of a carriage mid-story, on the pretext that accidents must be taken into account? (Maupassant [1888] 2001: 8)[1]

The sentiments expressed here are at odds with the Barthesian view of the 'reality effect', the use of otherwise irrelevant contingent details to create the illusion of a transcribed reality, an effect which Barthes finds in Balzac and Flaubert. They are, though, *avant la lettre*. strikingly similar to Ghosh's comments on 'the calculus of probability', which I have returned to throughout this book. In *The Great Derangement*, Ghosh contends that 'within the pages of a novel an event that is only slightly improbable in real life – say, an unexpected encounter with a long-lost childhood friend – may seem wildly unlikely' (2016: 24). In such a view, then, fact outmanoeuvres fiction to the extent that what can pass with little or no comment when it happens in real life is seen as incredible in fiction. Three years after *The Great Derangement*, Ghosh published *Gun Island*, where the narrative seems to refute what he had earlier said about plausibility in fiction, since it is peppered with unlikely meetings and, complementing this, the novel also refutes his remarks on fiction's capacity to represent the supposed improbability of climate disasters, by taking its protagonist, Dinanath, on a picaresque journey from Bengal to California to Italy and the Mediterranean, and having him experience a series of climate-triggered disasters in quick succession.

The inference is that the hitherto improbable is the new normal and from this it follows that just as unprecedented weather events rewrite the rules of meteorological likelihood, anthropogenic climate change infringes the supposed laws of probability with regard to what can reasonably be included in fiction. New phenomena demand new strategies of representation, and so rather than arguing, with the Ghosh of *The Great Derangement*, that realist fiction is unsuited to representing climate change, it seems more useful to suggest that a reconfigured notion of realism is necessary. When the hitherto abnormal becomes the norm, realist fiction needs to reimagine its boundaries and, varied though they are, most of the novels discussed in this study appear to be doing this. Paranormal elements infiltrate the otherwise rigorous realism of *The Rapture* and *Gun Island*, *Flight Behaviour* opens with Dellarobia Turnbow experiencing an epiphany, when the swathe of monarch butterflies that she is witnessing on an Appalachian hillside seem akin to Moses' burning bush and Ezekiel's vision of God, and *The Overstory* entwines its multiple human tales with the fortunes of trees that emerge as the main protagonists of the text. And virtually all the novels redefine the remit of the realist novel by undermining the notion that humankind occupies a privileged sovereign space, apart from the lives of all the other species on the planet. So, the new realist novel exists in various sub-forms, which remain close to the parent plant, but its rhizomes characteristically travel in directions that move outside the social parameters that circumscribe the worlds of Richardson and Fielding, Dickens and Thackeray, Stendhal and Balzac, Flaubert and Maupassant, to include the asocial and the ahuman. Concerned as they are with the long present, the novels discussed here mostly – *Solar* is again an exception – embody a realist aesthetic that journeys beyond the *Comédie humaine*.

In *The Overstory*, Richard Powers repeats the mantra that 'the best arguments in the world won't change a person's mind. The only thing that can do that is a good story' ([2018] 2019: 420, 607) and while this assertion may seem to be overblown in its neglect of other forms of argument, story is certainly a powerful conduit for engaging and augmenting audiences' ethical investment in understanding and combating climate change. Needless to say, Powers' broadbrush statement remains subjective without evidence to support it and recent years have seen the expanding field of empirical environmentalism begin to address readers' responses to the depiction of anthropogenic climate change in fiction. Pioneering articles such as Matthew Schneider-Mayerson's 'The Influence of Climate Fiction' offer an attempt to test the 'celebration [by] authors, activists, ecocritics, and environmental humanists ... of climate fiction as a source of affectively potent proenvironmental narratives' (Schneider-Mayerson 2018: 495) through qualitative surveys.[2] Schneider-Mayerson contends that 'much of the recent cultural, critical, and pedagogical interest in climate change fiction has been related to its potential psychological and ecopolitical influence' (2018: 475), and he distances himself from the position of commentators like Greg Garrard (2013b), which he characterizes as embodying the 'perspective of most traditional literary critics – that aesthetics and not influence should be the focus of the humanities' (Schneider-Mayerson 2018: 475, n. 12). However, the dichotomy between aesthetics and influence that is suggested here seems reductive, since aesthetically accomplished fiction is far more likely to be influential than poorly executed didactic fiction. So one returns to Powers' advocacy of storytelling as a mode of persuasion. His emphasis on the power of 'a good story' seems warranted, albeit with the caveat that stories that promote climate literacy and activism are not confined to fiction. They are to be found in the narrativization of climate, wherever it occurs: in cinema, social media, television documentary, political discourse, art and music and numerous other discursive modes, as well as in the novel.

All of the novels I have been discussing are realistic, but at the same time several of them foreground the activity of storytelling. In *MaddAddam*, Atwood writes, 'There's the story, then there's the real story, then there's the story of how the story came to be told. Then there's what you leave out of the story. Which is part of the story too' ([2013] 2014: 70). *Oil on Water* revolves around the journalist Rufus's quest for 'what is almost a perfect story' (2011: 135). In *The Healer*, Tapani is a poet, while his wife Johanna, like Habila's Rufus, is an investigative journalist. In *Animal's People*, Animal prefaces his narrative by explaining how he came to use a tape recording for his testimony. *The Overstory*'s assertion that story is the only medium that can change minds is first voiced by the character 'Maidenhair' (Olivia), who gives an account of her own redemption in a ceremonial context that invokes Native American oral narrative traditions. The extent to which narrative shapes events is even emphasized in *Solar*, where many readers will want to read against the grain, when Beard is said to be suspicious of 'people who kept on about narrative ..., believing all versions of it to be of equal value' (147). The narrative technique of *Clade*, with its postmodern resistance to closure and its self-conscious use of lacunae comes close to postmodern metafiction, but each of the individual chapters is realistic in itself and in an interview Bradley has been very explicit about the structure as a response to climate change:

> Stories demand we break reality up into manageable chunks by selecting particular sequences of events and identifying beginnings, middles and ends. But climate change resists that process by demanding we recognize how interconnected everything is, meaning any attempt to parcel reality up making [*sic*] us uncomfortably aware of the artificiality of the process, and of narrative more generally. (Brady 2017)

And *The Man with the Compound Eyes* comes closest of all to undercutting its realism, when it emerges that Alice is the author of two fictions that have the same title as the novel itself. Yet, here too, as in *Clade*, realism rubs shoulders with metafiction, and the sections that depict the impact of climate change and the exploitation of Taiwan's east coast lose none of their force as a consequence of the novel's self-reflexive elements. The effect of the fusion of modes is rather to initiate readers into compound vision and, again, one way of reading the novel's admixture of realism and metafiction is to see this as a response to the changed realities, climatic and more general, that necessitate the adoption of new ways of seeing.

In each case, realism remains, but, under the onslaught of climate change, it is not as we knew it. The new realism of the long-present climate novel insists on confronting the realities of the here-and-now and, taken together as a group the novels discussed here strike a hortatory note. The past is gone – we live on Eaarth, not Earth – and the future is unknown. So the present becomes not just a crucial, but also the only possible moment for engaging with its threat. In *The Overstory*, Mimi Ma's mother cites an old Chinese proverb to her father, Winston. The proverb asks, 'When is the best time to plant a tree?' and it provides an answer, 'Twenty years ago'. It is followed by a second question, which also has its own answer: 'When is the next best time? Now' (Powers [2018] 2019: 37). Winston has never previously planted anything, but galvanized by the proverb, he reflects that 'Now, that next best of times is long and rewrites everything' (37). It is a message that informs the mode of the climate fiction novels discussed in this book. Without overt didacticism, they direct attention to the immediacy and the gravity of the crisis, and in so doing, they imply that the long-present of the new realist novel can play a part in 'rewrit[ing] everything'.

Notes

Introduction: Writing to the moment

1 The year 2007 is Bloom's own dating for his coinage of the term. He used it in the publicity blurb for Jim Laughter's novel *Polar City Red* (2012), which attracted little attention when it was first published. The term subsequently achieved broad recognition, after National Public Radio and the *Christian Science Monitor* popularized it in 2012 (Glass 2013). More recently, Bloom has moved beyond the term 'cli-fi' in favour of what he calls ETF, 'end times fiction', a shift which reflects increasing engagement with apocalyptic scenarios (Bloom 2021).
2 For example, Hitchens (2003: x). Lynskey (2019: 167) is among a number of Orwell's biographers who point out that this belief is unsubstantiated.
3 In some of these cases, the trope of 'grandchildren' is supplemented by 'children'; in one, a comment by Joe Lieberman (McKibben 2010: 12), 'great-grandchildren' are added.
4 See too Trexler and Johns-Putra (2011: 186), and Milner and Burgmann (2020: 3).
5 See Trexler and Johns-Putra (2011), Irr (2017) and Goodbody and Johns-Putra (2019) for further introductions to climate fiction. Leikam and Leyda (2017) is a useful bibliography of American cli-fi.
6 The folkloric wisdom is that a frog thrown into boiling water will jump out, but if it is inserted into water that is gradually brought to the boil, it will be cooked to death. Bradley is one of a number of commentators who have used it as a trope for the dangers of ignoring gradualist climate change.
7 See Chapter 4, where I discuss this aspect of *Barkskins* more fully.
8 Ursula Heise concludes her review of Morton's *Hyperobjects* by saying that it contains 'so many self-cancelling claims about hyperobjects that coherent argument vanishes like the octopi that disappear in several chapters in their clouds of ink, Morton's favorite metaphor for the withdrawal of objects from the grasp of human knowledge. What the reader is left with is – well, ink and cloudiness' (Heise 2014).
9 Ghosh's *The Circle of Reason* (1986) and *The Calcutta Chromosome* (1995), which have respectively been seen to draw on magic realism and science-fiction, are exceptions.
10 Towards the end of *The Great Derangement*, Ghosh writes that when he tries to think of 'literary novelists writing in English' who depict 'accelerating changes in our environment … "only a handful of names" come to mind: J. G. Ballard,

Margaret Atwood, Kurt Vonnegut Jr., Barbara Kingsolver, Doris Lessing, Cormac McCarthy, Ian McEwan, and T. Coraghessan Boyle', going on to concede that 'no doubt many other names could be added to the list' (2016: 124–5).

11 Cf. Voltaire's satire of the convention in *Candide*, where towards the end his ingenuous protagonist remarks, 'I find that a man often meets people that he never expected to see again' ([1759] 1968: 117).

12 Others who point out the limitations of Ghosh's view include Milner and Burgmann, who say that his 'argument remains complicit with the binary opposition between "literary" and "genre" fiction it promises to undermine' (2020: 2).

13 I use the term (my coinage) by analogy with Gayatri Chakravorty Spivak's notion of 'strategic essentialism' (1988: 205).

14 See also Letter to Lady Branshaigh, 9 October 1756 (Carroll 1964: 326).

15 The three parts of Margaret Atwood's *MaddAddam* trilogy (2003–13), which moves between post-apocalyptic and pre-apocalyptic time frames, also use the present for the action set in the later period.

16 Maupassant is not discussed by Auerbach, but his advocacy of verisimilitude makes him an important addition to the trinity of Stendhal, Balzac and Flaubert. I return to this in the conclusion.

17 As Furst (1992: 30) points out, the phrase '*All is true*' is rendered in English, with emphasis, in the original French text.

18 It particularly informs the realism of three of the novels I discuss: *Oil on Water*, *The Healer* and *Gun Island*.

19 In his introduction to the Penguin edition, Angus Calder suggests that, along with other later Dickens novels, *Great Expectations* has affinities with the detective story (Dickens [1860–61] 1971: 16).

1 'Weather as everything': Social realism in Barbara Kingsolver's *Flight Behaviour*

1 Cf. Kingsolver's comments on this in interviews given at the time of the novel's publication: 'I had a hunch that we decide first what we believe and then we collect evidence to support it' (Young 2012); and 'First we decide whom we trust, then we believe what they say, then we look for supporting evidence. So I went looking into the literature of cognitive psychology' (Walsh 2012).

2 Subsequent references to the novel are to this edition.

3 Heather Houser views the novel as *centrally* concerned with science. She reads it as 'a fiction *of* science', which 'pushes at the seams of "fiction" and focuses analysis on creative climate writing writ large' (2020: 61–2; emphasis in original).

4 Cf. 'Like a patient etherised upon a table' (Eliot 1972: 11).
5 Viz. Exod. 3.2-3 and Isa. 1.13.
6 In her acknowledgements, Kingsolver explains that the key ingredients of her narrative are 'unfortunately true'. Only the relocation to southern Appalachia is fiction ([2012] 2013: 598).
7 See Milner and Burgmann, who begin their book on science-fiction and climate change with a discussion of Gilgamesh and Noah, arguing that 'treatments of catastrophic climate change … have tended to be organised around three main tropes: the new ice age, the burning world and the drowned world; or, more succinctly ice, fire and flood', and continue by saying that of these only flood 'has a deep history in the Western mythos' (Milner and Burgmann 2020: 3).
8 In 2010, two years before *Flight Behaviour* was published, unprecedented rainfall and mudslides devastated Angangueo, causing at least thirty deaths, leaving more than a thousand homeless and necessitating the evacuation of many more of the area's residents. The town is a tourist centre, located in the Monarch Butterfly Biosphere Reserve. The monarchs continue to return to the same mountainsides; tourism continues to threaten the area. Again, see Kingsolver's acknowledgements (2012: 598).
9 A 2019 NASA report says, 'The concentration of carbon dioxide in Earth's atmosphere is currently at nearly 412 parts per million (ppm) and rising. This represents a 47 percent increase since the beginning of the Industrial Age, when the concentration was near 280 ppm, and an 11 percent increase since 2000, when it was near 370 ppm' (Buis 2019).
10 Cf. the protracted us of Ovidian themes relating to transformation in Powers' *The Overstory*, discussed in Chapter 5.
11 Notable examples include Mary Shelley's *The Last Man in the World* (1826), Richard Matheson's *I Am Legend* (1954) and, particularly relevant in the context of the present study, the opening of Atwood's *Oryx and Crake* (2003), discussed in Chapter 10.

2 Seeking 'the perfect story': Metajournalistic realism in Helon Habila's *Oil on Water*

1 Both represent and interrogate the 'naturalization of oil' (Worden 2012: 441) as the basis of American society, and both have been adapted into highly successful films: *There Will Be Blood* (2007) and *Giant* (1956).
2 See particularly the story 'Night Ride' (Saro-Wiwa [1986] 1995: 111–19). Oil is not prominent in the collection as a whole, though Saro-Wiwa was, of course, an activist who led a non-violent campaign against the damage being inflicted on his

homeland and his people, the Ogoni, by foreign oil companies. See Saro-Wiwa (1992). He was executed by the Nigerian government in 1995.
3 Others include Isidore Okpewho's *Tides* (1993), Bina Nengi-Ilagha's *Condolences* (2002), Kaine Agary's *Yellow-Yellow* (2006) and Anthony Abagha's *The Children of Oloibiri* (2008), which are discussed by C. C. Ugwu in *Ecological Degradation in Selected Niger Delta Novels*, Unpublished PhD Thesis, University of Nigeria, Nsukka (2014), cited by Edebor (2017).
4 See, Chapter 10, where I discuss oil excavation and the 'Church of PetrOleum' in Margaret Atwood's *MaddAddam*.
5 See Balkan and Nandi (2021) and Balkan (2022) for further examples of petrofiction.
6 Subsequent references to the novel are to this edition.
7 In an earlier version of this passage, which appeared in the *Virginia Quarterly Review*, Habila also referred to a film that is very obviously *Waterworld*, but without mentioning it or its star, Kevin Costner, by name (Habila 2010). In the novel, the use of Costner's name identifies the film as *Waterworld*, though the title is not mentioned here either.
8 For example, Apsden (2010), and Nicol (2010). Fernández-Vázquez (2020) offers a more extended treatment of the relationship.
9 *Blood Diamond* is more obviously a thriller, albeit one concerned with an implied critique of 'conflict diamonds', diamonds mined and sold illegally to finance fighting in warzones.
10 This is not to dispute the view that in *Heart of Darkness* 'the colonizer's advancement appears to be defeated by the power inherent in nature' (Mayer 2010: 179).
11 Cf. Ayi Kwei Armah's extended treatment of 'Mame Water' in *Fragments* ([1970] 1974). I discussed this in Thieme (1980).

3 Apocalypse now? Visceral realism in Liz Jensen's *The Rapture*

1 *The Rapture* was published in January of 2009.
2 Subsequent references to the novel are to this edition.
3 Such temperatures were reached in England in 2022, when there was a new record high of 40.3°C in Coningsby, Lincolnshire, on 19 July.
4 In addition to Kahlo and van Gogh, Gabrielle also makes reference to a number of other artists whose work questions habitual modes of perception. These include

Bosch, mentioned in the context of the devastated landscape of Rio after it is hit by the earthquake (Jensen 2009b: 80); the Munch of the *The Scream* (21), a seminal expression of modern psychological angst and Turner, whose style is invoked to describe the submarine avalanche and tsunami likely to be caused by unleashing large amounts of methane (228).

5 'Because of its sludgy composition, mining and refining tar sands oil demands an enormous amount of energy. Tar sands generate 17 percent more carbon emissions than conventional oil' (Greenfield 2015).

6 Jensen was not the first novelist to write about a global disaster caused by methane released from the seabed: John Barnes in *The Mother of Storms* (1994), where the methane is unleashed by a pre-emptive nuclear missile strike, and Ian Irvine in *The Life Lottery* (2004), where it is triggered by major seismic activity, had both preceded her in writing fictional accounts of how the clathrate gun hypothesis (the hypothesis that increases in sea temperature could lead to the release of methane hydrates from the seabed, and that these would in turn generate further temperature rises and further releases of methane in an escalating cycle that would cause climate breakdown) could bring about just such a disaster. However, both of these novels are set in an apocalyptic future and so in this respect too, Jensen's locating her action in a period recognizably close to the present and for the most part resisting speculative fantasy makes the situation she describes immanent.

7 See, for example, Hitchcock's use of iconic landmarks such as Mount Rushmore (in *North by Northwest*, 1959), the Statue of Liberty (in *Saboteur*, 1942) and the Albert Hall (in *The Man Who Knew Too Much*, 1934 and its remake 1956).

8 *Pace* Mundler, who says Gabrielle is 'without her wheelchair, which is lost in the escape by helicopter' (2012: 157).

9 See Johns-Putra's discussion in 'Borrowing the World: Climate Change Fiction and the Problem of Posterity', particularly

> The figure of the child furnishes environmentalist discourse with a convenient signifier: … it is a synecdochic representation of future generations and readily conjures up an impulse toward protection, shelter, and guardianship. It thus embodies the floating concerns and anxieties that surround environmental issues, or, more accurately, it functions as an imaginary object and recipient of such concerns. Moreover, the association of children with innocence and hence with the 'natural' allows additional slippage between children and the nonhuman, especially between children and charismatic animals. (2017: 6)

10 See Lovelock (1991).

4 Tracing genealogies: Circumstantial realism in Annie Proulx's *Barkskins*

1 Subsequent references are to this edition.
2 One of the characters in *Barkskins*, George Pickering, is fascinated by the ethos of castaway narratives and, when he receives a copy of *Robinson Crusoe*, he is said to be 'enamored for weeks and read[s] the book over and over' (Proulx [2016] 2017: 226).
3 Proulx says the novel took her five years to write and prior to this she had been collecting material on landscape, forests and forestry for decades (Leyshon 2016).
4 Asked in an interview about the meaning of the term 'barkskins', Proulx answered, '*Barkskins* refers to people involved with trees in any way, from lumberjacks and timber workers to empire builders. It can also refer to insensitive, thick-skinned humans who ignore everything in life but their own goals' (Clay 2017). Elsewhere she was ambivalent about the provenance of the word and whether she had coined it:

> I don't know if I first saw the word or if I made it up. It is possible that I came across it in some old woodsman's memoir or such, but most likely I cobbled together 'bark' and 'skins' to make a descriptive occupation. There are bark-eaters (loggers or sawmill hands), barkies (a pole with the bark on), bark-markers (those who branded log ends with the company mark), and many more uses of 'bark'. A bald-headed fellow has obviously been 'barked'. (Owens 2016)

> In the dedication to the novel itself, Proulx says it is 'for barkskins of all kinds – loggers, ecologists, sawyers, sculptors, hotshots, planters, students, scientists, leaf eaters, photographers, practitioners of shinrin-yoku [Japanese for forest bathing or being in harmony with the atmosphere of the forest], land-sat interpreters, climatologists, wood butchers, picnickers, foresters, ring counters and the rest of us' (Proulx [2016] 2017: vii).

5 This is not confined to the New Zealand sections; there is something of the same in the background details Proulx provides when characters travel to France, the Low Countries and, in scenes that evoke *River of Smoke* (2011) and *Flood of Fire* (2015), the second and third parts of Amitav Ghosh's *Ibis Trilogy*, the Chinese trading hub of Guangzhou (Canton).
6 The way the figure of the therianthrope can challenge anthropocentric exclusivism is considered more fully in my discussion of Indra Sinha's *Animal's People* in Chapter 7.
7 Proulx has spoken of having had to cut 150 pages from her original draft, itself a foreshortened version of what she had first intended (Leyshon 2016; Owens 2016).

5 'Trees are social creatures': Encyclopaedic realism in Richard Powers's *The Overstory*

1 Cf. Margaret Atwood's widely quoted comment in a review of Powers's earlier novel, *The Echo Maker*: 'If Powers were an American writer of the 19th century, which writer would he be? He'd probably be the Herman Melville of *Moby-Dick*. His picture is that big' (Atwood 2006). Reviewers of *The Overstory*, who drew an analogy with *Moby Dick* include Markovits (2018) and Bate (2018).
2 In an interview at Paris's Shakespeare and Company Bookshop, Powers said that his 'original desire was to make the trees the real protagonists and actually have them as the heroes of the book, but there were some technical difficulties', and he indicated that the 'overture' to the novel, where he uses trees as the 'focalizers, if not to say the protagonists' is not 'representative' of its narrative voice, which is mainly in the hands of human intermediaries (Powers 2018).
3 The park in question is Mission Dolores Park in San Francisco.
4 An approach to forest management developed in the US Pacific North-West, which works to maintain biodiversity and old-growth forest and to strike a balance between timber operations and ecological concerns, with the latter taking precedence.
5 A three-month campaign to prevent timber companies from logging old-growth Redwoods in Northern California. Its tactics included tree-sits, the obstruction of the timber companies' trucks and activists' chaining themselves to trees.
6 Cf. a similar use of the trope in *The Man with the Compound Eyes*: 'A few years ago people were fond of saying that if you metaphorically compress the history of the world into a single day, humans only appear a few seconds before midnight' (Wu Ming-Yi [2011] 2014: 175–6).
7 The adage, which originated with the sophist Protagoras, has been alluded to earlier in the novel (278).
8 Called the Global Seedbed Germplasm Vault, its name evokes the world's largest seedbank, the Svalbard Global Seed Vault on the Norwegian island of Spitsbergen. The Svalbard Vault holds duplicates of seed samples stored in the world's genebanks as a safety back-up. According to its website, on 2 March 2022, it had eighty-nine depositors, 5,934 species and 1,145,693 seed samples.
9 Powers acknowledges his debt to her in his Shakespeare and Company interview (2018).
10 See Simard's *Finding the Mother Tree* (2021) for details of her career.
11 In addition to setting the two quotes as verse, Powers also transforms the second by rendering the last five words as upper case.

12 Cf. Liz Jensen's *The Rapture* (Chapter 3) where the character Harish Modak is an adherent of Lovelock's belief in 'the notion of Gaia, the planet as a self-regulating organism with its own "geophysiology"' (Jensen 2009b: 36).
13 Powers has altered Lovelock's wording slightly. The original reads, 'Earth *might be in certain ways* be [*sic*] alive – not as the ancients saw her, a sentient goddess with purpose and foresight – *more* like a tree' (Lovelock 1991: 12; emphasis added).
14 Based on John Ramsey MacKinnon's *The Ape Within Us* (1978).
15 It was shortlisted for the 2018 Man Booker Prize and won the 2019 Pulitzer Prize for fiction.
16 For example, Jordison (2018) and Kemp (2018).
17 Ghosh has himself seen *The Overstory* as a breakthrough in the novel's capacity to deal with climate issues (Ghosh 2019b and Ghosh 2019c). See Chapter 11.
18 Evocative of Ernest Callenbach's *Ecotopia* (1975), where the self-declared nation of the title, established in Northern California, Oregon and Washington, has seceded from the United States and offers a vision of an ecologically sustainable future.
19 This passage encourages the idea that Mimi Ma is linked with Mimas, a parallel also suggested in the similarity in their names.
20 In an intriguing article that offers evidence for another instance of arboranthropy in the novel, Susan Balée (2019) argues that Olivia is the chestnut tree that the Brinkmans imagine as their daughter.

6 It's not funny: Comic realism in Ian McEwan's *Solar*

1 Subsequent references are to this edition.
2 Cf. Greg Garrard's fine essay on *Solar*, which argues a similar case at greater length, while also providing an account of the circumstances leading up to the publication of the novel and the disappointment with which it was received, when it first appeared. Garrard concludes, 'McEwan's mild satirical reproof to Michael Beard's bumbling destructiveness teeters on the brink of the dizzyingly savage indictment the crisis more truly requires' (2013a: 136). See also Garrard (2013b: 180–2).
3 Tony Tanner ([1971] 1976: 141) includes Updike in a list of seven American writers of the 1950s and 1960s, who use the word 'entropy', adding that the notion of 'everything running down' (Susan Sontag's phrase; qtd. Tanner 141) is to be found in many more. McEwan uses the term in *Solar* in the context of the Spitsbergen climate group's appropriation of others' belongings in the boot room, where they have been required to leave their outer layers of clothing. He has Beard reflect,

Four days ago the room had started out in orderly condition, with all gear hanging on or stowed below the numbered pegs. Finite resources, equally shared, in the golden age of not so long ago' and go on to ask 'How were they to save the earth – assuming it needed saving, which he doubted – when it was so much larger than the boot room?' (78).

7 'I used to be human once': Testimonial realism in Indra Sinha's *Animal's People*

1 The Bhopal disaster occurred in December 1984 at the Union Carbide plant in the city. Estimates of the death toll vary between just under 4,000 and 16,000. More than half a million people are believed to have suffered injuries from their exposure to methyl isocyanate gas and other chemicals.
2 Subsequent references are to this edition.
3 Sinha himself was involved in a highly successful *Guardian* campaign to raise money for a similar clinic, which over the course of a dozen years had, in 2007, succeeded in providing free treatment to nearly 30,000 people (Sinha 2007b).
4 Mukherjee (2011) discusses this in terms of debates about the legal rights of animals. Cf. *The Overstory*, where Ray Brinkman 'wants trees to be rewarded for their intellectual property' (Powers [2018] 2019: 309), while another lawyer, Olivia Vandergriff's father, counters her comment that 'You can't own the rights to a living thing!', by saying, 'You can, you should' (202).
5 See, for example, Brigitte Rath, who provides a salutary antidote to views of the novel that close down the distance between the 'elite' author, Sinha, and his invented subaltern, Animal, arguing that the novel offers 'the hallucination of a subaltern voice' (2013: 180).
6 On the spoof website that Sinha devised for Khaufpur, an article entitled 'Controversial "Novel" Kicks up Political Storm' includes the following: 'Preview copies of "Animal's People" have been circulating among the movers and shakers in the Mantralaya. Sources close to Chief Minister's office termed the tome, penned by journalist Indra Sinha, as "a filthy and vile poison, full of bad language and sexy frolics" and informed that action would be forthcoming to ban it from sale in the state' (*Khaufpur Gazette* 2007).
7 Sections of the site, such as the item quoted in the previous note, remained available in May 2022, with a different URL (*Khaufpur Gazette* 2007). See the references.
8 Soyinka's poem 'Abiku' glosses its title with the epigraph: '*Wanderer child. It is the same child who dies and returns again and again to plague the mother* – Yoruba belief' (Soyinka 1968: 28; emphasis in original).
9 See, for example, Ashaolu (1977).

8 Nordic noir: Urban realism in Antti Tuomainen's *The Healer*

1 Subsequent references are to this edition.
2 Cf. Tzvetan Todorov in his essay 'The Typology of Detective Fiction':-

> We might say that at a certain point detective fiction experiences as an unjustified burden the constraints of this or that genre and gets rid of them in order to constitute a new code, The rule of the genre is perceived as a constraint once it becomes pure form and is no longer justified by the structure of the whole. Hence in novels by Hammett and Chandler, mystery had become a pure pretext, and the thriller which succeeded the whodunit got rid of it, in order to elaborate a new form of interest, suspense, and to concentrate on the description of a milieu. (Todorov [1971] 1977: 52)

3 See introduction, note 10, where details are included.
4 See, for example, McKibben (2010: 90–7).

9 'Boiling the frog'? Gradualist realism in James Bradley's *Clade*

1 Subsequent references are to this edition.
2 See Johns-Putra (2017) and my remarks at the end of Chapter 3. Discussing 'loss lit' on his own website, Bradley says. 'Certainly it's not accidental so many writers fall back on stories about lost parents and missing children when they seek to articulate their feelings about climate change, devices that capture something of the rupture and grief which suffuses the contemporary condition' (2015b).
3 In the penultimate chapter, '1420 MHz', there is a reference to mineral mines in the North-West Cape area of Western Australia that were operational until 'half a century ago', having closed after 'the world's economies shuddered and cracked through the twenties and thirties' (Bradley [2015] 2017: 254–5). This would suggest that the chapter is set around 2080. The action of the final chapter, 'Shimmer', is presumably slightly later.
4 In his Penguin press release on the title of the novel, Bradley writes:

> Given the way the story moves from the present into the future there seemed to me to be a sleek and slightly chilly edge to the word, a sense in which it captures something of the strangeness and otherness of the world to come. … I think – I hope – the novel itself captures some of this: part of the reason I decided not to

define the word in the book was because I wanted to preserve some of this sense of mystery and strangeness. (Bradley 2015a)

5   I am indebted to Pierce (2015) for directing me to this.
6   Cf. 'The world keeps on turning' (Tuomainen ([2010] 2013): 195).
7   A reference that anticipates the Bangkok Climate Change talks that were held in September 2018, three years after the publication of *Clade*.
8   When he first appears at this point, Adam sees Noah as 'seven, maybe eight' (108). Later he will say he did not know he 'existed until he was seven' (209).
9   A radio signal in the frequency range of 1,420 MHz was discovered in 1977 by the astronomer Jerry Ehman, since when controversy has raged as to its possible source (Schulze-Makuch 2017).

10 'Everything change': Speculative realism in Margaret Atwood's *MaddAddam* trilogy

1   Cf. her comment 'Science fiction has monsters and spaceships; speculative fiction could really happen' (Atwood 2003).
2   For example, Atwood (2004: 513).
3   David Bennett received the heart at the University of Maryland Medical Centre in Baltimore on 7 January 2022 and died two months later on 8 March (Salam 2022).
4   Swift addresses the reader as 'thee'. Atwood modernizes this to 'you'. The 'you' after the word 'inform' is an addition to Swift's original.
5   A reference in *Oryx and Crake* to humankind's 'arboreal ancestors' who '*used to shit on their enemies from above while perched in trees*' (Atwood [2003] 2004: 417; emphasis in original) is strongly redolent of the Yahoos. See Swift [1726] 1976: 182.
6   Nicholson and Mohler (1937) provide a detailed account of the relationship between the experiments performed in the Grand Academy of Lagado and actual experiments performed at the Royal Society. Atwood discusses the third book of *Gulliver's Travels* and its influence on B Movie mad scientists in 'On The Madness of Mad Scientists: Jonathan Swift's Grand Academy' (Atwood [2011] 2012: 194–211). The Lagado scientists offer a prototype for Crake in *Oryx and Crake*.
7   Atwood could be referring to Ira Levin's novel (1972), or either or both of the cinematic adaptations: the 1975 film, dir. Brian Forbes, or the 2004 film, dir. Frank Oz.
8   For examples relating to the trilogy, see Kohler (2017).

11 'Outside the range of the probable'? Picaresque realism in Amitav Ghosh's *Gun Island*

1. Here referred to in the singular, though *Gun Island* and Ghosh's earlier novel *The Hungry Tide* (2004) follow the more widely used form of 'The Sundarbans', which, for the sake of consistency I am using here. There is no distinction in Bengali. Some critics appear to use 'Sundarban', when referring solely to the Indian part of the region and 'Sundarbans' for the Indian and Bangladeshi. It may be that Ghosh deserts the plural form in *Jungle Nama*, because he is retelling a pre-colonial tale as an 'insider'. I am grateful to Asis De for this suggestion and for advising me on the issue more generally.
2. Dokkhin Rai is mentioned as a 'folk hero' of the same order as Chand Sadagar in *Gun Island* (Ghosh [2019] 2020: 5).
3. Subsequent references are to this edition.
4. Cf. the following passage in *The Hungry Tide*: 'Piya remembered a study that had shown there were more species of fish in the Sundarbans than could be found in the whole continent of Europe. ... [The] proliferation of environments was responsible for creating and sustaining a dazzling variety of aquatic life forms – from gargantuan crocodiles to microscopic fish' (Ghosh 2004: 125).
5. From the Italian 'Acqua Alta', the standard term used to refer to the periods when Venice floods.
6. Having earlier rendered the title of the rare text as '*Hypnerotomachia Poliphili*', here Ghosh refers to it as '*Hypnerotomachia Polyphili*'.
7. See De (2021) on how Dinanath's encounters with the affective uncanny reshape his 'structures of feeling'.
8. The museum in question is the Getty Museum in Los Angeles. It was threatened by a wildfire similar to the one described in *Gun Island* in 2019, though Ghosh says *this* was 'uncanny', because he wrote this part of the book several months earlier (Ghosh 2019a).
9. At the Indian book launch of the novel in Delhi in June 2019, Ghosh commented that one cannot write a novel to a 'prescription', adding 'I wouldn't say it's climate change. It's not just that. It's something much more complicated. It's the reality that we live in, and the reality that we live in today is so fractured, it's so sort of strange that there's something so uncanny about the way the world is changing' (Ghosh 2019d).
10. The Italian word '*stormo*' conveys more than the English 'storm' and when Cinta uses it at this point, Dinanath explains that it refers to 'a flock of birds in flight' and indicates its appropriateness for what they are witnessing: 'a storm of living beings, *bhutas*' (Ghosh [2019] 2020: 307).

11 On the earlier occasion, the translation is very slightly different: 'From the origin salvation comes' (Ghosh [2019] 2020: 244).
12 Cf. the similarly gnomic emphasis on 'mystery' at the end of Ghosh's second novel *The Shadow Lines*, where the narrator's closing words refer to his having been given a glimpse of 'a final redemptive mystery' (Ghosh 1988: 246).

12 'Innumerable ommatidia': Multi-realism in Wu Ming-Yi's *The Man with the Compound Eyes*

1 I have opted for the adjectival form 'Taiwanese' rather than 'Taiwan' after consulting Chun-yen Chen's 'Editor's Note' to *Ex-position*, 41, in which she explains that while 'Taiwan' may seem ungrammatical, 'Taiwanese' 'could be confusing as there is also a group of writers who write in the local language Hokkien, which is often called "Taiwanese"' (Chun-yen 2019: iii).
2 Wu has also been influenced by Italian cinematic neo-realism. As the title suggests, his novel *The Stolen Bicycle* ([2015] 2017) owes a debt to Vittorio De Sica's *Bicycle Thieves* (1948).
3 Subsequent references are to this edition.
4 The novel's translator, Darryl Sterk, has indicated that Haven is his translation of 'H. City' (Sterk 2013: 256), so the irony in the English translation is of his making. Corey Byrnes says that 'H. County'/Haven is 'a lightly fictionalized stand-in for Hualian County and City on the eastern coast of Taiwan' (Byrnes 2014).
5 The following passage in the first of these chapters establishes beyond doubt that this is Thom, since it repeats precise details about his past that have been provided early in the novel ([2011] 2014: 46): 'In his younger days, he cycled around Africa, piloted a sailboat across the Atlantic, ran an ultra-marathon across the Sahara, and even took part in an interesting sleep experiment, spending fully half a year thirty metres underground' (223). This is followed by information about his relationship with Alice.
6 Wu says as much in a Q&A session with the journal *Ex-position*: 'Today, thanks to social media and the Internet, every day we seem to be "watching" the world change. … The human mind has never watched the world with so many pairs of eyes and in so many layers' (2019: 144).
7 'Building the system … was almost "Mission Impossible". The tunnel cuts through Taiwan's central mountain range and was plagued by problems because of the complex geology of the site. There were dozens of floods and collapses; many workers died; and some experts doubted it would ever be finished' (Gluck 2006).

8 Prior to the publication of *The Man with the Compound Eyes*, Wu Ming-Yi also wrote a short story with the same title. Darryl Sterk summarizes the plot (2013: 253–4).
9 See my introduction, where I argue for the importance of strategic realism in an ethically committed approach to climate change and related environmental issues.
10 Translation by Lily Chen, Wu has also published *The Book of Lost Butterflies* (2000).

Conclusion: A new realism?

1 I am indebted to Marta Dvořák for directing me to this passage.
2 Schneider-Mayerson surveyed 161 readers of nineteen works of fiction, including four of those discussed in this book (*Flight Behaviour*, *Solar*, *The Healer* and *The Rapture*) and, perhaps predictably, arrived at the conclusion that these readers were generally from a younger and more liberal demographic than non-readers of climate fiction. His article includes an invaluable survey of work in the field up to the date of its publication.

References

Abani, C. (2004), *GraceLand*, Johannesburg: Picador Africa.
Achebe, C. (1988), *Hope and Impediments: Selected Essays: 1965–87*, Oxford: Heinemann.
Ameel, L. (2019), 'Antti Tuomainen's *The Healer* (2013) – Nordic Crime Cli-Fi', in A. Goodbody and A. Johns-Putra (eds), *Cli-Fi: A Companion*, 165–70, Oxford: Peter Lang.
Amis, M. ([1984] 2005), *Money*, London: Vintage.
Apsden, R. (2010), '*Oil on Water* by Helon Habila', *The Observer*, 29 August. Available online: https://www.theguardian.com/books/2010/aug/29/oil-on-water-helon-habila (accessed 26 May 2022).
Armah, A. ([1970] 1974), *Fragments*, London: Heinemann.
Ashaolu A. (1977), 'Allegory in *Ti-Jean and His Brothers*', *World Literature Written in English*, 16 (1): 203–11.
Atwood. M. ([1972] 1975), *Surfacing*, London: Virago.
Atwood, M. (1972), *Survival: A Thematic Guide to Canadian Literature*, Toronto: Anansi.
Atwood, M. ([1985] 1987), *The Handmaid's Tale*, London: Virago.
Atwood, M. ([2003] 2004), *Oryx and Crake*, London: Virago.
Atwood, M. (2003), 'Light in the Wilderness', *The Guardian*, 6 April. Available online: https://www.theguardian.com/books/2003/apr/26/fiction.margaretatwood (accessed 27 April 2022).
Atwood, M. (2004), '*The Handmaid's Tale* and *Oryx and Crake* in Context', *PMLA* 119: 513–17.
Atwood, M. (2006), 'In the Heart of the Heartland', review of *The Echo Maker* by Richard Powers, *New York Review of Books*, 21 December. Available online: https://www.nybooks.com/articles/2006/12/21/in-the-heart-of-the-heartland/ (accessed 5 February 2022).
Atwood, M. (2007), 'Introduction', in Aldous Huxley , *Brave New World*, Toronto: Vintage: vii–xvi.
Atwood, M. ([2009] 2010), *The Year of the Flood*, London: Virago.
Atwood, M. ([2011] 2012), *In Other Worlds: SF and the Human Imagination*, London: Virago.
Atwood, M. ([2013] 2014), *MaddAddam*, London: Virago.
Atwood, M. (2015), 'Interview' by Ed Finn, *Slate*, 6 February. Available online: https://slate.com/technology/2015/02/margaret-atwood-interview-the-author-speaks-on-hope-science-and-the-future.html (accessed 2 May 2022).

Atwood, M. (2019), *The Testaments*, London: Chatto & Windus.
Auerbach, E. ([1953] 2003), *Mimesis: The Representation of Reality in Western Literature*, trans. W. Trask, Princeton, NJ: Princeton University Press.
Austin, P. (2020/21), 'A Rustling in *The Overstory*: More-than-Human Storytelling in Richard Powers's Novel', *Sensus Historiae*, 38: 13–28.
Aw, T. (2013), Review of *The Man with the Compound Eyes*, *The Guardian*, 28 September. Available online: https://www.theguardian.com/books/2013/sep/28/man-compound-eyes-wu-mingyi-review (accessed 10 March 2022).
Bacigalupi, P. ([2009] 2010), *The Windup Girl*, London: Orbit.
Balée, S. (2019), 'Another Story in *The Overstory*: One of Richard Powers's Trees Has a Human Avatar', Politicsslashletters, 29 June. Available online: http://politicsslashletters.org/features/another-story-in-the-overstory-one-of-richard-powerss-trees-has-a-human-avatar/ (accessed 28 February 2022).
Balkan, S. (2015), 'Rogues in the Postcolony: Chris Abani's *GraceLand* and the Petro-Picaresque', *The Global South*, 9 (2): 18–37.
Balkan, S. (2022), *Rogues in the Postcolony: Narrating Extraction and Itinerancy in India*, Morgantown: West Virginia University Press.
Balkan, S., and S. Nandi, eds (2021), *Oil Fictions: World Literature and Our Contemporary Petrosphere*, Philadelphia: University of Pennsylvania Press.
Ballard, J. G. ([1962] 2008), *The Drowned World*, London: Harper Perennial.
Ballard, S., and P. Hudson, eds (2003), *Listen Here: Women Writing in Appalachia*, Lexington: University Press of Kentucky.
Barthes, R. (1968) 'L'effet de réel' ['The Reality Effect'], *Communications*, 11: 84–9. Available online: https://www.persee.fr/doc/comm_0588-8018_1968_num_11_1_1158 (accessed 30 June 2022).
Barthes, R. ([1973] 2002), *S/Z*, trans. R. Miller, Oxford: Basil Blackwell.
Bate, J. (2018), 'Review: *The Overstory* by Richard Powers – *Moby-Dick* with Tree-Huggers', *The Times*, 24 March. Available online: https://www.thetimes.co.uk/article/review-the-overstory-by-richard-powers-mobydick-with-treehuggers-pl9w2fb7d (accessed 14 February 2022).
Belsey, C. ([1980] 1989), *Critical Practice*, London and New York: Routledge.
Bicycle Thieves (1948), [Film] Dir. Vittorio de Sica, Italy: ENIC.
Blood Diamond (2006), [Film] Dir. Edward Zwick, USA: Warner Brothers.
Bloom, D. (2021) #endtimesfiction, [Twitter] 23 December. Available online: https://twitter.com/hashtag/endtimesfiction?src=hash/ (accessed 14 October 2022).
Bouteron, M. (1951), *La Comédie humaine*, vols. 1 and 2, Paris: Gallimard.
Bradley, J. ([2015] 2017), *Clade*, London: Titan Books.
Bradley, J. (2015a), 'Choosing the Book Title "Clade"', *Penguin Random House Australia*, 21 January. Available online: https://medium.com/@PenguinBooksAus/choosing-the-book-title-clade-f4d16baa6e87 (accessed 18 December 2021).
Bradley, J. (2015b), 'The End of Nature and Post-Naturalism: Fiction and the Anthropocene', *City of Tongues*, 30 December. Available online: https://cityoftongues.

com/2015/12/30/the-end-of-nature-and-post-naturalism-fiction-and-the-anthropocene/ (accessed 28 December 2021).

Brady, A. (2017), 'How Will Climate Change Affect Your Grandchildren: Interview with James Bradley', *Chicago Review of Books*, 24 October. Available online: https://chireviewofbooks.com/2017/10/24/burning-worlds-james-bradley-clade-interview/ (accessed 18 December 2021).

Buis, A. (2019), 'The Atmosphere: Getting a Handle on Carbon Dioxide', NASA Global Climate Change', 9 October. Available online: https://climate.nasa.gov/news/2915/the-atmosphere-getting-a-handle-on-carbon-dioxide (accessed 24 September 2021).

Bunyan, J. ([1678] 1968), *The Pilgrim's Progress*, Harmondsworth: Penguin.

Butler, O. ([1993] 2019), *Parable of the Sower*, London: Headline.

Byrnes, C. (2014), Review of *The Man with the Compound Eyes*, MCLC Resource Centre, Ohio State University, October. Available online: https://u.osu.edu/mclc/book-reviews/byrnes/ (accessed 10 March 2022).

Byrnes, C. (2019), 'Chinese Landscapes of Desire', *Representations*, 147: 124–60. Available online: https://www.academia.edu/41660992/Chinese_Landscapes_of_Desolation?email_work_card=abstract-read-more (accessed 10 March 2022).

Callenbach, E. ([1975] 2014), *Ecotopia*, 2nd edn, Berkeley, CA: Heyday.

Carroll, J., ed. (1964), *Selected Letters of Samuel Richardson*, Oxford: Clarendon.

Chamoiseau, P. ([1992] 1998), *Texaco*, trans. R. Myriam-Réjouis and V. Vinokurov, London: Granta.

Chandler, R. (1950), 'The Simple Art of Murder', *Saturday Review of Literature*, 15 April. Available online: https://ae-lib.org.ua/texts-c/chandler__the_simple_art_of_murder__en.htm (accessed 22 May 2022).

Channon, M. (2017), 'Could Canaries Volcano Really Cause a Mega-tsunami that Would Wipe out Plymouth?' *The Plymouth Herald*, 14 October. Available online: https://www.plymouthherald.co.uk/news/could-canaries-volcano-really-cause-628169 (accessed 2 May 2022).

Charles, R. (2018), 'The Most Exciting Novel about Trees You'll Ever Read', *Washington Post*, 3 April. Available online: https://www.washingtonpost.com/entertainment/books/the-most-exciting-novel-about-trees-youll-ever-read/2018/04/03/bb388a4e-3686-11e8-8fd2-49fe3c675a89_story.html (accessed 7 March 2022).

Chun-yen, C. (2019), 'Editor's Note', *Ex-position*, 41: i–iv.

Clark, T. (2015), *Ecocriticism on the Edge: The Anthropocene as a Threshold Concept*, London: Bloomsbury.

Clay, D. (2017), 'Imprint Author Interview: Annie Proulx', *Houston Public Media*, 23 January. Available online: https://www.houstonpublicmedia.org/articles/arts-culture/2017/01/23/184828/inprint-author-interview-annie-proulx/ (accessed 9 November 2021).

Coleridge, S. (1813), 'Notes on Tom Jones', *Literary Remains*. Available online: https://www.gutenberg.org/files/8533/8533-h/8533-h.htm#link2H_4_0095 (accessed 9 June 2022).

Conrad, J. ([1900] 1962), *Lord Jim*, Harmondsworth: Penguin.
Conrad, J. ([1902] 1980), *Heart of Darkness*, Harmondsworth: Penguin.
Conrad, J. ([1904] 1974), *Nostromo*, Harmondsworth: Penguin.
Cook, B., Anchukaitis, K., Touchan, R., Meko, D., and Cook, E. (2016), 'Spatiotemporal Drought Variability in the Mediterranean over the Last 900 Years', *JGR Atmospheres*, 121 (5): 2161–77. Available online: https://agupubs.onlinelibrary.wiley.com/doi/full/10.1002/2015JD023406 (accessed 23 April 2022).
Cowley, J. (2010), '*Solar* by Ian McEwan', *The Guardian*, 14 March. Available online: https://www.theguardian.com/books/2010/mar/14/solar-ian-mcewan (accessed 21 August 2022).
Cummins, A. (2016), '*Barkskins* Review – A Grisly Tale of Chopping Down People and Trees', *The Guardian*, 19 June. Available online: https://www.theguardian.com/books/2016/jun/19/barkskins-annie-proulx-review (accessed 22 August 2022).
De, A. (2021), 'Human/Non-Human Interface and the Affective Uncanny in Amitav Ghosh's *Gun Island*', *Revista Interdisciplinar de Literatura e Ecocritica*, 7 (1): 64–80. Available online: https://asle-brasil.com/journal/index.php/aslebr/article/view/165/118 (accessed 27 February 2022).
De Bruyn, B. (2016), 'Learning to Be a Species in the Anthropocene: On Annie Proulx's *Barkskins*', *Frame*, 29 (2): 71–90.
Defoe, D. ([1719] 1965), *Robinson Crusoe*, Harmondsworth: Penguin.
Defoe, D. ([1722] 1962), *A Journal of the Plague Year*, London: Dent.
Defoe, D. ([1722] 1978), *Moll Flanders*, Harmondsworth: Penguin.
Dickens, C. ([1849] 1966), *David Copperfield*, Harmondsworth: Penguin.
Dickens, C. ([1860–1] 1971), *Great Expectations*, Harmondsworth: Penguin.
Drewal, H. (2008), 'Mami Wata: Arts for Water Spirits in Africa and its Diasporas', *African Arts*, 41 (2): 60–83.
Dryden, J. ([1681] 1962), 'Absalom and Achitophel', in *The Poems and Fables of John Dryden*, ed. J. Kinsley: 188–216, London: Oxford University Press.
Edebor, S. (2017), 'Rape of a Nation: An Eco-critical Reading of Helon Habila's *Oil on Water*', *Journal of Arts & Humanities*, 6 (9): 41–9. Available online: https://www.academia.edu/34732898/Rape_of_A_Nation_An_Eco_critical_Reading_of_Helon_Habilas_Oil_on_Water (accessed 31 August 2021).
Ehrenpreis, I. (1964), *Tom Jones*, London: Edward Arnold.
Eliot, T. S. (1972), *Selected Poems*, London: Faber and Faber.
Elkin, P. (1973), *The Augustan Defence of Satire*, Oxford: Clarendon Press.
Emerson, R. ([1836] 1911), *The Conduct of Life, Nature and Oher Essays*, London: Dent.
Erdman, J. (2017), 'Florida's Drought Has Worsened so much that Airboats in the Everglades Are Getting Stuck', *The Weather Channel*, 20 April. Available online: https://weather.com/climate-weather/drought/news/everglades-airboat-stuck-florida-drought-april-2017 (accessed 2 May 2022).
Fernández-Vázquez, J. (2020), 'Into the Heart of Nature: Conradian Echoes in Helon Habila's *Oil on Water*', *Research in African Literatures*, 51 (4): 103–22.

Fielding, H. ([1742] 1964), *The Adventures of Joseph Andrews*, London: Oxford University Press.

Fielding, H. ([1749] 1969), *The History of Tom Jones: A Foundling*, Harmondsworth: Penguin.

Fiskio, J. (2021), *Climate Change, Literature, and Environmental Justice: Poetics of Dissent and Repair*, Cambridge: Cambridge University Press.

Foster, A. (1901), *Bunyan's Country; Studies in the Bedfordshire Topography of the Pilgrim's Progress*, London: Virtue.

Furst, L., ed. (1992), *Realism*, London: Longman.

Garner, D. (2016), 'Annie Proulx's *Barkskins* is an Epic Tale of Logging and Doom', *The New York Times*, 16 June. Available online: https://www.nytimes.com/2016/06/17/books/annie-proulx-barkskins-review.html (accessed 9 November 2021).

Garrard, G. (2013a), '*Solar*: Apocalypse Not', in *Ian McEwan: Contemporary Critical Perspectives*, ed. S. Groes: 123–36, London: Bloomsbury.

Garrard, G. (2013b), 'The Unbearable Lightness of Green: Air Travel, Climate Change and Literature', *Green Letters: Studies in Ecocriticism*, 17 (2): 175–88.

Garrard, G. (2016), 'Conciliation and Consilience: Climate Change in Barbara Kingsolver's *Flight Behaviour*', in M. Middeke, G. Rippl and H. Zapf (eds), *Handbook of Ecocriticism and Cultural Ecology*, vol. 2, 295–312. Berlin and Boston: De Gruyter. Available online: https://doi.org/10.1515/9783110314595-017 (accessed 16 September 2021).

Gee, M. (2004), *The Flood*, London: Saqi Books.

Ghosh, A. (1986), *The Circle of Reason*, New Delhi: Roli.

Ghosh, A. (1988), *The Shadow Lines*, London: Bloomsbury.

Ghosh, A. ([1992] 2005), 'Petrofiction: The Oil Encounter and the Novel', in *Incendiary Circumstances: A Chronicle of the Turmoil of Our Times*, 138–51, Boston: Houghton Mifflin.

Ghosh, A. (1995), *The Calcutta Chromosome*, London: HarperCollins.

Ghosh, A. ([2000] 2001), *The Glass Palace*, London: HarperCollins.

Ghosh, A. (2004), *The Hungry Tide*, London: HarperCollins.

Ghosh, A. (2016), *The Great Derangement: Climate Change and the Unthinkable*, Chicago and London: University of Chicago Press.

Ghosh, A. (2019a), 'Amitav Ghosh: National Book Festival, Library of Congress'. Available online: https://www.loc.gov/item/Available onlinecast-8824/ (accessed 28 January 2022).

Ghosh, A. (2019b), 'Amitav Ghosh – Reading and Conversation on *Gun Island*', Institute of the Humanities and Global Cultures, University of Virginia. Available online: https://www.youtube.com/watch?v=pixQalTh0xQ (accessed 22 January 2022).

Ghosh, A. (2019c), 'In Venice I Heard Bangla Everywhere: Amitav Ghosh on *Gun Island*'. Available online: https://www.youtube.com/watch?v=r5RbdChKMv4 (accessed 27 January 2022).

Ghosh, A. (2019d), 'University of Chicago Humanities Fall Festival 2019'. Available online: https://www.youtube.com/watch?v=MPsj_lstkBs (accessed 22 January 2022).
Ghosh, A. ([2019] 2020), *Gun Island*, London: John Murray.
Ghosh, A. (2021a), *Jungle Nama: A Story of the Sundarban*, London: John Murray.
Ghosh, A. (2021b), *The Nutmeg's Curse: Parables for a Planet in Crisis*, Gurugram: Penguin/Allen Lane.
Ghosh, A. (2021c), *Uncanny and Improbable Events*, London: Penguin.
Giant (1956), [Film] Dir. George Stevens, USA: Warner Brothers.
Glass, R. (2013), 'Global Warning: The Rise of "Cli-fi"', *The Guardian*, 31 May. Available online: https://www.theguardian.com/books/2013/may/31/global-warning-rise-cli-fi (accessed 1 September 2021).
Gluck, C. (2006), 'Asia's Longest Road Tunnel Opens', BBC News Channel, 16 June. Available online: http://news.bbc.co.uk/1/hi/world/asia-pacific/5086548.stm (accessed 11 April 2022).
Goodbody, A., and A. Johns-Putra, eds (2019), *Cli-Fi: A Companion*, Oxford: Peter Lang.
Greenfield, N. (2015), '10 Threats From the Canadian Tar Sands Industry', NRDC (National Resources Defense Council), 13 August. Available online: https://www.nrdc.org/stories/10-threats-canadian-tar-sands-industry (accessed 16 October 2021).
Habila, H. ([2010] 2011), *Oil on Water*, London: Penguin.
Habila, H. (2010), 'Irikefe Island', *VQR*. 86 (1). Available online: https://www.vqronline.org/fiction/irekefe-island (accessed 4 September 2021).
Habila, H. (2012), 'Conversations with African Poets and Writers: Helon Habila'. Available online: https://www.youtube.com/watch?v=K8eHI2NmWzA (accessed 26 May 2022).
Hay, L. (n.d.), 'Criminally Good: Interview with Author Antti Tuomainen'. Available online: http://lucyvhayauthor.com/criminally-good-interview-with-author-antti-tuomainen/ (accessed 22 May 2022).
Heise, U. (2014), Review of Timothy Morton, *Hyperobjects: Philosophy and Ecology after the End of the World*, *Critical Inquiry*, 4 June. Available online: https://criticalinquiry.uchicago.edu/ursula_k._heise_reviews_timothy_morton (accessed 23 July 2022).
Heise, U. (2019), 'Science Fiction and the Time Scales of the Anthropocene', *ELH*, 86 (2): 275–304.
Hill, J. (2000), *The Legacy of Luna*, San Francisco: HarperSanFrancisco.
Hitchens, C. (2003), 'Introduction' to *Animal Farm* and *1984*, Boston: Houghton Mifflin Harcourt.
Holland, R. (2019), *Contemporary Fiction and Science from Amis to McEwan: The Third Culture Novel*, London: Palgrave Macmillan.
Houser, H. (2020), *Infowhelm: Environmental Art and Literature in an Age of Data*, New York: Columbia University Press.
Huxley, A. ([1932] 1974), *Brave New World*, Harmondsworth: Penguin.

Iovino, S. (2010), 'Ecocriticism and a Non-Anthropocentric Humanism: Reflections on Local Natures and Global Responsibilities', in L. Volkmann, N. Grimm, I. Detmer, and K. Thomson (eds), *Local Natures, Global Responsibilities: Ecocritical Perspectives on the New English Literatures*, 29–53, Amsterdam: Rodopi.

IPCC (2021), Intergovernmental Panel on Climate Change Summary for Policymakers. Available online: https://www.ipcc.ch/report/ar6/wg1/downloads/report/IPCC_AR6_WGI_SPM.pdf (accessed 14 June 2022).

Irr, C. (2017), 'Introduction to Climate Fiction in English', in P. Rabinowitz (ed.), *Oxford Research Encyclopedia of Literature*, Oxford: Oxford University Press. Available online: http://literature.oxfordre.com/view/10.1093/acrefore/9780190201098.001.0001/acrefore-9780190201098-e-4 (accessed 6 June 2022).

IUCN (International Union for Conservation of Nature and Natural Resources) (2021–23), 'Red List of Threatened Species'. Available online: http://www.iucnredlist.org/initiatives/mammals/analysis/red-list-status (accessed 29 April 2022).

Jensen, L. ([2004] 2010), *The Ninth Life of Louis Drax*, London: Bloomsbury.

Jensen, L. (2009a), '*The Rapture* – Bookbits Author Interview', 3 November. Available online: http://www.radio4all.net/files/bookbits@rogers.com/3937-1-ljensen09.mp3 (accessed 10 October 2021).

Jensen, L. (2009b), *The Rapture*, London: Bloomsbury.

Jensen, L. (2012), '*Flight Behaviour* by Barbara Kingsolver – Review', *The Guardian*, 2 November. Available online: https://www.theguardian.com/books/2012/nov/02/flight-behaviour-barbara-kingsolver-review (accessed 2 October 2021).

Jensen, L. (2020), 'Storytellers and the Climate Crisis', *Wales Arts Review*; Jensen interviewed by Holly McElroy, 12 November. Available online: https://www.walesartsreview.org/storytellers-and-the-climate-crisis-with-liz-jensen/ (accessed 7 October 2021).

Johnson, S. ([1781] 1986), 'Life of Cowley' in *Selected Writings*, ed. P. Cruttwell: 403–6. London: Penguin.

Johns-Putra, A. (2017), 'Borrowing the World: Climate Change Fiction and the Problem of Posterity', *Metaphora* 2: 1–16. Available online: https://metaphora.univie.ac.at/volume2-johns-putra.pdf (accessed 1 October 2021).

Johns-Putra, A. (2019), *Climate Change and the Contemporary Novel*, Cambridge: Cambridge University Press.

Jordison, S. (2018), 'How Could *The Overstory* Be Considered a Book of the Year?', *The Guardian*, 18 December. Available online: https://www.theguardian.com/books/2018/dec/18/how-could-the-overstory-be-considered-a-book-of-the-year-richard-powers (accessed 4 March 2022).

Juchau, M. ([2015] 2016), *The World without Us*, London: Bloomsbury.

Kemp, P. (2018), 'Review: *The Overstory* by Richard Powers', *The Times*, 1 April. Available online: https://www.thetimes.co.uk/article/the-overstory-richard-powers-review-szhrp963h (accessed 4 March 2022).

Kermode, F. ([1967] 2000), *The Sense of an Ending: Studies in the Theory of Fiction*, Oxford: Oxford University Press.

Kerridge, R. (2019), 'Ian McEwan's *Solar* (2010) – British Comic Cli-Fi', in A. Goodbody and A. Johns-Putra (eds), *Cli-Fi: A Companion*, 159–64, Oxford: Peter Lang.

Khaufpur Gazette (2007), 'Controversial "Novel" Kicks Up Political Storm', 13 March. Web: https://khaufpur.wordpress.com/2007/03/13/controversial-novel-kicks-up-political-storm/ (accessed 16 May 2022).

Kingsolver, B. ([1995] 1997), *High Tide in Tucson: Essays from Now or Never*, London: Faber and Faber.

Kingsolver, B. (]2012] 2013), *Flight Behaviour*, London: Faber and Faber.

Kingsolver, B. (2018), 'The Heroes of this Novel Are Centuries Old and 300 Feet Tall', *New York Times*, 9 April. Available online: https://www.nytimes.com/2018/04/09/books/review/overstory-richard-powers.html (accessed 4 March 2022).

Kohler, J. (2017), 'Margaret Atwood Mesmerizes Every Generation with Prescient Writing', *St. Louis Post-Dispatch*, 15 September. Available online: https://www.stltoday.com/entertainment/books-and-literature/margaret-atwood-mesmerizes-every-generation-with-prescient-writing/article_974d6831-ce05-5f7c-86b2-34eae7f4c1cd.html (accessed 14 August 2022).

Leikam, S., and Leyda, J. (2017), 'Cli-Fi in American Studies: A Research Bibliography', *American Studies Journal*, 62. Available online: http://www.asjournal.org/62-2017/cli-fi-american-studies-research-bibliography/ (accessed 24 June 2022).

Lever, S. (2015), 'Going with the Floe', *Inside Story*, 12 March. Available online: https://insidestory.org.au/going-with-the-floe/ (accessed 28 December 2021).

Levin, I. (1972), *The Stepford Wives*, New York: Random House.

Leyshon, C. (2016), 'This Week in Fiction: Annie Proulx Discusses Her Upcoming Novel, *Barkskins*', *New Yorker*, 14 March. Available online: https://www.newyorker.com/books/page-turner/fiction-this-week-annie-proulx-2016-03-21 (accessed 23 July 2022).

Lovelock, J. (1991), *Gaia: The Practical Science of Planetary Medicine*, London and Stroud: Gaia Books.

Lowdon, C. (2021), '"When Gravity Isn't Enough": Review of Richard Powers' *Bewilderment*', *Sunday Times*, 5 September, Culture Section: 28.

Lukács, G. ([1950] 1964), *Studies in European Realism*, New York: Grosset & Dunlap.

Lynas, M. (2020), *Our Final Warning: Six Degrees of Climate Emergency*, London: 4th. Estate, 2020.

Lynskey, D. (2019), *The Ministry of Truth: The Biography of George Orwell's 1984*, New York: Doubleday.

Macdonald, G. (2017), '"Monstrous Transformer": Petrofiction and World Literature', *Journal of Postcolonial Writing*, 53 (3): 289–302.

MacKinnon, J. (1978), *The Ape Within Us*, New York: Holt, Rinehart & Winston.

Maeterlinck, M. ([1901] 2006), *The Life of the Bee*, Mineola, NY: Dover.

Man Who Knew Too Much, The (1934), [Film] Dir. Alfred Hitchcock, UK: Gaumont British.

Man Who Knew Too Much, The (1956), [Film] Dir. Alfred Hitchcock, USA: Paramount Pictures.

Manwaring, K. (2019), '*The Overstory*: A Review', *The Bardic Academic*, 1 October. Available online: https://thebardicacademic.wordpress.com/2019/01/10/the-overstory-a-review/ (accessed 10 January 2022).

Markovits, B. (2018), 'The Wisdom of Trees: review of *The Overstory* by Richard Powers', 23 March. Available online: https://www.theguardian.com/books/2018/mar/23/the-overstory-by-richard-powers-review (accessed 10 February 2022).

Mars-Jones, A. (2016), 'Chop and Burn'; review of Annie Proulx, *Barkskins*, *London Review of Books*, 28 July. Available online: https://www.lrb.co.uk/the-paper/v38/n15/adam-mars-jones/chop-and-burn (accessed 6 November 2021).

Maupassant, G. de ([1888] 2001), *Pierre et Jean*, trans. J. Mead, Oxford: Oxford University Press.

Mayer, M. (2010), 'When Trees Become Kings: Nature as a Decolonizing Force in Conrad's *Heart of Darkness*', in L. Volkmann, N. Grimm, I. Detmer, and K. Thomson (eds), *Local Natures, Global Responsibilities: Ecocritical Perspectives on the New English Literatures*, 179–88, Amsterdam: Rodopi.

McCarthy, C. (2006), *The Road*, London: Picador.

McEwan, I. ([2010] 2016), *Solar*, London: Vintage.

McKibben, B. (2010), *Eaarth: Making a Life on a Tough New Planet*, New York: Times Books.

McKibben, B. (2020), *Falter: Has the Human Game Begun to Play Itself Out?* London: Wildfire.

Milner, A. and J. Burgmann (2020), *Science Fiction and Climate Change: A Sociological Approach*, Liverpool: Liverpool University Press.

Morris, P. (2003), *Realism*, London and New York: Routledge.

Morton, T. (2013), *Hyperobjects: Philosophy and Ecology after the End of the World*, Minneapolis: University of Minnesota Press.

Mukherjee, P. (2011), '"Tomorrow There Will Be More of Us": Toxic Postcoloniality in *Animal's People*', in E. DeLoughrey and G. Handley (eds), *Postcolonial Ecologies: Literatures of the Environment*, 216–31, Oxford and New York: Oxford University Press.

Mundler, H. (2012), 'Liz Jensen's *The Rapture*: Journeying to Bethanyland', in C. Bazin and G. Leduc (eds), *Littérature Anglo-Saxonne au féminin: Renaissances et Horizons, 18–20 siècles*, 145–58. Paris: L'Harmattan.

Munif, A. ([1984] 1987), *Cities of Salt*, trans. P. Theroux, New York: Random House.

Munif, A. ([1986] 1991), *The Trench*, trans. P. Theroux, New York: Pantheon.

Nicol, P. (2010), '*Oil on Water* by Helon Habila', *The Sunday Times*, 1 August. Available online: https://www.thetimes.co.uk/article/oil-on-water-by-helon-habila-9vfx385q5jv (accessed 26 May 2022).

Nicolson, M., and Mohler, N. (1937), 'The Scientific Background of "Voyage to Laputa",' *Annals of Science*, 2 (3): 299–334.

Nixon, R. (2011), *Slow Violence: The Environmentalism of the Poor*, Cambridge, MA and London: Harvard University Press.

Nolè, L. (2020), 'Understanding the Fabric of the Natural World: The Role of the Collective Protagonist in Annie Proulx's *Barkskins*, *Journal of American Studies in Italy*, 3: 69–86. Available online: https://www.academia.edu/44348405/Understanding_the_Fabric_of_the_Natural_World_The_Role_of_the_Collective_Protagonist_in_Annie_Proulxs_Barkskins_ (accessed 30 March 2022).

North by Northwest (1959), [Film] Dir. Alfred Hitchcock, USA: Metro-Goldwyn-Mayer.

O'Shea, R. (2017), 'Canary Islands Face Volcano Eruption and Tsunami', *The Independent*, 25 October. Available online: http://www.independent.co.uk/travel/news-and-advice/canary-islands-volcano-eruption-tsunami-warning-cumbre-vieja-tenerife-a8018776.html (accessed 2 May 2022).

Owens, J. (2016), 'Powell's Interview with Annie Proulx, Author of *Barkskins*', *Powell's Books*, 23 September. Available online: https://medium.com/@Powells/powells-interview-with-annie-proulx-author-of-barkskins-8ca93f943797 (accessed 9 November 2021).

Pierce, P. (2015), 'The Catastrophe Business: *Clade* by James Bradley', *Sydney Review of Books*, 20 March. Available online: https://sydneyreviewofbooks.com/review/clade-james-bradley/ (accessed 6 December 2021).

Plantz, K. (2015), 'As the Weather Shifts, "Cli-fi" takes Root as a New Literary Genre', *Thomson Reuters Foundation News*, 10 April. Available online: https://news.trust.org/item/20150410094252-x7we9/ (accessed 24 June 2022).

Powers, R. ([2018] 2019), *The Overstory*, London: Vintage.

Powers, R. (2018), 'Richard Powers on *The Overstory*', Interview at Shakespeare and Company Bookshop, 1 October. Available online: https://www.youtube.com/watch?v=1JFoiOn0XkI (accessed 5 March 2022).

Proulx, A. ([2016] 2017), *Barkskins*, London: 4th. Estate.

Prystash, J. (2018), 'Speculative Realism, Daoist Aesthetics, and Wu Ming-Yi's *The Man with the Compound Eyes*', *ISLE: Interdisciplinary Studies in Literature and Environment*, 25 (3): 510–28. Available online: https://doi.org/10.1093/isle/isy049 (accessed 20 August 2021).

Puchner, M. (2022), *Literature for a Changing Planet*, Princeton, NJ and Oxford: Princeton University Press.

Rath, B. (2013), ' "His Words Only?" Indra Sinha's Pseudotranslation: *Animal's People* as Hallucinations of a Subaltern Voice', *AAA: Arbeiten aus Anglistik und Amerikanistik*, 38 (2): 161–83. Available online: https://www.academia.edu/30705456/_His_words_only_Indra_Sinhas_Pseudotranslation_Animals_People_as_Hallucinations_of_a_Subaltern_Voice (accessed 22 August 2022).

Richardson, S. ([1740] 1962), *Pamela*, vol 1, London: Dent.

Richardson, S. ([1753] 1812), *The History of Sir Charles Grandison*, vol. 1, London: Suttaby, Evance and Fox.

Rosenthal D. (2020), 'Climate Fiction and Poverty Studies: Kingsolver's *Flight Behavior*, Diaz's "Monstro" and Bacigalupi's "The Tamarisk Hunter"', *ISLE: Interdisciplinary Studies in Literature and Environment*, 27 (2): 268–86. Available online: https://academic.oup.com/.../doi/10.1093/isle/isz105/5637809 (accessed 18 September 2021).

Saboteur (1942), [Film] Dir. Alfred Hitchcock, USA: Universal Pictures.

Salam E. (2022), 'First Person to Receive Heart Transplant from Pig Dies, Says Maryland Hospital', *The Guardian*, 9 March. Available online: https://www.theguardian.com/us-news/2022/mar/09/first-person-heart-transplant-pig-dies-david-bennett (accessed 28 April 2022).

Saro-Wiwa, K. ([1986] 1995), *A Forest of Flowers*, Harlow: Longman.

Saro-Wiwa, K. (1992), *Genocide in Nigeria: The Ogoni Tragedy*, London, and Port Harcourt: Saros.

Save the Amazon Rainforests (2022). Available online: https://www.savetheamazon.org/rainforeststats.htmhttps://www.savetheamazon.org/rainforeststats.htm (accessed 29 April 2022).

Schneider-Mayerson, M. (2018), 'The Influence of Climate Fiction: An Empirical Survey of Readers', *Environmental Humanities*, 10 (2): 473–500. Available online: https://read.dukeupress.edu/environmental-humanities/article/10/2/473/136689/The-Influence-of-Climate-FictionAn-Empirical (accessed 28 May 2022).

Schulze-Makuch, D. (2017), 'Forty Years Later, SETI's Famous Wow! Signal May Have an Explanation', *Air & Space Magazine*, 8 June. Available online: https://www.airspacemag.com/daily-planet/forty-years-later-setis-famous-wow-signal-may-have-explanation-180963628/ (accessed 29 December 2021).

Seaman, D. (2016), Review of *Barkskins*, *Booklist*, 15 June. Available online: https://www.booklistonline.com/Barkskins-Annie-Proulx/pid=8054186 (accessed 7 March 2022).

Shklovsky, V. ([1929] 1968), 'A Parodying Novel: Sterne's *Tristram Shandy*', trans. W. Georg Isaak, in J. Traugott (ed.), *Sterne: A Collection of Critical Essays*: 66–89, Englewood Cliffs, NJ: Prentice Hall.

Simard, S. (2021), *Finding the Mother Tree: Discovering the Wisdom of the Forest*, New York: Alfred A. Knopf.

Sinha, I. ([2007] 2008), *Animal's People*, London: Simon and Schuster.

Sinha, I. (2007a), 'The Only Way to Deal with Tragedy Is to Laugh at It', *The Guardian*, 25 September. Available online: https://www.theguardian.com/books/2007/sep/25/bookerprize2007.thebookerprize (accessed 14 August 2022).

Sinha, I. (2007b), 'Bhopal: A Novel Quest for Justice', *The Guardian*, 10 October. Available online: https://www.theguardian.com/world/2007/oct/10/india-bhopal (accessed 14 August 2022).

Snow, C. (1959), *The Two Cultures and the Scientific Revolution*, Cambridge: Cambridge University Press.

Soyinka, W. ([1963] 1977), *A Dance of the Forests*, in *Wole Soyinka, Collected Plays, 1*, 1–77, Oxford: Oxford University Press.

Soyinka, W. (1968), *Idanre and Other Poems*, New York: Hill and Wang.

Spivak, G. (1988), *In Other Worlds: Essays in Cultural Politics*, New York and London: Routledge.

Steinbeck, J. ([1939] 1963), *The Grapes of Wrath*, Harmondsworth: Penguin.

Sterk, D. (2013), 'What I Learned Translating Wu Ming-Yi's *The Man with the Compound Eyes*', *Compilation and Translation Review*, 6 (2): 253–61. Available online: https://ctr.naer.edu.tw/v06.2/ctr060242.pdf (accessed 10 March 2022).

Sterk, D. (2016), 'The Apotheosis of Montage: The Videomosaic Gaze of *The Man with the Compound Eyes* as Postmodern Ecological Sublime', *Modern Chinese Literature and Culture*, 28 (2): 183–222. Available online: https://www.academia.edu/33981474 (accessed 10 March 2022).

Stepford Wives, The (1975), [Film] Dir. Brian Forbes, USA: Columbia Pictures.

Stepford Wives, The (2004), [Film] Dir. Frank Oz, USA: Paramount Pictures.

Sterne, L. ([1759–67] 2003), *The Life and Opinions of Tristram Shandy*, London: Penguin.

Svalbard Global Seed Vault (2022). Available online: https://seedvault.nordgen.org/ (accessed 2 March 2022).

Swift, J. ([1726] 1976), *Gulliver's Travels and Other Writings*, ed. L. Landa, London: Oxford University Press.

Tanner, T. ([1971] 1976), *City of Words: American Fiction, 1950–1970*, London: Jonathan Cape.

There Will Be Blood (2007), [Film] Dir. Paul Thomas Anderson, USA: Paramount Vantage and Miramax.

Thieme, J. (1980), 'Myth, Society and the African Artist in Ayi Kwei Armah's *Fragments*', *Gulliver-German English Yearbook*, 53–67, Berlin: Gulliver.

Thieme, J. (2001), *Postcolonial Con-Texts: Writing Back to the Canon*, London and New York: Continuum.

Thieme, J. (2017), 'Therianthropes Past and Future: Transformative Figures in Colonial and Postcolonial Writing', in B. Neuman and S. Frenzel (eds), *Ecocriticism – Environments in Anglophone Literatures*, 151–67, Heidelberg: Universitätsverlag Winter.

Thomas-Corr, J. (2019), '*Gun Island* by Amitav Ghosh review – a Bengali Da Vinci Code', *Sunday Times*, 16 June. Available online: https://www.thetimes.co.uk/article/gun-island-by-amitav-ghosh-review-miracles-myths-and-a-mystical-tour-round-india-q07v796xx (accessed 14 January 2022).

Thoreau, H. ([1849] 1961), *A Week on the Concord and Merrimack Rivers*, New York: Signet.

Thoreau, H. ([1862] 1996), *Autumnal Tints*, Carlisle, MA: Applewood Books.

Todorov, T. ([1971] 1977), *The Poetics of Prose*, trans R. Howard, Ithaca, NY: Cornell University Press.

Trexler, A. and Johns-Putra, A. (2011), 'Climate Change in Literature and Literary Criticism', *Wiley Interdisciplinary Reviews*, 2: 185–200. Available online: https://www.academia.edu/3188021/Climate_Change_in_Literature_and_Literary_Criticism (accessed 6 June 2022).

Tuomainen, A. ([2010] 2013), *The Healer*, trans. L. Rogers. London: Harvill Secker.

Tuomainen, A. (2013), 'In Conversation … Arne Dahl, Antti Tuomainen and Stuart Neville', NoAlibis TV. Available online: https://www.youtube.com/watch?v=jCN-xkclKN4&t=173s (accessed 22 May 2022).

Urquhart, J. (2010), '*Solar*, by Ian McEwan', *The Independent*, 14 March. Available online: https://www.independent.co.uk/arts-entertainment/books/reviews/solar-by-ian-mcewan-5527479.html?r=59747 (accessed 5 July 2022).

Voltaire ([1759] 1968), *Candide or Optimism*, trans. J. Butt, Harmondsworth; Penguin.

Wagner-Martin, L. (2014), *Barbara Kingsolver's World: Nature, Art, and the Twenty-First Century*, New York: Bloomsbury.

Walcott, D. ([1957] 1970), *Ti-Jean and His Brothers*, in *Dream on Monkey Mountain and Other Plays*, 81–166, New York: Farrar, Straus and Giroux.

Walonen, M. (2016), *Contemporary World Narrative Fiction and the Spaces of Neoliberalism*, London: Palgrave Macmillan.

Walsh, B. (2012), 'Barbara Kingsolver on *Flight Behavior* and Why Climate Change Is Part of Her Story', *Time*, 12 November. Available online: https://entertainment.time.com/2012/11/08/barbara-kingsolver-on-flight-behavior-climate-change-and-the-end-of-doubt/ (accessed 24 September 2021).

Walton, K. (1990), *Mimesis as Make-Believe: On the Foundations of the Representational Arts*, Cambridge, MA: Harvard University Press.

Waterworld (1995), [Film] Dir. Kevin Reynolds, USA: Universal Pictures.

Watt, I. ([1957] 1963), *The Rise of the Novel*, Harmondsworth: Penguin.

White, L. (1967), 'The Historical Roots of our Ecological Crisis', *Science*, 155: 1203–7.

Whitman, W. ([1855] 1957), *Leaves of Grass*, London: Dent.

Wohlleben, P. ([2015] 2017), *The Hidden Life of Trees: What They Feel, How They Communicate: Discoveries from a Secret World*, trans. J. Billinghurst, London: William Collins.

Worden, D. (2012), 'Fossil Fuel Futurity: Oil in *Giant*', *Journal of American Studies*, 46 (2): 441–60.

Wu, M-Y. ([2011] 2014), *The Man with the Compound Eyes*, trans. D. Sterk, London: Vintage.

Wu, M-Y. ([2015] 2017), *The Stolen Bicycle*, trans. D. Sterk, Melbourne: Text.

Wu, M-Y. (2019), 'Q&A: Wu Ming-Yi', *Ex-position*, 41: 137–45.

Wyndham, J. (1951), *The Day of the Triffids*, London: Michael Joseph.

Wyndham, J. (1953), *The Kraken Wakes*, London: Michael Joseph.

Young, R. (2012), 'Barbara Kingsolver Sets a Fire', *Interview Magazine*, 7 November. Available online: https://www.interviewmagazine.com/culture/barbara-kingsolver-flight-behavior (accessed 30 November 2021).

Index

Note: Page numbers in **bold** indicate passages of central importance for the main texts and authors being discussed.

Abani, Chris, *GraceLand* 34
Accelerated Colony Collapse Disorder (ACCD) 122
Achebe, Chinua 38
Age of the Anthropocene **3**, **5**, **38**, **52**, **71**, 87
  Anthropocene exceptionalism, Anthropocene exclusivism 25, 58, 63, 70, 72, 85, 96, 135, 155, 158, 164, 167, 169, 171–2
alder trees 63
alternative vision, compound vision 78, 84, 102, 125–6, 149–50, 152, 155–6, 160, 163–9, 176 (*see also* ommatidia)
Amazon, Amazonas, Amazon rainforest 90, 105, 117
Ameel, Lieven 107, 108, 112
Amis, Kingsley 89
Amis, Martin 89
  Money 92
animal hybrids 134, 137, 172 (*see also* therianthropes)
animist, animism (*see also* hylozoism) 58, 64, 71, 77, 78, 82, 148, 150, 154, 160, 162, 164
Antarctic, Antarctica 117–18, 120, 122, 125
anthropogenic climate change 16, 48, 57, 65, 89, 171, 174, 175
apiology (*see* bees)
apocalypse, apocalyptic 3, 20, 29, 35, 45, 46, 47, 51–3, 56, 84, 104, 115, 117, 129, 142, 168, 177 n.1, 181 n.6
  Apokalis 97–8, 102
Appalachia, Appalachians 17, 20, 26, 27, 171, 174, 179 n.6
Appleseed, Johnny (John Chapman) 76
Arabian Nights, The 145
arboranthropy, arboranthropic 77, 156, 184 n.20

Arctic, Arctic permafrost 2, 5, 65, 67, 69, 72, 89–91
Artificial Intelligence (AI) 84, 156, 172
Asplund, Erik Gunnar 158
Atwood, Margaret 3, 7, 69, **127–38**, 172, 175, 178 n.10, 183 n.1, 187 nn.1, 2, 7
  Brave New World, Introduction 134
  The Handmaid's Tale 128, 136
  In Other Worlds 127, 128, 130, 135–6
  MaddAddam (2013) 127–8, 130–1, 136–7, 175
  MaddAddam trilogy (2003–13) 127–38, 172, 178 n.15
  Oryx and Crake 127, 128–35, 137, 179 n.11
  Surfacing 137
  Survival 69
  The Testaments 136
  The Year of the Flood 127, 128, 130–2, 134
Auerbach, Erich *Mimesis* 9–10, 13, 87, 178 n.16

Bacigalupi, Paolo *The Windup Girl* 2
Ballard, J. G. 177 n.10
  The Drowned World 3–4
Balzac, Honoré de 9–10, 12–15, 16, 87, 106, 173, 174, 178 n.16
  Comédie humaine 10, 12–13, 14, 88, 174
  Le Père Goriot 13
  Sarrasine 14
banyan tree, banyan-like 73, 78, 81
Barnes, Julian 89
Barthes, Roland 5, 13–14
  S/Z 14
  The Reality Effect (L'effet de réel) 5, 15, 60–1, 70, 173
bees, apiology, apiological 122–3, 126, 130
beetles (*see* insects)
Belsey, Catherine 9, 14

Bhopal, Bhopal chemical disaster 95–8, 100, 185 n.1
bhuta 146, 150, 153, 188 n.12
biodiversity 65, 113, 114, 140, 142, 183 n.4
bioengineering (*see* genetic engineering)
birch, white birch trees 63, 69, 85
Blood Diamond 37, 180 n.9
Bloom, Dan 1, 45, 177 n.1
boiling the frog 4, 114–15, 120, 121, 177 n.6
Bo tree, Buddha's Bo Tree 74, 84
Boccaccio, Giovanni *The Decameron* 45
Bradley, James *Clade* 4, 5, 12, 84, **113–26**, 150, 155, 156, 164, 172, 176, 187 n.7
Bridge, The 103
Bunyan John *Pilgrim's Progress* 11
Butler, Octavia E. *Parable of the Sower* 3–4
butterflies, monarch butterflies 17, 22–7, 30, 53, 74, 85, 123, 155, 160, 162–3, 169, 171–2, 174, 179 n.8, 190 n.10

Callenbach, Ernest *Ecotopia* 3–4, 184 n.18
capitalism, corporate capitalism 13–14, 102, 122, 136, 150, 171
Cervantes, Miguel de *Don Quixote* 7, 88, 154
Chamoiseau, Patrick *Texaco* 34
Chandler, Raymond 106–7, 111, 186 n.2
  The Long Goodbye 106
  'The Simple Art of Murder' 107
Chapman, John (*see* Appleseed, Johnny)
chestnut trees 72–5, 83, 184 n.20
  Hundred-Horse Chestnut, Hoel chestnut 73–5
children, grandchildren (*see* parentage, trope of)
Christian fundamentalism, fundamentalist cults 48, 52, 128, 136
Christie, Agatha 14
'clade', the term 115–16, 186–7 n.4
Clark, Timothy 29, 54
classic realism (*see* realism)
clathrate gun hypothesis 181 n.6 (*see also* methane)
clear-cutting 20, 27–8, 73, 82 (*see also* deforestation)
'cli-fi', the term 1, 45, 121, 127, 139, 150, 177 n.1
climate change denial 18, 24, 27, 31, 93, 118, 136, 171

climate talks
  Bangkok climate talks 118, 187 n.7
  Copenhagen climate summit 46
coastal erosion 119, 156, 168
Coleridge, Samuel Taylor 10
collective protagonist 62, 70, 81
comic epic (*see* epic)
comic realism 4, 87–9
compound vision (*see* alternative vision)
confirmation bias 18, 26, 66, 79, 178 n.1
Conrad, Joseph 36, 41, 158
  Heart of Darkness 36, 41, 180 n.10
  Lord Jim 158
  Nostromo 158
crime fiction, detective fiction 14, 15, 36, 103, 105–7, 186 n.2
crop failures, crop sustainability 20, 40, 119, 127, 133

Dahl, Arne 103
Daoism, Daoist thinking 169
Defoe, Daniel 7, 10–12, 13, 62, 87
  A Journal of the Plague Year 124
  Moll Flanders 11
  Robinson Crusoe 7, 11, 58, 128, 129, 182 n.2
deforestation 5, 65, 66, 70, 81–3 (*see also* clear-cutting)
Descartes, René 10–11
desertification 3, 132
detective fiction (*see* crime fiction and Todorov)
Dickens, Charles 88, 174
  David Copperfield 8
  Great Expectations 8, 14, 178, n 19
disability 48, 50, 53, 78, 96, 163
dolphins 142, 146, 152, 172
Douglas-firs 73
drought 90, 132, 133 (*see also* desertification)
Dryden, John 88, 92
Durkheim, Emile 79
Dylan, Bob 'A Hard Rain's a-Gonna Fall' 168
dystopia, dystopian fiction 2–4, 16, 45–6, 92, 102, 104, 130, 135, 136 (*see also* utopia, 'ustopia')

Eaarth (*see* Bill McKibben)
earthquake, earthquakes 6, 49, 51, 53, 154, 156, 158, 167, 181 n.4

'ecological gaze' 160, 162
eco-poverty, poverty studies 20
eco-terrorism 84, 103, 105, 108
Eliot, T. S. 'The Love Song of J. Alfred Prufrock' 21, 179 n.4
Elkin, P. R. 92
Emerson, Ralph Waldo 'Nature' 74–5
empirical environmentalism 175
Enlightenment
   (European) Enlightenment 64, 76, 149, 154, 160, 172
   pre-(European) Enlightenment 9, 76, 141, 145, 150, 153
   spiritual Enlightenment, Buddhist Enlightenment 74, 84
entropy 50, 91, 111, 117, 184 n.3
epic, epic narratives 3, 62, 85, 87–8, 141
   comic epic 88
Epic of Gilgamesh, The 3, 179 n.7
eschatological **51–2**
extinction, Great Extinctions 52–3, 89, 108, 116, 133, 168
   Extinction Rebellion 45
   Sixth Great Extinction 71–2
extraterrestrial intelligence 114, 122, 124, 126
Ezekiel 22, 53, 174

fabulation 8, 140–1, 147, 153, 158 (*see also* fantasy)
fantasy 7, 35, 120, 145, 152, 155, 181 n.6 (*see also* fabulation)
Ferber, Edna *Giant* 34
Fielding, Henry 87–8, 154, 174
   Joseph Andrews 88
   Tom Jones 7, 88, 154
film noir (*see* Nordic noir)
fish, declining fish stocks 42, 118–19, 130–1, 142, 152, 188 n.4
Flaubert, Gustave 9, 12, 61, 173, 174, 178 n.16
   Madame Bovary 61
   'Un coeur simple' 61
flood, floods 3, 6, 27–30, 120, 129–32, 135, 137, 160
   Old Testament Flood 22, 179 n.7
   (*see also* Atwood, *The Year of the Flood*)
forest ecology 159, 161
forest fires (*see* wildfires)
formal realism (*see* realism)

Foucault, Michel 79
Fukushima nuclear disaster 28, 31
fundamentalist cults (*see* Christian fundamentalism)
Furst, Lilian R. 8, 13, 178, n.17

Garrard, Greg 23, 175, 184 n.2
Gee, Maggie *The Flood* 4
Genesis, Book of 9, 129
genetic engineering, bioengineering 120, 121, 122, 128, 131, 134–6
Ghosh, Amitav 6–8, 16, 18, 23, 33–4, 47, 80, 104, 115, 121, **139–54**, 153, 173–4
   The Calcutta Chromosome 177 n.9
   The Circle of Reason 34, 177 n.9
   Flood of Fire 182 n.5
   The Glass Palace 34
   The Great Derangement 6–8, 18, 23, 33–4, 47, 80, 104, 115, 121, 137, 139–41, 144–6, 153, 173–4, 177–8, n.10
   Gun Island 8, 133, **139–54**, 155–6, 172, 173, 174, 178 n.18, 188 nn.2, 6, 8–9
   The Hungry Tide 140, 142, 188 n.4
   Jungle Nama 140–1
   The Nutmeg's Curse 140–1
   'Petrofiction' 33, 137
   River of Smoke 182 n.5
   The Shadow Lines 189 n.12
   Uncanny and Improbable Events 139, 140, 144
Ginkgo biloba (Maidenhair) tree 73–4
global warming 1–5, 6, 7, 23–7, 47, 51, 53, 65, 89, 103, 105, 122, 125, 132, 134, 139–40, 143, 148, 154. 167, 171
gradualism, gradualist views of climate change 6–7, 47, 104, 113–26, 139, 143, 164, 177 n.6
greenhouse gases, greenhouse effect 53, 71, 89, 93, 171

Habila, Helon *Oil on Water* 4, **33–43**, 95, 105, 108, 156, 171–2, 175, 178 n.18, 180 n.7
habitat loss 27, 121, 148
Heise, Ursula K. 62, 177 n.8
Hill, Julia 'Butterfly' *The Legacy of Luna* 74
Homer 9, 88
   Iliad 87

hurricane, hurricanes 49–50, 115, 120
Huxley, Aldous *Brave New World* 134–6
hylozoism, hylozoist 155, 169
hyperobjects, hyperreal 6, 35, 177 n.8
Hypnerotomachia Polyphili 141, 145, 172, 188 n.6

insects, insectile, insect vision 122, 164–5 (*see also* bees, butterflies)
  beetles 142–3, 152, 162–3
  spiders 140, 148, 150, 152, 172
Intergovernmental Panel on Climate Change (IPCC) 3
'interspecies literature' 30
Iovino, Serenella 30

James, Henry *The Aspern Papers* 149–50
Jensen, Liz
  The Ninth Life of Louis Drax 54
  The Rapture 4, 12, **45–56**, 104, 117, 156, 172, 174, 181 n.6, 184 n.12, 190, n.2
  review of *Flight Behaviour* 45
Johnson, Samuel 11, 92
  The Life of Cowley 11
Johns-Putra, Adeline 29–30, 163, 181, n.9, 186 n.2
Juchau, Mireille *The World without Us* 123

Kahlo, Frida 48, 180 n.4
kauri tree 63
Kermode, Frank *The Sense of an Ending* 52
Kerridge, Richard 90–1
Kingsolver, Barbara 2, 7, 81, 85, 178 n.1
  Flight Behaviour 16, **17–31**, 45, 50–1, 53, 89, 123, 155, 156, 171, 172, 174, 190 n.2
  'The Forest in the Seeds' 27
  review of *The Overstory* 81

landslides (*see* soil erosion)
Larsson, Stieg 103
Le Sage, Alain-René *Gil Blas* 7, 154
Leopold, Aldo 6, 74
linden 73, 7
Little Ice Age 142, 149
Locke, John 10
loggers, logging 5, 18, 23, 25, 27–8, 62, 70, 72, 74, 77, 79, 84, 182, n.4, 183 n.5

long present 2, 4–5, 46, 57, 114, 129, 137, 174, 176
Lovelock, James 76, 156, 169, 181 n.10, 184 nn.12, 13
  Gaia 55, 76
  The Revenge of Gaia 76
Lukács, György *Studies in European Realism* 13–14

McCarthy, Cormac 2, 178 n.10
McEwan, Ian 7, 89, 178, n.10
  Solar 4, 16, **87–93**, 156, 173, 174, 175, 184, nn.2, 3, 190 n.2
McKibben, Bill *Eaarth* 2–3, 16, 25, 108, 115, 177 n.3, 186, n.4
MacKinnon, John 184 n.14
Mankell, Henning 103
Maeterlinck, Maurice *The Life of the Bee* 123
Maidenhair (*see Ginkgo biloba*)
Malthusianism 133 (*see also* population growth)
Manifest Destiny 58
Māori 60
maple, maple trees 63, 73, 77
Matthew, Book of 136
Maupassant, Guy de 12, 173, 174, 178 n.16
Melville, Hermann *Moby Dick* 69, 183 n.1
metafiction, metafictive 15, 35, 131, 155, 166, 176
metajournalism 4, 37, 40, 43
methane 53, 55, 90, 117, 134, 156, 167, 181 nn.4, 6 (*see also* clathrate gun hypothesis)
Mi'kmaw, Mi'kmaq 5, 58–66
migration (*see also* species migration) 3, 23, 34, 106, 110, 122, 123, 133, 150–4
millenarism, millenarianist 52
Modernism 81
monarch butterflies (*see* butterflies)
monsoon activity 118
Moore, Charles J. 167
More, Sir Thomas *Utopia* 136
Morris, Pam 13
Morton, Timothy 6, 177 n.8
Moses 21–2, 174
Muir, John 6, 74–5
Mukherjee, Pablo 95, 99, 185 n.4
mulberry 73, 77

multinationalism, multinational companies 33, 36–7, 95–6, 99 (*see also* neocolonialism)
Munif, Abdelrahman
Cities of Salt 33
The Trench 33

neo-Classicism, neo-Classical 11, 62
neocolonialism, neocolonial 35, 41, 95, 98, 101, 140, 171, 172 (*see also* multinationalism)
neo-realism (in Italian cinema) 189 n.2
new forestry 70, 183 n.4
New Zealand/Aotearoa 60, 63, 182 n.5
Niger Delta 33–43, 95, 180 n.3
Nixon, Rob 104
Nordic noir, film noir 103, 112
North West Passage 168

oak trees 73, 77, 78
oceanic 'dead zones', 'Great Dead Zones' 131, 142
oil, oil excavation and extraction 4, 33–43, 55, 95, 108, 133, 136–7, 150, 156, 179 nn.1, 2, 181 n.5 (*see also* petrofiction, petronovels)
Old Tjikko 74
ommatidia 156, 162–3, 165 (*see also* alternative vision)
organic farming, organic gardening 20, 27, 127, 130–1
Orwell, George *1984* 2, 177 n.2
over-population (*see* population growth)
Ovid *Metamorphoses* 29, 76, 77, 83

Pacific Trash Vortex 6, 158–9, 167
pandemics, plague 104, 114, 122, 123–4, 129
paranormal, preternatural knowledge 45, 49, 141–6, 150, 153, 160, 174 (*see also* uncanny, the)
parentage, trope of 2–3, 114, 118, 163, 177, n.3, 186–9 n.2
people trafficking 133, 151
permafrost (*see* Arctic)
petrofiction, petronovels 33–4, 137, 180 n.5
photosynthesis 84, 89, 91
picaresque 7, 88, 145–7, 151, 154, 174
pines 29, 63, 84, 85

plague (*see* pandemics)
population growth, over-population 117, 121, 132, 133, 156, 168 (*see also* Malthusianism)
postmodern, postmodernism 35, 36, 43, 81, 169, 176
Potter, Beatrix 92
Powers, Richard 69–85
The Echo Maker 183 n.1
The Overstory 4, 12, 18, 30, 55, 65, **69–85**, 89, 96, 139, 150, 155, 162, 164, 172, 174–6, 179 n.10, 183 nn.2, 9, 11, 185 n.4
prescience, preternatural foreknowledge 4, 54, 124, 136, 138, 146, 154
Proulx, Annie *Barkskins* 4, 5, 18, **57–67**, 69, 70, 80, 82, 113–14, 156, 172, 182, nn.2–5, 7
Prystash, Justin 169

Queensland Bottle Tree 73
Querini Stampalia 141, 145, 150, 152

realism, realisms 1–16, 85, 171–6
classic realism 9, 13, 16, 46, 81, 166, 169
formal realism 9, 46, 99, 147
multi-realism 155–69
new realism, new realisms 5, 16, 171–6
urban realism 103–12
(*see also* neo-realism – Italian cinema)
redwood trees 63, 70, 74
Redwood Summer 70, 183 n.5
reforestation 57, 66–7, 73
refugee, refugees 24, 40, 104, 105, 122, 150, 152, 168
Revelation, Book of 53, 85, 97
Richardson, Samuel 11–12, 16, 46, 87, 174
Pamela 12
Sir Charles Grandison 11–12, 46
Rosenthal, Debra J. 20, 29–30
Royal Society, The 128

Salgari, Emilio *The Mystery of the Black Jungle* 149–50, 153
Saro-Wiwa, Ken 179, n.2, 180 n.1
Forest of Flowers 34
Genocide in Nigeria 179, n.2
satire, satirical 18, 21, 25, 28, 87–8, 91–3, 128, 130, 131, 145, 178 n.11, 184 n.2

Saussure, Ferdinand de, post-Saussurean linguistics 9
science fiction, sci-fi 1, 2, 3, 7, 104, 120, 127–8, 177 n.9, 179 n.7, 187 n.1
sequoia 71
Sequoia National Park 6, 74
Shakespeare, William
Macbeth 73
The Merchant of Venice 149
The Tempest 136
Shklovsky, Viktor 15, 165–6
Simard, Suzanne 75 *Finding the Mother Tree* 183 n.10
Sinclair, Upton *Oil!* 34
Sinha, Indra *Animal's People* 4, 23, 55–6, 76, **95–102**, 135, 137, 155, 171–2, 175, 182 n.6, 185, nn.3–7
slow violence 104
Smollett, Tobias 87, 88
snakes, serpents 98, 140, 141, 146–50, 152, 172
Snow, C. P. *The Two Cultures* 89
soil erosion 16, 18, 20, 23, 27–8, 156
Soyinka, Wole
'Abiku' 101, 185 n.8
A Dance of the Forests 101
species migration, species loss 16, 17, 19, 121–3, 127, 131, 136–7, 142–3, 148, 152, 168
speciesism 64, 76, 77, 136, 173
speculative, speculative fiction **127–38**, 167, 169, 181 n.6, 187 n.1
spiders (*see* insects)
Spitsbergen 91, 183 n.8, 184, n.3
Spivak, Gayatri Chakravorty 178, n.13
spruce trees 63, 69, 74, 85
Steinbeck, John *The Grapes of Wrath* 3
Stendhal 9, 12, 87, 174, 178 n.16
Stepford Wives, The 136
Sterk, Darryl 156, 160, 163–4, 169, 189 n.4, 190 n.8
Sterne, Laurence *Tristram Shandy* 14–15, 165–6
strategic realism 8, 166, 178 n.13, 190 n.9
Stubb, Alexander 107–8
subaltern, subaltern experience 43, 98, 99, 185 n.5
suicide tree (*tachigali versicolor*) 83

Sundarban, Sundarbans 140, 142–3, 145, 148–9, 152, 188 n.1, 188 n.4
Svalbard Global Seed Vault 183 n.8
Swift, Jonathan 92
Gulliver's Travels 128, 136, 187 nn.4–6

Tellus 103
Thackeray, William Makepeace 88, 174
therianthropes, therianthropic 64, 76–7, 96, 102, 135, 137, 152, 156, 168, 172
Thieme, John 58, 76, 180 n.11
'third culture novel' 89
Thoreau, H. D.
A Week on the Concord and Merrimack Rivers 75
Autumnal Tints 75
350.org campaign group 2–3, 25 (*see also* McKibben, Bill)
Todorov, Tzvetan 14, 186 n.2
Tolstoy, Leon
Anna Karenina 81
War and Peace 81
tornado, tornadoes 132, 143–4, 152
trafficking (*see* people trafficking)
Transcendentalism 75–**6**
transplant surgery 128
Trash Vortex (*see* Pacific Trash Vortex)
tsunami, tsunamis 6, 47, 51, 55, 132, 142, 154, 156, 168, 181 n.4
Tuomainen, Antti *The Healer* 4, **103–12**, 118, 156, 172, 175, 178 n.18, 190 n.2

uncanny, the 46, 121, 124, 139–40, 144, 146, 150, 154, 156, 188 nn.7, 8, 9
(*see also* paranormal)
Union Carbide 185 n.1
Updike, John *Rabbit is Rich* 91, 184 n.3
urban realism (*see* realism)
utopia, utopian, 'ustopia' 128, 130, 134–6

van Gogh, Vincent 49, 54, 180 n.4
Venice 141, 143–54, 188 n.5
verisimilitude 11, 15, 17, 46, 61, 67, 124, 173, 178 n.16
virtual reality 75, 114, 121–2, 124–5
volcano, volcanic eruptions 119, 163
Canary Islands volcano 132
Voltaire *Candide* 145–**6**, 154, 178 n.11

Walcott, Derek *Ti-Jean and His Brothers* 101
Walton, Kendall 8
water dependency, water supplies 69, 109, 127, 131–2 (*see also* drought)
water pollution 40–2, 108, 142, 156
Waterworld 35, 180 n.7
Watt, Ian *The Rise of the Novel* 9, 10, 13
Waugh, Evelyn 89
White, Lynn Jr. 'The Historical Roots of Our Ecological Crisis' 64
Whitman, Walt *Leaves of Grass* 76
wildfires 142, 148, 154, 188 n.8
willow trees 63, 85
Wohlleben, Peter *The Hidden Life of Trees* 70, 75

Writers Rebel group 45
'writing to the moment' 1–16, 46
Wu Cheng'en, *Journey to the West, The* 145
Wu Ming-Yi *The Man with the Compound Eyes* 6, 30, 55, 96, 135, 137, **155–69**, 171, 172, 176, 183 n.6, 189, n.6, 190 n.8
  The Dao of Butterflies 169
  The Stolen Bicycle 189 n.2
Wyndham, John
  The Kraken Wakes 3
  The Day of the Triffids 120

Yggdrasil 74
Yosemite National Park 6, 74

www.ingramcontent.com/pod-product-compliance
Lightning Source LLC
Chambersburg PA
CBHW052111300426
44116CB00010B/1629